Teletherapy Toolkit™:
Therapist Handbook for Treating Children and Teens

by Dr. Roseann Capanna-Hodge

Dedication

To all my fellow therapists –

You are navigating this teletherapy journey, and you've got this!

To my amazing team of therapists at Dr. Roseann & Associates –

You have been part of the mission to "change the way we view and treat children's mental health," and I love you all.

Roseann Capanna-Hodge

Contents

Chapter 10 – Teletherapy Techniques for Anxiety and Worry 223

Chapter 11 – Teletherapy Techniques: OCD 245

Endorsements

Teletherapy Toolkit™: Therapist Handbook for Treating Children and Teens

"This first-of-its-kind book should be in the hands of every therapist as he or she leaps into tele-therapy."

Lauren Micalizzi, Ph.D.
Brown University

"Dr. Roseann, in her book, The Teletherapy Toolkit™, marries her innovative thinking and clinical expertise with very practical therapeutic activities adapted for use in virtual health practices. This book is not only a "must read," but an easy to apply "must use" for therapists, teachers, and parents to support and foster children and teens' mental health and well-being."

Joan Rosenberg, PhD
Psychologist / Speaker
Author, 90 Seconds to a Life You Love

"Dr. Roseann is a consummate professional, and her book will be an excellent reference for any psychotherapist in this day and age."

Mitch Sadar, PhD
Psychologist

"A timely book for every therapist as we face our own fears of transitioning to online therapy. Jam-packed with specific ways to interact with your clients while using an online format. A must for every clinician!"

Kimberly Morrow, LCSW
Anxiety Treatment Specialist, Author, Co-Owner of AnxietyTraining

"Dr. Roseann offers unique and effective methods that facilitate lifelong skills."

Angelika Y. Sadar, MA
Licenced Psychologist
BrainARC America
2020 Joel F. Lubar award recipient for contributions to the field of neurofeedback

Foreword

My name is Dr. Cleopatra. I am the world's leading fertility strategist, and as such, am known as The Fertility Strategist. I am a scientist and university professor who pioneered the field of fertility biohacking and the use of the science of epigenetics to create 'superbabies' (using tools that we have available right in our own homes). To date, I have received three million dollars in support of my research program, and I have been cited in 1000 studies in the past five years alone.

I first met Dr. Roseann Capanna-Hodge through the Mindshare Mastermind led by NY Times best-selling author JJ Virgin. This community is home to some of the most influential doctors and health professionals in the world. Within the Mindshare community, and every community of which Dr. Roseann is a part, she is a beloved colleague and friend. She is the foremost pediatric mental health expert and the founder and director of the Global Institute on Children's Mental Health. Since Dr. Roseann and I first met, we have had the privilege and blessing of sharing many incredible and enriching experiences—including meeting mental health idol, Oprah Winfrey.

COVID-19, the disease caused by the SARS-CoV-2 coronavirus, has left an indelible mark on our world and on children's mental health. Due to its novel and highly infectious nature, COVID-19 has required people worldwide to reduce their physical interactions. Increased physical and social isolation has led to an amplified need for mental health services while simultaneously decreasing physical access to mental health services—a dangerous combination. By default, COVID-19 is demanding change in the way mental health services are deployed. This change is likely here to stay, even post-pandemic.

Teletherapy is a critical answer to the immediate and longer-term challenges we now face. It allows therapists to continue to work with and support children when in-person visits are not possible, whether due to pandemic or more routine factors, including inclement weather and busy family schedules.

Dr. Roseann is revolutionizing the way we understand and treat children's mental health. Forbes has called her *"a thought leader in children's mental health"* for precisely that reason. I have yet to meet a clinician who understands children's mental health so thoroughly and has nearly universal success helping to reduce and reverse mental health symptoms among children.

Teletherapy Toolkit™: Therapist Handbook for Treating Children and Teens is the first of its kind and is urgently timely. It is a must-have handbook of virtual therapeutic activities that all therapists need on their shelves. It gives therapists exactly what they need to provide quality and effective therapy to children virtually.

Today, therapists find themselves in a position where they need to reinvent and reimagine their services in a hurry. Therapists who work with children need easy-to-use and highly effective techniques that will keep children engaged while ensuring they meet their therapeutic goals. **The Teletherapy Toolkit™** is packed with dozens of activities and informational sheets.

Dr. Cleopatra Kamperveen

The Fertility Strategist

Dr. Roseann-Capanna-Hodge

Associate Professor (with tenure), University of Southern California

National Institutes of Health-funded scientist

Executive Director, The Fertility & Pregnancy Institute

September 7, 2020

Los Angeles, CA

Chapter 1 – My Calling

I remember it like yesterday.

I was playing on the front stoop with my dolls on a hot summer's day. I couldn't have been more than five years old. My Italian-speaking family friend, Angeline, bent down to ask me what I wanted to be when I grew up. With my hands on my hips and a big, proud smile on my face, I announced, *"A psychiatrist!"*

Angeline's eyes fluttered, and she turned to my mom. Giving her a judgy up-and-down once-over, she exhaled an "ah." I didn't understand then, but later, I realized she was thinking what most people thought in the 1970's about the world of mental health: it was full of "crazy" people. She likely assumed that the only way a five-year-old girl could know what a psychiatrist even was is if someone in our family went to one. Incidentally, that couldn't have been further from the truth (although who among us couldn't use a little therapy?).

The reality was that psychiatry was my calling. Despite having no idea what a psychiatrist really did, it was literally a "knowing" that I was destined to become one. This was something I was *compelled* to do.

As I grew older, I knew I wanted to help people through conversations. Talking was something I loved to do … just ask my tenth grade teacher, Mr. Bear, who made me sit in the corner for it. Yep!

As a teenager, I was the girl my friends came to for advice. And I loved it! I couldn't believe I could actually counsel people all day long *and get paid for it.* Sign me up!

Around that time, I also realized that psychiatrists were largely medication prescribers, so my dream shifted a bit—I wanted to be a *psychotherapist.*

I've now spent almost 30 years in the mental health field, and I have worn a *lot* of hats: mental health worker, therapist, school psychologist, evaluator, neurofeedback therapist, mentor, supervisor, founder and director, author, speaker, corporate trainer, and media expert. And I have worked in a *lot* of places, too: residential centers, substance abuse centers, schools, businesses, and of course, as the director of my incredibly successful center, Dr. Roseann and Associates.

The one thing I never saw coming in all these years is to be where we are right now—in the middle of a global pandemic. The world is so *different*, isn't it? And because of it, the field of mental health may be changed forever.

Is teletherapy here to stay? My guess is it is. People have gotten really cozy with technology like Zoom, which has made therapy so convenient and accessible that I am not sure clients will ever want to sit in a wait room again.

This pandemic isn't going away anytime soon, and therapists need new tools to continue helping people in these vastly different circumstances. As I watched my own team of highly skilled therapists attempt to reinvent the wheel, I too scoured Amazon looking for tools, activities, and really, *this* book.

I know what therapists need right now is an easy-to-use prescriptive therapy "recipe" book. So that's what I decided to write.

This book, along with our therapist course (that offers American Psychological Association sponsoring of continuing education credits) is all about upleveling teletherapy. Its goal is to teach others how to use techniques that we know work and have adapted for the virtual world. It's a springboard to foster creativity and guide children and teens in reducing and reversing mental health issues.

And that's more important now than ever.

Keep this recipe-style therapy activities book handy. You can also go to www.teletherapytoolkit.com/PDF for a free PDF copy of all the activity infographics contained in The Teletherapy Toolkit™ to use with clients and info-graphic sheets to share with parents. You just need to enter your email address and show proof of purchase, so have a picture of (or scanned) receipt ready, and you will receive a FREE copy of the activities and information sheets to use with clients.

Chapter 2 – Mental Health Issues on the Rise

Long before this pandemic, children and teens across the globe have struggled with mental health. In the United States, one in two children, or 54.2 percent (Bethell et. al, 2011), have a physical or mental health problem. And things aren't that different in Europe, where rates of youth mental health problems were already at an all-time high (Kovess et. al, 2015).

The bottom line is that kids are in crisis, and parents don't know how to help them. More and more children are struggling with serious mental health issues, and this isn't going away.

In fact, more and more children are dealing with chronic clinical issues that, sadly, we are missing until it is much later in their lives. The 2016 National Survey of Children's Health data published online in JAMA Pediatrics indicated that as many as one in six U.S. children between the ages of six and seventeen have a treatable mental health disorder such as depression, anxiety problems, or Attention-Deficit/Hyperactivity Disorder (ADHD) (Whitney & Peterson, 2019). That same study also found that nearly half of children with these disorders did not receive counseling or treatment from a mental health professional such as a psychiatrist, psychologist, or clinical social worker. According to The National Alliance on Mental Illness (NAMI), the average delay between onset of mental illness symptoms and treatment is 11 years (2019). And while parents may not know the signs of the disorders, they are clearly seeking help, because according to research, 30% of general physician consultations concern child behavior problems and established behavior problems (Ryan, O'Farrelly, & Ramchandania, 2017).

When I started out in my profession, I had a few complex and layered cases. You know, kids with ADHD, anxiety, dyslexia, and allergies. But today, that is the standard. I wondered what was happening to create this increase. I knew it wasn't better diagnostics, because not much has changed there. Autism rates skyrocketed during this time … heck, mostly in the last 10 years.

Kids are struggling more than ever, and so are their parents.

The pandemic has thrown the world into a tailspin, and parents and children are feeling it. Working from home, virtual learning, and social distancing have all led to overwhelm, frustration, disappointment, isolation, and a whole lot of anxiety—even feelings of panic. These long, stressful months and ongoing uncertainty has caused those with and without a history of mental health issues to struggle with so many emotions. Parents were already so overwhelmed and scared for their children's future, and this pandemic has only heightened those fears.

That overwhelm is exactly what compelled me to form The Global Institute of Children's Mental Health in January of 2020. Professionals and parents need tools to help reduce and reverse children's mental health issues. They simply don't know how effective therapies and tools such as psychotherapy, nutrition, and brain-based therapies can be.

The good news is that research supports the effectiveness of psychological therapies *across all ages* and settings—from private practices to community centers to day hospitals. Psychotherapy clearly has a universal appeal.

This pandemic may have thrust you into the world of teletherapy, but it's actually been around for a long time. And because of that, there is also a lot of research that supports its efficacy. In Hilty et. al (2013), they note, *"Telemental health is effective for diagnosis and assessment across many populations (adult, child, geriatric, and ethnic) and for disorders in many settings (emergency, home health), and appears to be comparable to in-person care."*

Further, teletherapy can be as effective as in-person therapy for a variety of conditions (Turgoose, Ashwick & Murphy, 2018; Varker et.al, 2019) *and,* as an added "bonus," clients are less likely to drop out of therapy (Mohr et. al, 2012).

Are There Factors That Influence the Effectiveness of Psychotherapy?

We know psychotherapy works. We also know that there are factors that influence treatment outcomes. The quality and effectiveness of the therapy results from not only client motivation and willingness to take action, but from the expertise and skills of the therapist (Beutler, 1997; Fairburn & Cooper, 2011). Therapists need to be skilled and have access to the tools and techniques to address the core issues our children and teens face today.

And that is what this book provides.

Additional factors that influence the effectiveness of psychotherapy are:

- Patient Characteristics

- Hawthorne Effect

- Hope and Positive Expectations

- Therapeutic Alliance

- Therapist Variables and Behaviors

- Therapy Quality and Therapist Competence

(Feinstein, Heiman & Yager, 2015; Fairburn & Cooper, 2011; Wampold, 2015)

Benefits of Teletherapy

One of the greatest benefits of teletherapy is that you don't even need to leave your home to get help. Clients don't have to worry about whether or not the nosy PTA president will somehow find out they're seeking help. Plus, it enables people to access help *no matter where they are.* Teletherapy also has reduced stigmatization, increased convenience for patients, and improved provider efficiency and timeliness.

Additional benefits include:

- Accessibility

- Ease of use of technology

- Convenience

- Affordability

- Greater flexibility

- Reduced wait times

- Increased availability

- Access for college students

- Access for those in remote areas

- Access for the disabled

- Better access to highly experienced therapists

- Access despite feeling unwell or sick, or weather-induced restrictions

- Availability during times of pandemic/shelter in place orders

- No travel or transportation concerns

- Increased privacy

- Client support between visits

- Countered stigma

Challenges Related to Teletherapy

While there are many benefits to teletherapy/telemental health, there are also challenges:

- Therapists don't have access to visual cues like body language or facial expressions that can help guide a therapeutic session.

- The client's issues can make it difficult to interpret his or her own body language.

- The client may have social concerns.

- Age and cognitive factors may be an issue.

- The client may be resistant to the process.

- Clients may have distractions at home that make it hard for them to engage with a therapist.

- For some patients, like those with serious mental health disorders, direct care is required.

- Insurance does not always cover telehealth services.

- Client may have little to no access to technology and internet connection.

Clearly, online therapy may not be a suitable solution for everyone. Virtual sessions simply aren't ideal in complex situations when symptoms are not managed, or when a client just doesn't want to engage. Sometimes, resistance to the process is exacerbated by the physical distance.

You've likely had a session or two during which the child or teen literally leaves the room, right? I recall three or four years ago, one of my mentees called to tell me about her teen client who politely said he needed to go and get something to eat. He proceeded to get into his car, grab his takeout, and not come back. At his next session, when the therapist asked what happened, he said, *"I told you I had to get some food."* Oh, did we laugh about this for years!

Again, teletherapy isn't for everyone, and we have an ethical responsibility to suggest in-person sessions when we believe that to be the case.

With all of teletherapy's pros and cons, one thing is certain: it is here to stay.

And like me, you want to provide the best therapy possible, whether in-person or virtually, right?

I'm so glad you've found this book to help you do so.

Research Citations

Bethell, C. D., Kogan, M. D., Strickland, B. B., Schor, E. L., Robertson, J., & Newacheck, P. W. (2011). A national and state profile of leading health problems and health care quality for US children: key insurance disparities and across-state variations. *Academic pediatrics*, 11(3 Suppl), S22–S33. https://doi.org/10.1016/j.acap.2010

Beutler, L. E. (1997). The psychotherapist as a neglected variable in psychotherapy: An illustration by reference to the role of therapist experience and training. *Clinical Psychology: Science and Practice*, 4(1), 44-52. https://doi.org/10.1111/j.1468-2850.1997.tb00098.x

Fairburn, C. G., & Cooper, Z. (2011). Therapist competence, therapy quality, and therapist training. *Behaviour Research and Therapy*, 49(6-7), 373–378. https://doi.org/10.1016/j.brat.2011.03.005

Feinstein, R., Heiman, N., & Yager, J. (2015). Common factors affecting psychotherapy outcomes: some implications for teaching psychotherapy. *Journal of Psychiatric Practice*, 21(3), 180–189. https://doi.org/10.1097/PRA.0000000000000064

Hilty, D. M., Ferrer, D. C., Parish, M. B., Johnston, B., Callahan, E. J., & Yellowlees, P. M. (2013). The effectiveness of telemental health: a 2013 review. *Telemedicine Journal and E-health : The Official Journal of the American Telemedicine Association*, 19(6), 444–454. https://doi.org/10.1089/tmj.2013.0075

Kovess, V., Carta, M. G., Pez, O., Bitfoi, A., Koç, C., Goelitz, D., Kuijpers, R., Lesinskiene, S., Mihova, Z., & Otten, R. (2015). The School Children Mental Health in Europe (SCMHE) Project: *Design and First Results. Clinical practice and epidemiology in mental health* : CP & EMH, 11(Suppl 1 M7), 113–123. https://doi.org/10.2174/1745017901511010113

Mohr, D. C., Ho, J., Duffecy, J., Reifler, D., Sokol, L., Burns, M. N., Jin, L., & Siddique, J. (2012). Effect of telephone-administered vs face-to-face cognitive behavioral therapy on adherence to therapy and depression outcomes among primary care patients: a randomized trial. *JAMA*, 307(21), 2278–2285. https://doi.org/10.1001/jama.2012.5588

National Alliance on Mental Illness – NAMI (2019). Mental health by the numbers. https://www.nami.org/mhstats

Ryan, R., O'Farrelly, C., & Ramchandani, P. (2017). Parenting and child mental health. *London journal of primary care*, 9(6), 86–94. https://doi.org/10.1080/17571472.2017.1361630

Turgoose, D., Ashwick, R., & Murphy, D. (2018). Systematic review of lessons learned from delivering tele-therapy to veterans with post-traumatic stress disorder. *Journal of Telemedicine and Telecare*, 24(9), 575–585. https://doi.org/10.1177/1357633X17730443

Varker, T., Brand, R. M., Ward, J., Terhaag, S., & Phelps, A. (2019). Efficacy of synchronous telepsychology interventions for people with anxiety, depression, posttraumatic stress disorder, and adjustment disorder: A rapid evidence assessment. *Psychological Services*, 16(4), 621–635. https://doi.org/10.1037/ser0000239

Wampold, B. E. (2015). How important are the common factors in psychotherapy? An update. *World Psychiatry: Official Journal of the World Psychiatric Association (WPA)*, 14(3), 270–277. https://doi.org/10.1002/wps.20238

Whitney, D. G., & Peterson, M. D. (2019). US National and State-Level Prevalence of Mental Health Disorders and

Disparities of Mental Health Care Use in Children. *JAMA pediatrics*, 173(4), 389–391. https://doi.org/10.1001/jamapediatrics.2018.5399

Chapter 3 – Becoming a Teletherapy Rockstar

Even if you've done a virtual therapy session here and there in the past, you likely never imagined being a full-time virtual therapist. Whether you're used to working in a school, agency, or office, you are now literally in people's homes, offices, and cars as you try to help children and teens face whatever challenges they are dealing with.

And let's face it … some of us are winging it.

It may remind you of when you first started out and were thrown into your first job. Your degree in hand, you were excited to change the world!

I know I was. What I didn't know was that I was there to make the other two psychologists' lives easier, and I wasn't going to get supervision unless I asked for it. There were no regularly scheduled guidance sessions, or anything of the sort. It was just me asking and looking for reassurance that I was doing the right thing. Now, I realize that's not always the case. Some are lucky enough to receive great, supportive supervision. I know I make it a point to give my therapists at my Ridgefield, CT center weekly individual and group supervision. In addition, we train deeply on one topic per year, which provides so much depth of knowledge and skills development.

Rockstar therapists don't just happen; they are created, nurtured, and cultivated through training and experience. I know that. You know that. But here we are, thrown into the world of teletherapy, largely without support.

You may be loving it, or you may be hating it. Either way, you realize the need to "figure it out," because again, it isn't going anywhere anytime soon.

Just like you learned to be a rockstar therapist in person, you can pivot to teletherapy with the right tools. Consider this book the "cushion" you need to get your bearings. From the physical setting up of sessions to actual techniques, I've got you covered.

If you are feeling overwhelmed right now, like you don't have the bandwidth to add even one more thing to your plate, don't worry. I've intentionally kept the chapters short and actionable.

Keep this recipe-style therapy activities book handy. You can also go to **www.teletherapytoolkit.com/PDF** for a free PDF copy of all the activity infographics contained in The Teletherapy Toolkit™ to use with clients and infographic sheets to share with parents. You just need to enter your email address and show proof of purchase, so have a picture of (or scanned) receipt ready, and you will receive a FREE copy of the activities and information sheets to use with clients.

Even with just 10 minutes to spare, you'll benefit from the value of prescriptive activities herein that deal with many of the issues that are impacting the children, adolescents, and families you're working work with right now.

Chapter 4 – Preparing for Teletherapy Sessions

Now that you know how effective teletherapy sessions can be, let's get you ready for your first of hopefully many sessions.

Countless therapists are currently figuring out how to do virtual psychotherapy as they go. They aren't really sure what the parameters or best practices are. While we all may have similar therapist training, the world of teletherapy requires that you be prepared in different ways. There are disparities in everything from legal considerations and treatment consents to preparing for and engaging with clients in a session.

Legal and Ethical Considerations

More than a dozen years ago, one of my all-time favorite clients came bouncing into my office, plopped on the couch and said, *"I am moving to Washington State."* His mom trailed in behind, saying how they really wanted to continue seeing me. At first, I was glad. George had made so much progress over the eight years I had been seeing him on and off. He went from being a child his mom had to literally hang upside down to get him to focus enough for me to talk with him to being a teenager who could sit and chat with me for a full hour. His anxiety went from being a daily struggle to a once-in-a-while nuisance, and most of it centered around his very difficult sister who was constantly poking at him. I knew right away that George wasn't going to benefit from phone calls (I did say this was more than a dozen years ago!), and then, I realized that I also wasn't licensed in Washington State. I couldn't see a way to continue to support him.

At first, George was angry with me. But then I assured him that I would find the coolest therapist ever (despite his belief that *I* was the coolest ever … and I mean, of course he was right!). More importantly, I reminded him of the many tools he had gained and how much he had to look forward to.

I said goodbye to a skeptical George and sent him on his way with six stamped and addressed envelopes that he could use to write to me whenever he needed and an appointment time to see his new therapist. When I checked in on George, he reported loving being near his cousins and his new school, and that he felt good about his new therapist, Ms. Barbara. *I* felt good that I had done the right thing for George.

It was also the right choice in terms of legality, too.

Even though we might think of virtual therapy as vastly different than in-person therapy, we have the same ethical and legal considerations to make. Really, much of how we practice virtually is the same as practicing in the office. As far as ethics in teletherapy, you should follow your professional national organization, such as The American Psychological Association (APA), National Association of Social Workers (NASW), American Counseling Association (ACA), or Anxiety and Depression Association of America (ADAA).

While there is no legal certification requirement to perform telemental health therapy sessions, many professional mental health associations emphasize that therapists, psychologists, and mental health professionals be prepared, competent, and trained to provide therapy virtually.

Licensing and Practicing Over State Lines

In order to practice therapy and call yourself a "psychotherapist," you must be licensed in the state where you treat your client. In most states, this rule means that a clinician who holds a license in one state, Connecticut, for example, may not be legally allowed to treat a client who lives in another, such as Ohio. Mental health professionals should always check with the licensing board in the client's home state to identify their ethical and legal duties. It is essential to find out what your state requirements are for practicing therapy across state lines.

It is important to note that while there are rules and regulations about psychotherapy being practiced virtually and across state lines, coaching is not governed by the same rules. There is a definite distinction between psychotherapy and life coaching. The focus of therapy is working on clinical mental health and emotional issues while coaching focuses on goal setting, personal empowerment, motivation, and strategies to define and reach your dreams.

Resources for Checking State Requirements:

Epstein Becker Green - *Telemental Health Laws* survey of 50 states and the District of Columbia

- https://www.ebglaw.com/telemental-health-laws-app/

American Psychological Association (APA) - Telehealth guidance by state

- https://www.apaservices.org/practice/clinic/covid-19-telehealth-state-summary

Check Your Liability Insurance

When practicing teletherapy, you want to check your liability insurance to make sure you are allowed to do teletherapy. Confirm that teletherapy and cross-state services are covered under your policy before you get started. Be prepared that you may have to demonstrate competence in telehealth service delivery, including the possibility of getting certified.

Ensuring Privacy

The discussions you have with your clients contain protected health information (PHI), and it's your responsibility to keep that information safe, secure, and confidential. To practice online therapy, you'll need to make absolutely certain that the platform you are using protects your client's privacy. Ensure that the teletherapy platform, EHR software, and any other technology you are using is HIPAA compliant, and that you have a signed business associate agreement (BAA) in place. This applies to both private providers and those who work at agencies and schools.

Examples of HIPAA-compliant teletherapy platforms include:

- Doxy.me
- Simple Practice
- Theranest
- Therapy Notes
- Zoom (with the HIPAA-compliant add-on option)
- Vtconnect
- Vsee

- Thera-link

- Wecounsel

- TheraPlatform

- Virtual Therapy Connect

Check to Make Sure You Can Bill for Teletherapy Services

If you are a private clinician, then you need to learn what you need to bill for teletherapy services. That means checking or pre-certifying your clients prior to their first appointment as well as letting them know what their co-pay obligations are.

Reimbursement for teletherapy is often dependent on filling out the forms correctly. It is important to note that billing for telehealth sessions often requires the Place of Service Code 02 and specific modifier codes (usually 95 or GT), depending on the payer.

Patient Considerations for Teletherapy Health

As we've established, teletherapy isn't appropriate for every client, so it is important to take careful consideration of what is best for the client.

Here are some specifics:

- Type and level of care you can provide.

- The client's accessibility and comfort level with technology.

- The client's access to the right therapeutic items at home.

- Whether your client's specific issues really require in-person sessions.

- The clinical appropriateness of virtual therapy only versus a hybrid of teletherapy and in-person sessions.

- Accessibility to privacy.

- The client's age, attention span, and cognitive capacity.

- The client's engagement in and cooperativeness with treatment.

- Current and/or past difficulties with substance abuse and history of violence or self-injurious behavior (which may suggest the insufficiency of virtual therapy).

Get the Right Setup

Having the right space, technology, and supplies is very important for a great teletherapy session. ***See Parent Teletherapy Checklist.

Setting Up Your Office Space

Having a designated, secure space for your teletherapy sessions is important to keep sessions professional and for you to enter into "therapist mode." It also helps to keep you organized and get ready for work.

When setting up your office space, you want to consider:

- Privacy: Select a space for your online therapy sessions that is private and in which no one else can hear the conversation between you and your client.

- Potential Distractions: Your family can't barge in, you aren't having to deal with your dog barking, etc.

- Noise Level: Noises such a phone buzzing, television, or your washer spinning can really disrupt the flow of a session.

- Background: You want to look as professional as possible. Make sure whatever is behind you looks "businesslike" and uncluttered.

- Lighting: Invest in good lighting, so your face can be seen consistently throughout a session.

- Supplies: Have your therapy supplies right next to you for easy access. Getting a desk or small shelving unit that provides you with quick access to the things you need is important.

- A comfortable desk and chair.

 - A whiteboard and dry erase markers.

Get the Right Technology

Having the right hardware, software, internet access, digital privacy safeguards, and security precautions to help ensure client privacy are all critical to have in place and tested before you begin. Practice and get really familiar with the equipment and software. Send a practice link to a friend and ask him or her to run through the process with you, so you know what it looks like on his/her end, too. This also allows you to make sure all your equipment is working properly while providing you the opportunity to address any problems *before* your actual appointment. Lastly, it is also important to have a backup device in case you have equipment failure.

Therapist Teletherapy Equipment List:

- A computer with a high-resolution webcam and enough memory to support video sessions

- Computer, phone, or tablet with speaker, microphone, and camera

- An external camera or microphone (if your device does not have one of high quality)

- Headphones for additional privacy

- Pre-planned and created slides packed with psychoeducational materials

- Good lighting (such as a 10- or 12-inch selfie light on a tripod, or one with a clamp)

- Fast internet connection with enough bandwidth to support video

- An application that is safe and secure SSL or Secure Sockets Layer. Having an SSL connection means you are using a website or application that provides a secure channel for communication between two devices (yours and the device of the person you are counseling).

Client Therapy Equipment List:

- Computer, phone, or tablet with speaker, microphone, and camera

- Headphones for additional privacy

- Fast internet connection with enough bandwidth to support video

Prepare Your Clients for Teletherapy

Clients need to know what to expect from you and what their teletherapy session will look like. Paint the picture of what a typical session is like beforehand and provide the details about the platform you will use. You also want to assess their comfort level with technology and answer any questions about the platform. Having a frequently asked questions (FAQ) section in your email or website is an effective way to reduce client questions and stress.

Client Dos and Don'ts:

- Remind clients that you will need to verify their information via an ID or driver's license to ensure address and identity information.

- Suggest to clients or their parents that they find a space in their house that is private, quiet, and as free from distraction as possible.

- Ask parents to make sure the child isn't in a public space or distracted by toys or devices.

- Also ask parents to make sure that siblings or other family members do not interrupt or run through sessions.

- Stress to clients or their parents the importance of confidentiality and maintaining a private area for sessions.

- Encourage the use of a computer or high-quality tablet.

- Ask clients or their parent to close out other programs on the computer.

- Have clients or their parents turn off their phone ringer and any notifications.

- Adjust the volume and check equipment in advance of a session.

- Have earbuds or earphones ready to help maintain privacy and improve sound.

- Have a back-up plan ready should the video lag.

- Practice with equipment.

- Adjust client expectations and discuss how a first session can be awkward.

- Get creative and really go the extra mile to incorporate interesting games and topics (that's what this book is all about!).

Best Practices for Providing Teletherapy Sessions

There is no doubt a lot to consider when we venture into the world of virtual therapy!

Here is a summary of a therapist's best practices:

- Operate within the parameters of your state's licensure.

- Know the difference between psychotherapy and coaching, and be clear in your treatment consent if you are practicing one and not the other.

- Have signed consent forms in place before you begin working with the client.

- Learn about and practice with the technology.

- Have a contingency plan in case of technical issues, and make sure the client has it in writing.

- Have all your supplies ready and accessible.

- Remind clients that recording is not allowed.

- Be clear about the boundaries of a session, including who is supposed to be there or not.

- Always double-check that the client is in a confidential location, and be aware of anyone else's presence.

- Turn off distractions on your computer or phone.

- Make sure informed treatment consents are in place.

- Discuss your fees up front, including any charges for contact between regularly scheduled appointments,

- such as phone calls, emails, and texts.

- Have a written policy about emailing and texting.

- Predetermine whether insurance will cover the services provided as well as the client's/parents responsibility regarding insurance reimbursement.

- Make sure you have provided your "Cancellation/No-Show Policy."

- Dress professionally during virtual sessions.

- Maintain eye contact during your virtual sessions and explain to your clients why you are looking away when it is necessary.

Keep this recipe-style therapy activities book handy. You can also go to www.teletherapytoolkit.com/PDF for a free PDF copy of all the activity infographics contained in The Teletherapy Toolkit™ to use with clients and infographic sheets to share with parents. You just need to enter your email address and show proof of purchase, so have a picture of (or scanned) receipt ready, and you will receive a FREE copy of the activities and information sheets to use with clients.

Chapter 5 – Teletherapy Essentials
Checklists and Sample Consent Form

I recall getting my first treatment consent form a friend who got it from another friend. Along the way, that same consent form has been modified dozens of times as I learned more and more and my services changed. If you're anything like me, having something to work off of beats starting from scratch!

Recently, the father of one of my clients asked me, *"Why do I have to sign so many forms?"* I explained that I wasn't trying to destroy his eyesight, but that it was important to understand what therapy is and what our office policies and procedures are, so we could all be on the same page.

Because there is so much to consider and remember as you jump into the world of teletherapy, the following checklists provide you with a condensed version of what you read in the first four chapters. Printing these checklists out will help keep you organized and prepared for your sessions.

And now, *you* don't have to start from scratch!

Teletherapy Checklists

Therapist Physical Space Checklist—select a space according to the following considerations:

◻ Privacy: No one else can hear the conversation between you and your client.

◻ Free from Distractions: Your family can't barge in, you aren't dealing with your dog barking, etc.

◻ Noise Level: The flow of your session won't be disrupted by noises such as a phone buzzing, television, or your washer.

◻ Professional background: Whatever is behind you looks "businesslike" and uncluttered.

◻ Lighting: Your face can be seen consistently throughout a session.

◻ Supplies: Your therapy supplies are right next to you for easy access.

◻ Setup: A desk or small shelving unit, comfy chair, foot stool, etc.

◻ A whiteboard and dry erase markers.

Therapist Equipment Checklist:

◻ A technology platform that is consistent with HIPAA-compliant practices.

◻ A computer with a high-resolution webcam and enough memory to support video sessions.

◻ Computer, phone, or tablet with speaker, microphone, and camera (consider a big monitor wrist rest).

◻ An external camera or microphone (if your device does not have one of high quality).

◻ Headphones for additional privacy.

◻ Pre-planned and created slides packed with psychoeducational materials.

◻ Good lighting (such as a 10- or 12-inch selfie light on a tripod, or one that has a clamp).

◻ Blue blocker glasses to reduce the stress and activation of your nervous system.

◻ Fast internet connection with enough bandwidth to support video.

◻ A password-protected, secure internet connection (not public or unsecured WiFi).

◻ Up-to-date antivirus/antimalware protection to prevent being hacked.

◻ An application that is safe and secure (SSL or Secure Sockets Layer).

Client Equipment Checklist—ensure your client has:

- ▢ Computer, phone, or tablet with speaker, microphone, and camera.

- ▢ Headphones for additional privacy.

- ▢ Fast internet connection with enough bandwidth to support video.

Therapist Patient Considerations Checklist—determine/assess/obtain:

- ▢ The client's age, attention span, and cognitive capacity.

- ▢ The type and level of care you can provide to the client.

- ▢ Client's engagement level and cooperativeness with treatment.

- ▢ Current and past difficulties with substance abuse and history of violence or self-injurious behavior.

- ▢ Whether teletherapy sessions are appropriate and/or if in-person sessions are required.

- ▢ Parent/guardian permission and signed consent.

- ▢ The client's accessibility and comfort level with technology.

- ▢ Whether patient has the right therapeutic items/resources at home.

- ▢ The type of technology patient has at his/her disposal (computer, phone, etc.).

- ▢ Accessibility to privacy during a session (see below).

Therapist Patient Privacy and Treatment Considerations Checklist

You have:

- ☐ Implemented the foundational components of therapy: identify mutually agreed upon therapy goals, share written goals with the client, create a therapeutic treatment plan, and select means of measurement (pre- and post-session SUDS, Likert scale, formal ratings, etc.).

- ☐ Reviewed with parents your goals, overview of session (what a session will look like), and expectations of them, including: being clear that no one is allowed to participate in or disrupt sessions and that all recording devices will be turned off (including Alexa and home security devices).

- ☐ Confirmed with parents that a private, quiet space is available to the client for sessions, as free from distraction as possible, and identified it.

- ☐ Parents' cell phone numbers available in case you need to text them during a session.

- ☐ Identified whether client needs headphones, etc.

- ☐ Created a treatment plan with parents and client on how to handle dysregulated, upset, or volatile behaviors, as well as a safety plan if accessible.

- ☐ Ensured parents have access to the session space in case of distress (i.e. key available).

- ☐ Asked parents to check for and remove any items that could be used by high-risk clients for self-harm.

- ☐ Provided a code word to parents they can use should they need to unexpectedly discontinue a session due to an unplanned visitor or situation at home.

Therapist "Client Dos and Don'ts" Checklist:

- ☐ Remind clients that you will need to verify their information via an ID or driver's license to ensure address and identity information.

- ☐ Ask parent to make sure the child isn't in public during sessions.

- ☐ Ask parent to make sure the child isn't distracted by toys or devices.

- ☐ Ask parent to ensure siblings or other family members won't run through a session.

- ☐ Ask if client is in a confidential and private area during each session.

- ☐ Encourage the use of a computer or high-quality tablet.

- ☐ Ask parent to close out other programs on the computer.

- ☐ Ask parent to turn off phone ringers and any notifications.

- ☐ Ask parent to adjust volume and check (and practice with) equipment in advance of a session.

- ☐ Suggest accessibility to earbuds or earphones to help maintain privacy and improve sound.

- ☐ Review the back-up plan should video lag.

- ☐ Check in with the parent or caregiver to see what supplies are available to the client before you ask him or her to provide a long list of items and assess whether access is an issue or not.

- ☐ Check if parent has access to a printer—if he/she does, send PDF worksheets or information sheets in advance. If he/she does not, mail a packet with supplies in advance.

- ☐ Have a back-up plan in case the family you are working with doesn't have access to supplies (for example, send a packet, borrow from school or library, use more virtual tools, etc.).

- ☐ Practice using a higher level of verbal description in sessions (i.e. "Okay, next we are going to go to the white board. Click the green button on the bottom, then the arrow, and that will open up the white board.")

- ☐ Try to model visually as much as you can to avoid confusion/frustration.

- ☐ Work with what the child or teen has in terms of supplies and energy level. Be flexible and creative, and use movement as part of the session to maintain focus.

Therapist Client-Engagement Checklist:

Keeping a child/teenager engaged for a 45-50-minute teletherapy session can be difficult. Therapists should do their best to meet the child where he or she is, to help the child reduce symptoms and learn new ways of thinking, feeling, and behaving.

- Include two or three activities in every session.

- Make sure supplies are ready and accessible in your office and at the child's home.

- Create structure and routine.

- Keep directions simple and predictable.

- Ask the child or teen to re-explain the directions back or show understanding of what to do.

- Have a written breakdown of the structure of the session.

- Remind the parent and/or child or teen to turn off device notifications and close other open screens.

- Structure the sessions around how the child or teen processes best (visual, auditory, or kinesthetic learner).

- Modify the difficulty of the therapeutic activity based on attention level and processing skills.

- Break up sessions with different types of tasks.

- Use descriptive language and images to help with transitions.

- Go over session goals at the beginning of each session.

- Ensure a parent is accessible to support a teletherapy session if needed.

- Don't let a parent take over a session with a list of complaints.

- Use movement during every session at the beginning or for breaks.

- Get kids to connect to their body, so their nervous system is more alert.

- Pay attention to body language that indicates boredom.

- Reinforce when the child is engaged, contributes, or recognizes that paying attention is a challenge.

- Have the child earn rewards when on task (i.e. a certain amount of time to play a game).

- Get creative.

- Use real therapeutic techniques; don't just play games (see below).

- Include sensory items such as a fidget toys on your parent supply list.

Therapist Activity Decision Tree Checklist:

It is important for therapists to always evaluate if an activity is truly a therapeutic activity, or if it falls into the "fun" activity category without moving the dial therapeutically. The real question that must be answered at every session is, *"Will this activity support our treatment goal?"*

Don't get me wrong; therapeutic activities can definitely be fun. But the goal of therapy is to facilitate change. While rapport-building activities are important, they shouldn't be the only type of teletherapy activity. Both you and the client should have a clear understanding of what the treatment goals are, and just like in an in-person session, you should both be working toward those goals in every teletherapy session.

For many therapists, the world of teletherapy is uncharted waters, and planning for sessions and having the right activities may feel overwhelming. Never fear! This book is your roadmap to supporting the therapeutic needs of the children, teens, and families you are working with.

***Prior to each session:**

- ▢ Review goals.

- ▢ Review progress toward goals.

  - ▢ Evaluate Likert scale or other measures.

- ▢ Select an activity and determine:

  - ▢ Is this a therapeutic activity or not?

  - ▢ Is this rapport building?

- ▢ Decide if activity addresses therapeutic goals:

  - ▢ If yes, continue.

  - ▢ If no, then find a more appropriate activity.

- ▢ Assess success of activity toward reaching therapeutic goal.

Therapist Self-Care Checklist:

Doing therapy virtually has its pros and cons. While the benefits are many, sitting in front of a computer for extended periods of time can be draining. Here are some tips to help you integrate self-care into your daily routine.

Endurance:

- ▢ Schedule short, frequent breaks.

- ▢ Don't schedule long days of back-to-back sessions.

- Schedule time for lunch and snacks.

- Have nutrition/protein bars and nuts available for a quick "refuel" as needed.

- Stretch or do some yoga at least three times a day.

Alertness:

- Exercise in the morning to keep yourself alert and energized.

- Eat clean protein frequently and some healthy fats to fuel your brain.

- Take vitamin B12 for energy.

- Get up, move around, and release any tension in your body between every session.

Eye Fatigue:

- Take eye breaks after each session: close your eyes for a count of 10 and give yourself five seconds for your eyes to readjust.

- Use voice dictation for your notes to give your eyes a break.

- Reduce screen time outside of work.

- Lower the brightness of your screen.

- Wear blue light blocker glasses.

Lowering Stress:

- Practice meditation in the middle of your day and in the evening.

- Use biofeedback on yourself daily.

- Use EFT/Tapping.

- Practice a 4-7-8 breath several times a day.

- Use humor to lower stress levels.

- Take a magnesium bath or supplement with magnesium daily.

- Use Reiki to balance your nervous system.

General Wellness:

- Use essential oils in a diffuser.

- Use energy-clearing tools.

- Eat an anti-inflammatory diet.

- Get at least seven hours of sleep per night.

- Reduce stress in your personal life.

- ☐ Get regular supervision and connect with other therapists.

- ☐ Attend therapy sessions for yourself.

- ☐ Schedule vacations.

- ☐ Start/engage in a hobby.

- ☐ Get lots of hugs, and don't isolate.

- ☐ Remove toxic relationships from your life.

- ☐ Learn to say, "No."

- ☐ Create time boundaries.

- ☐ Always visualize the positive.

- ☐ Practice positive affirmations.

- ☐ Celebrate your wins.

- ☐ Work on your own limiting beliefs and negative thinking.

- ☐ Don't ignore body sensations—take the time to address them.

- ☐ Spend a little time in nature each day, even if it's in your backyard or neighborhood park.

Now that we've covered the essential checklists for you, here's one you can provide to your client/your client's parents to make sure your client is all set up to make the most out of your sessions.

Parent Teletherapy Checklist:

Hello parents! I want your child to have the best possible therapy experience, so setting aside a private space and time is important. Please go through this checklist to help ensure that he or she has what s/he needs.

Privacy:

- ☐ Select a space for your teletherapy sessions that is private, so no one else can hear the conversation.

- ☐ Avoid sessions in public places.

- ☐ Ask family members not to interrupt.

- ☐ Let your therapist know if anyone else is in the room.

Free from Distractions:

- ☐ Ask your family to keep noise levels down.

- ☐ Remove any non-therapy-related toys from the session area.

- ☐ Turn off other programs on the computer.

- ☐ Minimize noises such as a phone buzzing or your washer spinning since they can really disrupt the flow of a session.

- ☐ Turn off phone and computer notifications, as well as any other programs on the computer, etc.

Supplies:

- ☐ Check the supply list and make sure you have them ready and available.

- ☐ Have your therapy supplies (therapy toys, pens, paper, etc.) right next to your child for easy access.

- ☐ Print out any worksheets or handouts your therapist sent you (alternatively, if you don't have a printer, have the packet items sent to you beforehand accessible to your child).

- ☐ Have fidget and/or sensory toys available.

General:

- ☐ Arrive five minutes early.

- ☐ Make sure the therapist has your cell phone number and that you keep it near you during sessions.

- ☐ Make yourself available for the session in case you are needed.

- ☐ Let the therapist know if you at a different location than normal.

◻ Have your "code word" accessible in case there are any urgent needs that require you to stop the session quickly.

◻ Email the therapist any new information at least 24 hours before your child's scheduled session or ask to schedule a separate parent session.

Equipment:

◻ Computer, phone, or high-quality tablet with speaker, microphone, and camera.

◻ Earbuds or earphones to help maintain privacy and improve sound.

◻ Fast internet connection with enough bandwidth to support video.

◻ Adjust volume and practice with your equipment before sessions.

◻ Have the therapist's back-up phone number handy in case there are technical issues.

Next up … remember that treatment consent form I mentioned at the beginning of the chapter? Here's one for teletherapy that you can use and modify as you see fit!

Keep this recipe-style therapy activities book handy. You can also go to **www.teletherapytoolkit.com/PDF** for a free PDF copy of all the activity infographics contained in The Teletherapy Toolkit™ to use with clients and infographic sheets to share with parents. You just need to enter your email address and show proof of purchase, so have a picture of (or scanned) receipt ready, and you will receive a FREE copy of the activities and information sheets to use with clients.

Teletherapy Consent Form:

Overview:

Teletherapy-based services require access to certain services and tools. In order to participate in teletherapy services, patients need to give their consent via signature. Security, benefits, and risks of the service are explained below in detail.

What Is Teletherapy?

Teletherapy is an online therapy service that provides psychological counseling and support to patients via the internet, video conferencing, telephone, and chat.

Benefits and Risks of Teletherapy:

- Teletherapy services are delivered via the internet and video conferencing software.

- Because sessions are reliant on internet technology, there may be disconnections and other technical difficulties as a direct result of low-speed internet.

- Teletherapy services enable patients and specialists to communicate if patients have barriers such as transportation or illness, especially during the pandemic.

Teletherapy Session Communication Plan:

- Desired communication for teletherapy services is via videoconferencing technology.

- We will email you a private link to your appointment.

- Connect 5-10 minutes prior to the appointment time and check whether the internet speed, webcam, and microphone work properly and as expected.

- While we make every effort to be on time, we will notify you if we are running late. Please make sure that you are on time, as well. Sessions will be ended if you are not present within 15 minutes of start time.

- If there are connection problems because of low-quality video, low internet speed, or any other technical difficulties, your therapist will call your provided phone number.

Security and Privacy:

The software used in online appointments is protected and secure.

If patients have concerns about the security of the records that will be transmitted via the electronic record system, they should share concerns with the therapist.

My Rights and Responsibilities Under Teletherapy:

- I understand that I have the right to discontinue therapy at any time.

- I will respect any cancellation policies and give notice at least 24 hours prior to the appointment.

- I understand that there are risks, benefits, and consequences associated with teletherapy, including but not limited to, disruption of a session due to technology failures, interruption and/or breaches of confidentiality by unauthorized persons, and/or limited ability to respond to emergencies.

- I understand that during a teletherapy session, we could encounter unexpected technical difficulties resulting in session interruptions. If this occurs, the session will be ended and restarted. If we are unable to reconnect within ten minutes, please call me at_____ to discuss a possible re-schedule.

- I understand that my therapist will follow all privacy laws and will be conducting the teletherapy session in a confidential location. I will participate in my session from as private a location as possible that is also as quiet and free from distraction as possible and let my therapist know if any other parties are present.

- I understand that there will be no recording of any of the virtual, video, or phone sessions by either party. All information disclosed within sessions and written records pertaining to those sessions are confidential and may not be disclosed to anyone without written authorization except as required by law.

- I understand that the privacy laws that protect the confidentiality of my protected health information (PHI) also apply to teletherapy unless an exception to confidentiality applies (i.e. mandatory reporting of child, elder, or vulnerable adult abuse; danger to self or others; I raise mental/emotional health as an issue in a legal proceeding).

- I understand that if I (*my child is) am having suicidal or homicidal thoughts, actively experiencing psychotic symptoms, or experiencing a mental health crisis that cannot be resolved remotely, it may be determined that teletherapy services are not appropriate and a higher level of care is required.

- Because teletherapy sessions are not in person, it is important to have an emergency plan in place. I understand that my therapist may need to contact my emergency contact and/or appropriate authorities in the case of emergency.

- The emergency contact person who my therapist may contact on my behalf in a life-threatening emergency only will come to my location or take me to the hospital in the event of an emergency. In case of an emergency, my location is:

_____

And my emergency contact person's name, address, phone number is:

_____

_____

I have read the information provided above and discussed it with my therapist. I understand the information contained in this form and all my questions have been answered to my satisfaction.

Patient Name   Patient Date of Birth

Guardian Name

Signature

Chapter 6 – Psychoeducation Resources for Parents: Information, Neuroscience, and Strategies

Psychoeducation: A Therapy Gamechanger

"We've never had someone explain this to us before," Chris and Jen expressed when we talked about why their son was paralyzed by anxiety. They could never understand how Cooper was a straight-A student and involved in a ton of extracurricular activities, but a hot mess at home. His room looked like a bomb had gone off; he had piles of books everywhere; and he was as pleasant as could be to everyone else, but angry and withdrawn at home. Chris and Jen had taken Cooper to no less than half-a-dozen therapists, asked his school administrators, teachers, and counselor for help, and tried your standard garden variety of pharmaceuticals to no avail.

As smart as Cooper is, he was rigid; even when therapy helped, he consistently fell back to old behaviors, and the stressed-out Cooper would reappear. By the time the family found my center, Cooper was breaking down physically and mentally. He wasn't sleeping, suffered from headaches, and was even cutting off his friends. His parents were beside themselves with worry.

After reviewing his QEEG brain map—which shows us the health of the brain while identifying over- and underactive areas—it was clear that Cooper was under chronic long-term stress. He had anxiety and executive functioning issues, as well.

I showed Chris and Jen the regions that were affected and explained how the communication system in Cooper's brain was in overdrive. Even more importantly, I talked to them about what happens to the brain of a stressed and anxious person and how it affects his behavior. In Cooper's case, his nervous system was stuck in a hyper state, and he experienced constant looping thoughts. Even though he could hold it together all day, he broke down at night because he was basically breaking down physiologically.

When I walked Chris, Jen, and Cooper through exactly what was causing Cooper to be anxious, unfocused, and angry as well as his physical symptoms, they understood that until they calmed his nervous system down, nothing was going to be different. Cooper was going to continue reverting to the same behaviors every time life got stressful. For the first time, they understood what was happening in his brain and why he was stuck behaviorally. Each was equally important in moving forward.

After doing some neurofeedback, Cooper began the process of learning new, healthy ways to cope with stress and problem-solve with his therapist.

Psychoeducation is such a powerful tool. Oftentimes, it is utilized as part of the first couple of therapy sessions, when really, it should be part of *every* session in some way or another. When you help a person and his or her family to understand how the brain and body are affected, you show them how much power they have in changing behaviors.

This chapter includes printable resources you can use time and time again to help parents understand the issues their children are facing.

Keep this recipe-style therapy activities book handy. You can also go to www.teletherapytoolkit.com/PDF for a free PDF copy of all the activity infographics contained in The Teletherapy Toolkit™ to use with clients and infographic sheets to share with parents. You just need to enter your email address and show proof of purchase, so have a picture of (or scanned) receipt ready, and you will receive a FREE copy of the activities and information sheets to use with clients.

Breath Work Info Sheet

What Is Breath Work?

The practice of intentful breathing is the most basic aspect of self-care and stress management. It helps calm the nervous system by creating a rhythmic breathing pattern.

How Does Breath Work Improve Brain Function?

Breathing regulates our brain and body, so when our breathing rate becomes elevated, a number of physiological changes begin to occur. Breathwork impacts the autonomic nervous system (ANS), which receives information from the environment and other parts of the body and regulates the activity of the organs, often at a subconscious level. The ANS is composed of the parasympathetic and sympathetic symptoms, both of which have a direct impact on how we manage stress. The body's fight-or-flight response is controlled by the sympathetic nervous system. The parasympathetic nervous system works to relax and slow down the body's response.

When you're stressed or anxious, your breathing often becomes irregular, and shallow breath affects our ANS. Breathing deeply allows for more carbon dioxide to enter your blood, which quiets down parts of the brain—the limbic system and amygdala—which are the emotional centers that handle your anxiety response. On the other hand, slow, deep breathing functionally resets the autonomic nervous system.

What Can I Do as a Parent to Help My Child Learn How to Practice Intentful Breathing?

The best way to help your child get into the habit of daily intentful breathing is to practice it together. Cueing him or her to use breathing techniques to calm anxiety signifies the importance of it.

Using a breathing technique such as the 4-7-8 breath cycle can be very beneficial for your child or teen. The 4-7-8 breathing technique is patterned breathing where you breathe in through the nose for four seconds, hold your breath for seven seconds, and exhale from your mouth for eight seconds. Repeat the 4-7-8 breath cycle at least three times in a row. Ideally, you want to do this two to four times a day. Since this breathing calms your body and mind so much, being seated or lying down is best.

Visualization Info Sheet

What Is Visualization?

Visualization is different from meditation. It's a practice of seeing yourself being successful, achieving something you want, solving a problem, and so on. Being mindful of our surroundings and using visualization to reduce stress are techniques that have long been used to improve health. Whether your goal is to better manage stress or address a specific issue, intentful visualization is a great way to create positive momentum by getting to the core of an issue and its resolution.

How Does Visualization Improve Brain Function?

When we visualize, our brain interprets what we imagine the same way it does real-life action. We can use the power of our mind to shape our brain, as visualization can create changes in the brain's structure and neural circuits. When we imagine and have the sensory experience of positive change, successful solutions, or change in general, our brain sees, feels, and believes it to be true.

What Can I Do as a Parent to Help My Child Learn How to Visualize?

Encouraging your child to visualize by using phrases such as, "What does it look like when you X?" or "Can you paint the picture?" helps him or her to focus on positive solutions instead of getting stuck in negative thinking or behaviors. You can ask your child to close her eyes and see herself successfully doing something, and spend a few minutes intently concentrating on the visualization.

Guided Visualization Info Sheet

What Is Guided Visualization?

A guided visualization is a technique that teaches one to focus on the mind-body connection. Through the use of guided imagery, a parent helps a child to create mental images that stimulate a sensory experience: one based on the smell, taste, sight, temperature, etc. of what he or she is imagining. A practitioner typically talks a client through a visualization that is designed to address a specific issue or sensation.

Guided visualizations are used to address unresolved issues, stressors, and fears. They have been shown to improve health, wellness, attitude, behavioral change, peak performance, stress levels, anxiety, and pain. Guided imagery has been used for decades to improve immune function and even to alter the activity of cancerous cells.

How Does Guided Visualization Improve Brain Function?

When we visualize, our brain interprets what we imagine the same way it does real-life action. We can use the power of our mind to shape our brain, as visualization can create changes in the brain's structure and neural circuits. When we imagine and have the sensory experience of positive change, successful solutions, or change in general, our brain sees, feels, and believes it to be true.

What Can I Do as a Parent to Help My Child Learn How to Visualize?

Encouraging your child to visualize by using phrases such as, "What does it look like when you X?" or "Can you paint the picture?" helps him or her to focus on positive solutions instead of getting stuck in negative thinking or behaviors. You can ask your child to close her eyes and see herself successfully doing something, and spend a few minutes intently concentrating on the visualization.

For example, a few days before taking a test, ask your child to close his or her eyes and see him/herself being relaxed, focused, and answering all the questions correctly. Have him take three deep breaths in through the nose and out through the mouth, so he can relax his busy mind and body. Ask him to notice what he sees, hears, tastes, and smells, so he can make a strong sensory and visual connection to help cue the subconscious mind to believe that he will do well on that exam. Have him take a few minutes every day seeing himself doing well and continue deep breathing with him. The power of visualization is that the subconscious brain knows no difference between what is real or imagined, so if we feed the brain the positive outcome, the brain will believe it.

Somatic Experiencing Info Sheet

What Is Somatic Experiencing?

Somatic experiencing is a trauma-informed therapy that involves a bottom-up approach to resolving trauma and working with the mind via focus on body sensations. This therapy also works with memories evoked from body experiences as the person focuses on what is going on with the body. It helps to reset a nervous system that has been holding in stress and trauma, which in turn stabilizes emotions.

It helps people become more aware of their body state and have more mastery and control over what is going on in their body as they learn how to step back and observe what is happening within instead of having to constantly re-experience stress activation.

Somatic experiencing teaches people to recognize and renegotiate what is going on in the body, so they can settle that uncomfortable feeling on their own. This helps individuals to feel less panicked by better identifying body sensations and their meanings, while using tools gained through therapy to manage stress.

Somatic experiencing can be especially useful for those with compounded chronic stressors—two or more stressors at the same time—such as death and divorce. Additionally, it can be used to help break fears and phobias and treat chronic pain.

How Does Somatic Experiencing Improve Brain Function?

By connecting to the body's sensation, one can reset his or her nervous system, reaching the activation levels in the sympathetic nervous system and impacting autonomic nervous system functions which can be influenced by unresolved trauma.

Somatic experiencing is also useful for dealing with chronic stress, because the body will experience fight, flight, or freeze reactions similar to those induced by physical trauma, causing one to either be hyper-aroused or to feel low, dissociated, or depressed.

What Can I Do as a Parent to Help My Child Use Somatic Experiencing?

Core to somatic experiencing is teaching children to focus on the body's sensations, so they can make a mind-body connection to their stressors, which in turn triggers them to use their tools to self-manage stress. As a parent, you teach and cue your child to pay attention to those body sensations and help him or her work through the uncomfortable sensations. Asking, *"Where in your body do you notice it?"* is a good place to start.

Executive Functioning Info Sheet

What Is Executive Functioning?

Executive functions are central processes that are most intimately involved in providing organization and order to our actions and behavior. They are the control center of the brain that allows us to do more complex cognitive functions. Executive functions involve planning for the future, strategic thinking, the ability to inhibit or delay responding, initiating behavior, and shifting between activities flexibly.

The major components of executive functioning include:

1. Organization: The ability to gather and order information to process it and organize materials.

2. Working memory: A system for temporarily storing and managing the information required to carry out complex cognitive tasks.

3. Regulation: Being able to take in your environment and control your response to it.

4. Inhibition: The ability to stop one's own behavior at the appropriate time, including actions and thoughts.

5. Shift: The ability to move freely from one situation to another and to think flexibly in order to respond appropriately to the situation. This can be within a task or between tasks.

6. Initiation: The ability to begin a task or activity and to independently generate ideas, responses, or problem-solving strategies.

People with executive functioning issues lack situational awareness—they can't read and organize the room, space, time, and objects, and often have problems with non-verbal working memory due to lack of internal self-talk.

How Does Executive Functioning Training Improve Brain Function?

When you teach the brain to alert differently, it can take action differently. Executive functioning is a complex cognitive process that impacts all your thinking. By starting with visualizing an outcome and working backward, we get the brain in an active state and are therefore more able to be engaged in learning and processing.

Most planning occurs in a different place in the brain than from where it is executed. By teaching how to visualize the finished product, one can plan steps, gather materials, and complete tasks more efficiently. Doing so allows us to address difficulties with time management, teaching novel concepts, calendar planning, and long-term assignment planning.

What Can I Do as a Parent to Help My Child Improve His/Her Executive Functioning?

Teaching and cuing your child to visualize the end product is the single most important thing a parent can do to help turn a child's executive functioning around.

EFT/Tapping Info Sheet

What Is EFT/Tapping?

Emotional Freedom Technique (EFT), also known as "tapping," works by tapping on different meridian points of the body while simultaneously making statements that are designed to change one's thinking, reduce discomfort, and release body sensations. With tapping, individuals are able to release negative emotions, regulate and process emotions more easily, and avoid becoming so triggered or activated by them.

With EFT, you begin by identifying negative emotions or sensations, and then tap on the meridian points. You start by focusing on a set-up statement while tapping. Next, you check in with yourself about the intensity of your fear or stressor (or do a SUDS check in). You begin at the side of the hand, saying the set-up statement three times, and then tap through nine different meridian points. As you tap through the points, you repeat your set-up statement while tapping three to five times on each meridian point. You cycle through one to two times, and then check in with yourself again about how intense your fear or stressor feels. The goal is to bring the intensity down.

For children, EFT can be used to address stressors or fears like being afraid of the dark. It is also helpful in dealing with perfectionism and can even be used to help with pain, as pain is often somatic and can be caused by emotions as well.

How Does EFT/Tapping Improve Brain Function?

Tapping allows the brain and body to release stress and negative emotions and to calm and regulate the Central Nervous System (CNS). People clear energy blocks by tapping on their stuck emotions, thereby moving information from the subconscious to the conscious. EFT is effective in removing stressors stuck in the emotional center of the brain, the amygdala, without causing individuals to relive them.

Stressful experiences and negative emotions can disrupt the path of energy in neurons, so tapping on meridian points can release blocked energy and allow proper energy flow to open up again. When you're able to bring the intensity of the emotions down, it also becomes easier to talk through emotions and experiences, and positive self-affirmations become more effective.

What Can I Do as a Parent to Help My Child Use EFT/Tapping?

After helping your child create a set-up statement, you can help him or her reduce the intensity of emotions or stressors that come up. Children are very open. Generally speaking, they aren't as held back by limiting beliefs, so they are open to the process and respond quickly to EFT/Tapping. When a younger child is feeling dysregulated, it can be helpful for parents to hold him or while gently tapping up and down the spine, which is often calming. Teaching these skills early on can help in normalizing tapping in later years as an effective coping mechanism. There are also ways to activate the meridian points discreetly, which can be helpful for school or work.

EFT Tapping Points

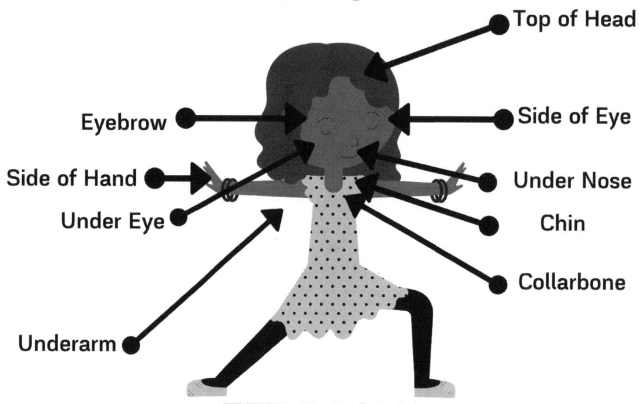

Top of Head

Side of Eye

Under Nose

Chin

Collarbone

Eyebrow

Side of Hand

Under Eye

Underarm

EFT BASICS

- Identify the problem that you are facing.
- Determine what level you are at on a scale of 1 to 10.
- Set up the statement, "Even though, I have X, I love and accept myself."
- Tap the points and complete three full cycles.
- Re-evaluate your level.

www.childrensmentalhealth.com

Exposure Response and Prevention Therapy for Obsessive-Compulsive Disorder (OCD) Info Sheet

What Is ERP Therapy?

Exposure response and prevention therapy (E/RP or ERP Therapy) is a combination of exposure therapy and cognitive behavioral therapy (CBT) that gradually exposes people to their trigger, so they learn how to be uncomfortable to the point where they can ignore the trigger. People are gradually and systematically exposed to their fears in a safe environment. ERP is proven to reduce intensity of obsessions and frequency of compulsions by empowering one to "talk back" to his or her anxiety and learn to tolerate the uncomfortable feelings and anxiety.

How Does ERP Improve Brain Function?

Before ERP begins, deep psychoeducation about how OCD impacts the brain and behavior is essential for both the child or teen and parent. Understanding the neuropsychological mechanisms of anxiety and OCD helps both the child and his or her family to move forward in therapy, because they understand the neuroscience behind how the habit forms, and how to use that science to "unlearn" obsessions and compulsions.

It teaches a child:

- How to manage thoughts and triggers.
- Skills to take back control over thoughts.
- How to break the cycle of seeking reassurance and repeated behaviors.
- About what is actually happening in the brain.

What Can I Do as a Parent to Help My Child with OCD?

Family members are involved in the process of gradual exposures at home while learning how to avoid accommodating the child's obsessional thinking, compulsive behaviors, and rituals. Parents help to increase tolerance to uncomfortableness by helping their child build coping skills and change their responses to anxiety.

Picky Eaters 101 Info Sheet

Powering up our children's and teen's brain with nutrient-dense food is a foundational component to physical and mental health. When kids eat food loaded with vitamins, minerals, healthy fats, and protein, their brain simply works better, which means they can more easily focus, regulate their mood, and learn. If you have been eating a standard American diet (SAD), then transitioning to a nutrient-dense anti-inflammatory diet may be a challenge, so start slowly and keep adding more and more foods. Following are Dr. Roseann's best tips for helping parents get picky eaters to not be so picky!

Shop with Your Kids

Kids and teens often become excited about food when they are involved in the shopping for ingredients for the food they want to prepare. With the clients at my center, or who I see virtually, I like to lay the ground rules first by saying something like, *"We need protein, vegetables, fat ..."* and so on. Involve your children in the entire process—from thinking about what to make (or by finding something fresh and on sale to create from there) to shopping to preparation.

Be Cognizant of How Food Looks

When we go to a fancy restaurant, they don't just toss food on the plate; they make it look just as good as it tastes. Add color by tossing in fruit, vegetables, or herbs your child likes, so it is more appealing.

Avoid Forcing It

I always say to my kids, *"Try it, and if you don't like it, you don't have to eat it."* Nine times out of ten, they wind up liking it. The fear children feel around not liking new foods can be very real. They seek having some control over what they eat, as well, so by giving them choices, you can reduce resistance.

Keep Exposing Your Child to New Foods

The belief is that it takes nine to eleven times of being offered a food for the average picky eater to be willing to try it. That means you need to be patient, because eventually, your kids *will* likely try new foods, and hopefully, like them!

Start with What They Like

Whenever you are trying to add new, healthier foods into your child's diet, start with what he or she likes and find healthier alternatives. Even though some parents go "cold turkey" with their food makeovers, doing so doesn't work for everyone. If your child loves sandwiches, for example, swap out the bread for an organic or gluten-free type and purchase nitrate-free meats. The good news is that there are some amazing products out there, and it is actually very easy to eat healthy.

Infuse Flavor

One of the biggest fallacies about healthy eating is that it doesn't taste good. For me and my family, it all starts with healthy ingredients that infuse a lot of flavor, including spices and herbs. Parents need not be afraid of cooking! Start with basic recipes that focus not just on nutrition, but on lots of flavor, too. Don't be afraid to be creative and explore different cuisines. For example, marinating meat for two to three days really ups the flavor game.

Think About Texture and Spicing

More and more children have issues with the texture of foods due to sensory-processing issues. For them, they react not to the food itself, but to things like temperature and consistency. When prepping food, you want to think about the foods your kids enjoy and build menus based on similar likes and preferences. The goal is to build from where they are comfortable.

Rotate Foods

When you eat the same things all the time, you get bored. And when you're bored, your palate narrows, and eating habits can become quite restrictive while causing resistance to new foods. Aside from boredom, when you don't rotate your foods, you can also develop food sensitivities, which can really derail health.

Invite Kids to Cook

I don't remember a time when my kids didn't cook! As soon as they could hold themselves up, I had them help me add spices into our food. And when they could stand and hold utensils, they helped cut things up and with food prep. It is really pretty simple, and when children prep their own meals, they're more likely to eat the food. It also helps them develop their own relationship with and excitement about food without a parent having to do anything besides enjoy a wonderful experience together.

Don't Keep Junk Food in the House

Here is the deal: If you don't have junk food in the house, your kids can't eat it. It is as simple as that. When you have tasty and healthy food choices in the house, that is what your family will eat. And don't worry; they won't starve, because they will have real, nutritious food available to them.

Be a Role Model

If you want your kids to eat healthy, then you have to, too. That means you don't get to have your "special drawer." Show your kids that you all love eating chicken, fish, veggies, avocado, and so on, and they will join you.

Expose Your Child and Their Friends to New Flavors

One of my favorite tricks was to make some of my best dishes when my kids' friends were over for a visit. Their friends (even the picky ones) would love the food so much, my kids would beam with pride. They came to really take pride in our healthy eating and always encouraged their friends to try new things, too. I loved hearing, *"Dude, you gotta try this!"*

Provide Choices

You can't force kids to eat spinach (although I have used a little hypnosis for that!), but you can give them a couple of choices. When we do, they feel empowered and in control. And kids are always striving for autonomy, so why not give them the power to make healthy food choices? When they feel like they are in control, they are more likely to eat things they might not normally.

Start Them Young

Who says you have to feed young children boring-flavored food? When I gave my infant rice pasta, I added in pureed spinach and garlic. I can still hear him humming with delight as he ate! We don't start out giving our kids french fries and hot dogs; we feed them vegetables and fruits, because they are filled with nutrients. Move from pureed foods to sautéed vegetables and meats with onions and garlic. There is no need to make separate meals of processed garbage! Just start them young, and see how doing so creates a love of healthy foods.

Talk Food Science

My kids know which nutrients are in most foods. Ever since they were little, I made a game of sorts out of guessing the nutrients in the food we ate. It gave them a deeper connection to the food as well as the "why" behind eating healthy. I didn't have to yell, *"You need more vegetables,"* because they already knew what vitamins A, C, D, and E did for the body and brain, and that those vitamins come from the food they eat. Keep in mind that you don't have to be a scientist to figure it which foods contain nutrients; that's what Google is for!

Focus on Nutrient-Dense Food

Most kids are eating a lot of fillers devoid of nutrients, like sugar, juice, soda, candy, sweets, bread, cereals, and so on. When you focus on giving your kids foods that are packed with nutrients, proteins, and fats, the body gets what it needs, and they will begin craving the good stuff instead of the junk. I can honestly say if my kids have the choice between a cookie or a steak, they will pick the steak every time.

Cut Back on Snacks

When your kids graze all day, they may not want to sit down and eat a healthy meal. On top of not really being hungry, those snacks may not be healthy or filled with nutrients.

Swap Out Soda for Seltzer

Everyone knows soda isn't ever a good idea for kids, right? Still, that memo is often missed! Sugar has NO nutritional value. On tap of that, it suppresses the immune system and alters taste buds. Swap it out for seltzer or fruit-flavored seltzers.

Use Restaurant Apps

When you are traveling, you can still eat healthy. Use the internet or restaurant apps to find healthy restaurants. I have been using the Find Me Gluten Free app for too many years to count. Even if you aren't gluten free, the restaurants that list themselves as such have healthier options and cater to restricted eaters.

Mindfulness Meditation Info Sheet

What Is Mindfulness Meditation?

Mindfulness meditation is a mental training practice that teaches you to slow down your inner thoughts, break negative chatter, and calm both your mind and body. Being "mindful" means becoming aware and attentive to what is happening around you as well as what is happening inside your own mind and body. Therefore, mindfulness-based strategies help to settle the nervous system and create a sense of relaxation and calm.

How Does Mindfulness Meditation Improve Brain Function?

Through meditation, one increases alpha brain waves and helps the nervous system go into a relaxed parasympathetic dominant state, which results in decreased stress, anxiety, and depression, lower blood pressure, improved immune function, decreased pain, and increased memory, executive functioning, attention, and grey matter.

What Can I Do as a Parent to Help My Child Learn Mindfulness?

As parents, we have to take a gentle, nonjudgmental peek in the mirror and ask ourselves an important question: Are *we* taking a few moments throughout the day to be mindful? Remember, we model for our children constantly. If you have not brought mindfulness-based activities and strategies into your home, now is the time to do so.

Mindfulness techniques and strategies are fun and easy to teach to children, and there are many resources available to help you do so. They are often simple to do (some require only one or two steps). Plus, children immediately experience the physical and emotional changes that take place in the brain and the body, which is positively reinforcing and motivating for them. Mindfulness techniques that incorporate movement of the body are especially exciting for children, and they strengthen the brain-body connection.

These techniques teach:

- Mindful breathing
- Mindful listening
- Mindful body scan
- Mindful movement

Play and Expressive Arts Therapy Info Sheet

What Is Play and Expressive Arts Therapy?

Play and expressive arts therapy is a well-established discipline based upon a number of psychological theories. In play therapy, toys are substituted for the child's words and play for the child's language. Therapists strategically utilize play therapy to help children express what is troubling them when they do not have the verbal skills to express their thoughts and feelings. Through play, therapists help children learn adaptive behaviors and gain tools for emotional and self-regulation, social skills, and executive functioning skills.

Research shows that play and expressive arts therapy is highly effective in improving children's emotional and behavioral wellness. It is also clear that early intervention is so critical in mental health, and play therapy is an effective tool for young children to learn new skills to manage feelings and learn to self-regulate.

How Does Play and Expressive Arts Therapy Improve Brain Function?

Play and art therapy helps the nervous system to regulate, which positively impacts emotional and behavioral regulation and subsequent responses. It also helps children put words to emotions and/or address issues they may not have the skills to communicate.

What Can I Do as a Parent to Help My Child Use Play and Art Therapy Techniques?

Connecting with your child through art and play is important in many ways: it builds an emotional connection between child and parent; it is a tool to facilitate communication; and it helps children connect their emotions to body sensations, as well as helping them connect to feelings they may lack awareness of. It is important for parents to be present and connect.

How Parents Can Build Mental Health Through Play

Have Fun

Play should always be fun. Since it is also the way children learn, it is a great opportunity to infuse learning. Through play, children can learn listening skills and turn-taking. It builds attachment and develops creativity, cognitive, memory, attentional, behavioral, sensory, and motor skills as well as social-emotional skills such as handling disappointment, interacting with others, recognizing feelings in themselves and others, self-control, affection, and positive self-image and self-esteem.

Let Kids Lead

Let them have fun and take control. Don't manage their play, because you will disrupt the flow. Play lets children problem-solve, role play, and test out being in control, which are all skills that help them in all areas of social-emotional development.

Be the Narrator

Repeat what they are saying, but don't criticize or question. Ignore behaviors such as whining or over-silliness.

Kids love when adults repeat what they are saying, because they feel attended to, which helps them build strong listening skills.

Use Feeling Words

Concentrate on feeling words that come up by repeating your child's statements. This will help alert them to emotions and help them become able to better label and understand their own and other's emotions.

Use Toys That Encourage Free Play

Toys like LEGOs or markers allow for children to be creative, which helps with the flow of thoughts and ideas as well as emotions. Unstructured play helps children to understand emotions, develop social skills, and explore physical characteristics, as well as build self-control.

Help Them Build Self-Control

While your child is having fun, play is also an opportunity for kids to build self-control. Parents can reinforce the play behaviors that demonstrate self-control (*"Bunny is using the blocks so nicely with his brother!"*), and they can simply model desired behaviors while playing (as in by showing your child how the two puppies are waiting their turn, etc.).

Fun Play Activities

Play and development go hand in hand! Ordinary household materials such as beads, rice, or dry pasta can easily turn into engaging and super-fun activities for you and your children. Scooping, sorting, or even shaking items in a bottle can provide children with sensory stimulation, motor development, and a creative outlet.

Cognitive Behavioral Therapy Info Sheet

What Is Cognitive Behavioral Therapy (CBT)?

CBT is a type of psychotherapy that emphasizes changing thinking patterns. Core principles of CBT are that issues and psychological problems are based on faulty or unhelpful ways of thinking and learned patterns of unhealthy behavior, and that one can learn better ways of coping with distress and/or problems, which will relieve symptoms.

CBT doesn't just address faulty ways of thinking, but also behaviors. It emphasizes learning to calm one's mind and body and facing fears instead of avoiding them. It also emphasizes role-playing, or other ways of practicing working out a problem, to assist independent problem-solving and confidence-boosting.

Even though traditional talk therapy has been shown to be clinically effective, it should not be the first therapy for a highly distressed or stressed individual or child. Talk therapy relies on rational thinking, so with the absence of a regulated nervous system, talk therapy is not only frequently ineffective, but it can actually contribute to further activation of the nervous system.

How Does Cognitive Behavior Therapy (CBT) Improve Brain Function?

For people who aren't activated by talk therapy, CBT can be a valuable tool for examining limiting beliefs, negative thoughts, or behaviors that get in the way of emotional, social, behavioral, and physical health. Role-playing helps a person see him or herself as successful while improving self-confidence.

What Can I Do as a Parent to Help My Child with Cognitive Behavioral Therapy (CBT)?

Being mindful of the statements a child makes, reinforcing positive statements, and helping a child who is negative or "stuck" to switch the dialogue is important. Role modeling positive statements, stress management, flexibility, and being kind to oneself is very important for children of all ages.

Anxiety Info Sheet

What Is Anxiety?

Stress is a healthy and natural response to challenges or frustrations. Anxiety, however, interferes with our daily functioning, because the anxious feelings or behavioral symptoms are disproportionate to the real or imagined worry or issue. It prevents children from concentrating in school, and even causes them to avoid talking to others or leaving the house. The source, whether real or imagined, can create significant issue causing distress. At this point, anxiety becomes a disorder. Since anxiety lingers, children or teens often experience looping or spinning thoughts, as well as uncomfortable body sensations such as shortness of breath, muscle tension, headaches, stomach aches, etc.

How Does Anxiety Affect Brain Function?

When we are under stress, these brain structures jump into action and prepare for a crisis, which then triggers the fight-or-flight response. The amygdala and hippocampus play a major role in emotional regulation and stress responses. They are part of the hypothalamic pituitary adrenal axis that can cause the CNS to react strongly to stimuli. The amygdala overrides the prefrontal cortex when involved with the fight-or-flight system. Without good prefrontal control, the amygdala hijacks the brain. That means we react in less-rational ways, because the brain has gone into survival mode. Calming the CNS is critical in reducing anxiety and depression.

What Can I Do as a Parent to Help My Child with Anxiety?

Follow Dr. Roseann's **It's Gonna Be OK**™ eight pillars of foundational health: daily self-care strategies, nutrition, nutrients and supplements, lifestyle support for genetic mutations, increased detoxification, improving sleep, using proven holistic therapies, and positive parenting. Focusing on the foundational pieces is so important for symptom reduction and reversal. For more information on the eight pillars, check out Dr. Roseann's **It's Gonna Be OK**™ book and the parent course, **The Get Unstuck Program**™: **The Step by Step Way to Change Your Child's Mental Health**, here: www.childrensmentalhealth.com/courses.

Being a role model for stress management and self-care is important. Emphasis on teaching and supporting your child's ability to manage his or her own stress is essential. Don't ignore the signs of anxiety; seek help from a licensed mental health professional. Proven natural techniques such as psychotherapy, neurofeedback, and biofeedback can really turn things around for an anxious child or teen.

Attention-Deficit Hyperactivity Disorder Info Sheet

What Is Attention-Deficit/Hyperactivity Disorder (ADHD)?

Attention-deficit/hyperactivity disorder (ADHD) is not simply an inability to stay focused. It is a chronic condition that affects millions of children and often persists into adulthood. ADHD children may present with a combination of problems, such as difficulty sustaining attention, hyperactivity, and impulsive behavior. They also have poor executive functioning, which impacts them academically, socially, and at home. One in 10 children will be identified with ADHD, and it is the second most common children's mental health issue.

Many people assume that the ADHD child cannot focus, but that is inaccurate. Not only can she focus, but she may also hyperfocus when interested in something, especially highly stimulating activities. This common misconception often causes parents to think, *"This kid can focus, so he doesn't have ADHD!"*

The reason children with ADHD can hyperfocus is because their brain receives the stimulation that keeps them engaged when they are excited or interested. That is why they can game for long periods of time or play LEGOS.

How Does ADHD Affect Brain Function?

Genetic and environmental factors contribute to ADHD. There are structural and functional differences in the brain of the ADHD child. Structurally, the ADHD child will show delayed cortical development, cortical thinning, reduced grey and white matter volume, and reduced volume in other brain regions. Functional differences include reduced connectivity of neurons in the prefrontal cortex, basal ganglia, and cerebellum. The frontal brain waves of the ADHD child have too much slow-wave activity and not enough fast-wave activity to allow them to stay engaged.

What Can I Do as a Parent to Help My Child with ADHD?

Follow Dr. Roseann's **It's Gonna Be OK™** eight pillars of foundational health: daily self-care strategies, nutrition, nutrients and supplements, lifestyle support for genetic mutations, increased detoxification, improving sleep, using proven holistic therapies, and positive parenting. Focusing on the foundational pieces is so important for symptom reduction and reversal. For more information on the eight pillars, check out Dr. Roseann's **It's Gonna Be OK™** book and the parent course, **The Get Unstuck Program™: The Step by Step Way to Change Your Child's Mental Health**, here: www.childrensmentalhealth.com/courses.

Obsessive-Compulsive Disorder Info Sheet

What Is OCD?

Obsessive-compulsive disorder (OCD) is a negative reinforcement cycle in which an individual experiences obsessions and compulsions.

Obsessions are images, thoughts, and urges that create distress, fear, anxiety, or discomfort.

Common obsessions can include (but are not limited to):

- Fear of being contaminated by germs or contaminating others.

- Fear of losing things or not having what you need.

- Fear of harming yourself or others.

- Order and symmetry.

Compulsions are the behaviors, which can range from hand washing to having to line items up to not wanting to touch something. This is the seeking-reassurance and enabling piece in the negative reinforcement cycle that leads to temporary relief.

Common compulsions include:

- Excessive hand washing.

- Excessive double-checking.

- Excessive ordering and arranging.

- Excessive counting, repeating words, tapping, etc.

How Does OCD Affect Brain Function?

OCD results from learned behaviors that get negatively reinforced coupled with genetic and environmental influences. With OCD, a person's nervous system is in a hyper state, which results in a reduced ability for rational thinking. An overactive nervous system is more likely to get and stay activated.

What Can I Do as a Parent to Help My Child with OCD?

Follow Dr. Roseann's **It's Gonna Be OK™** eight pillars of foundational health: daily self-care strategies, nutrition, nutrients and supplements, lifestyle support for genetic mutations, increased detoxification, improving sleep, using proven holistic therapies, and positive parenting. Focusing on the foundational pieces is so important for symptom reduction and reversal. For more information on the eight pillars, check out Dr. Roseann's **It's Gonna Be OK™** book and the parent course, **The Get Unstuck Program™: The Step by Step Way to Change Your Child's Mental Health**, here: www.childrensmentalhealth.com/courses.

It is also important for parents to avoid feeding into the negative reinforcement cycle of OCD. Instead, work to help children understand and recognize OCD behaviors. A useful tool for parents is to ask a child if he or she feels like s/he has "stuck" thoughts or behaviors when they notice certain behaviors ,which allows the child to identify and recognize when a behavior is due to OCD. Parents can often mistake OCD as a behavioral issue, seeing the problems as a power struggle or a fight, when in reality, there is true fear behind OCD-related behaviors.

Lyme Disease Info Sheet

What Is Lyme Disease?

Lyme and tick-borne diseases are complex and produce physical, cognitive, and psychiatric symptoms. One person may experience severe joint pain while another may have brain fog and anxiety; yet they both have a tick-borne illness. These symptoms can occur acutely, or they can wax and wane in a more long-term, chronic manner. Symptoms can appear immediately after a tick bite, or sometimes weeks, months, or even years later, which make diagnosis and treatment even more complex.

How Does Lyme Disease Affect Brain Function?

When Lyme disease affects the brain, it is frequently referred to as Lyme neuroborreliosis or Lyme encephalopathy. Neuroborreliosis is an infection within the brain that can mimic virtually any type of encephalopathy or psychiatric disorder and is often compared to neurosyphilis. Both are caused by spirochetes, are multi-systemic, and can affect a patient neurologically, producing cognitive dysfunction (memory, word-finding, attention problems) and organic psychiatric illness (anxiety, depression, OCD).

The causative agent of Lyme disease, Borrelia burgdorferi, is a highly neurotropic organism that can not only produce neurologic disease but can also remain dormant within the central nervous system (CNS) for long periods—even months or years. It is an evolved pathogen that uses several strategies to survive in both human and animal hosts, including utilizing a screw-like mechanism that allows the bacteria to embed in the cell's membrane.

There are multiple ways in which Lyme disease affects the brain and body and produces changes in the CNS that lead to mental health issues. The Lyme spirochete can burrow into the brain and nervous system, causing damage within the brain that leads to long-term issues. It causes brain swelling or inflammation that leads to psychiatric issues and immune reactions to the bacteria. It impacts the endocrine system and hormones, as well. Lyme can impact any area of the brain, including the emotional center: the limbic system. The bacteria in Lyme releases toxins in the brain and body, and these exotoxins are continuously released as waste material that may cause symptoms.

What Can I Do as a Parent to Help My Child with Lyme?

Follow Dr. Roseann's **It's Gonna Be OK™** eight pillars of foundational health: daily self-care strategies, nutrition, nutrients and supplements, lifestyle support for genetic mutations, increased detoxification, improving sleep, using proven holistic therapies, and positive parenting. Focusing on the foundational pieces is so important for symptom reduction and reversal. For more information on the eight pillars, check out Dr. Roseann's **It's Gonna Be OK™** book and the parent course, **The Get Unstuck Program™: The Step by Step Way to Change Your Child's Mental Health**, here: www.childrensmentalhealth.com/courses.

If your child has a history of unexplained medical and mental health symptoms, or hasn't gotten better with traditional therapies and psychotherapy, consider infectious disease as a possible source of the mental health issue. It is important to note that infectious disease takes many forms, and that while one may have a single illness, it is more likely that one is affected by more than one infection, including strep, virus, other bacteria, or environmental contaminants such as mold.

The first step is to find a Lyme-literate medical or mental health professional for proper diagnosis and treatment. The best way to do that is to seek a referral from a trusted friend or from Lyme organizations at the regional or national level, such as ILADS, your state Lyme organization, or www.aspire.care.

PANS/PANDAS Info Sheet

What Is PANS/PANDAS?

PANS and PANDAS are two distinct disorders that result from different infectious sources but produce similar neuropsychiatric and neurocognitive issues. They are clinical diagnoses given to children who have a dramatic and sudden onset of neuropsychiatric symptoms, including obsessive-compulsive disorder (OCD), tics, or an eating disorder. Children may display a high level of moodiness, irritability, and/or anxiety, have difficulty with school-work, and show regressive behaviors.

Symptoms can wax and wane over time with intense periods of psychiatric and behavioral issues. Even after treatment has lessened the behavior, or the behavior has normalized, infections and environmental sources can cause a flaring of symptoms that can be temporary or bring on a full resurgence of symptoms.

Obtaining a PANS/PANS diagnosis can be challenging because symptoms can mimic other diagnoses. Another problem with diagnosis is that when individuals present with psychiatric issues, most practitioners aren't trained to think about potential medical sources.

There is NO single test that can diagnose the syndrome. A clinical diagnosis of PANS/PANDAS syndrome in children is based on a combination of personal history, clinical examination, and laboratory tests. Prior to a PANS/PANDAS diagnosis, other syndromes and medical and clinical issues must be excluded.

How Does PANS/PANDAS Affect Brain Function?

In PANS and PANDAS, something mistakenly triggers the immune system to attack itself. More specifically, antibodies are triggered to attack a part of the brain called the basal ganglia, which is responsible for movement and behavior. This misguided reaction can result in inflammation in the brain, triggering an abrupt onset of symptoms.

What Can I Do as a Parent to Help My Child with PANS/PANDAS?

Follow Dr. Roseann's **It's Gonna Be OK™** eight pillars of foundational health: daily self-care strategies, nutrition, nutrients and supplements, lifestyle support for genetic mutations, increased detoxification, improving sleep, using proven holistic therapies, and positive parenting. Focusing on the foundational pieces is so important for symptom reduction and reversal. For more information on the eight pillars, check out Dr. Roseann's **It's Gonna Be OK™** book and the parent course, **The Get Unstuck Program™: The Step by Step Way to Change Your Child's Mental Health**, here: www.childrensmentalhealth.com/courses.

If your child has a sudden onset of OCD, tics, or food restriction, you need to consider PANS and PANDAS. A sudden onset of psychiatric issues isn't normal, and medical issues need to be considered. Ask your child's physician to run a rapid strep test and a blood culture. If they are positive, most experts agree on prescribing antibiotics.

In addition, if your child has been exposed to infections like the flu, mono, walking pneumonia, and so on, further lab work is recommended. Literate physicians often run a panel of blood work called the Cunningham Panel™ that gives more information. The absolute ideal thing to do is to seek out a PANS/PANDAS expert, but experts are generally hard to find. Lastly, always follow your parent gut and keep searching until you find the root cause.

Depression Info Sheet

What Is Depression?

Depression is a condition in which a child has a persistently depressed mood or loss of interest in activities causing significant impairment in daily life. Depression in children can show itself as weepiness, irritability, anger, behavioral issues, loss of interest, withdrawn behaviors, fatigue, and somatic complaints.

How Does Depression Affect Brain Function?

A combination of biological, psychological, and social sources of distress lead to depression. Chronic stress states due to anxiety and life stressors can also lead to depression. These factors cause changes in brain function, including altered neurotransmitter activity and brainwave communication.

What Can I Do as a Parent to Help My Child with Depression?

Follow Dr. Roseann's **It's Gonna Be OK™** eight pillars of foundational health: daily self-care strategies, nutrition, nutrients and supplements, lifestyle support for genetic mutations, increased detoxification, improving sleep, using proven holistic therapies, and positive parenting. Focusing on the foundational pieces is so important for symptom reduction and reversal. For more information on the eight pillars, check out Dr. Roseann's **It's Gonna Be OK™** book and the parent course, **The Get Unstuck Program™: The Step by Step Way to Change Your Child's Mental Health**, here: www.childrensmentalhealth.com/courses.

Being a role model for stress management and self-care is important. Emphasis on teaching and supporting your child's ability to manage his or her own stress not only helps you, but your child as well. Looking at life stressors or possible issues that could be causing your child to be sad, disengaged, or display behavioral issues is necessary. Don't ignore the signs of depression; seek help from a licensed mental health professional.

Autism Spectrum Disorder Info Sheet

What Is Autism Spectrum Disorder (ASD)?

Autism is a developmental disorder characterized by challenges with social skills, repetitive behaviors, speech, and nonverbal communication. There are a variety of symptoms that impact social, behavioral, and emotional functioning along a continuum from low to high. The diagnosis of autism spectrum disorder (ASD) is based on identifying observed and reported behaviorally defined clinical symptoms.

Many children with ASD also have co-occurring conditions, such as sleep disorders, seizures, ADHD, OCD, behavioral problems, mood issues, etc. Co-occurring conditions are common in children with ASD and may have great effects on child and family functioning and clinical management.

How Does Autism Affect Brain Function?

People with autism process information differently than those without autism, as their cortical networks are prone to both hyper communication and low communication. Moreover, certain structures within the brain don't process information in the same way.

What Can I Do as a Parent to Help My Child with Autism?

Follow Dr. Roseann's **It's Gonna Be OK™** eight pillars of foundational health: daily self-care strategies, nutrition, nutrients and supplements, lifestyle support for genetic mutations, increased detoxification, improving sleep, using proven holistic therapies, and positive parenting. Focusing on the foundational pieces is so important for symptom reduction and reversal. For more information on the eight pillars, check out Dr. Roseann's **It's Gonna Be OK™** book and the parent course, **The Get Unstuck Program™: The Step by Step Way to Change Your Child's Mental Health**, here: www.childrensmentalhealth.com/courses.

Early intervention, particularly with sensory and social functioning, is critical. It is also important for special-needs parents to be part of a community that understands them and their children; organizations such as Talk About Curing Autism (TACA) can be a great resource and place for connection.

Concussion Info Sheet

What Is a Concussion?

A concussion is a type of traumatic brain injury (TBI) caused by a blow to the head or body, a fall, or any injury that jars or shakes the brain inside the skull that can result in prolonged injury, and in some cases, death. Motor vehicle accidents, falls, and sports-related injuries are the primary causes of concussion.

Even though most people think there is a loss of consciousness with a concussion, upwards of 90 percent of concussions do not involve the loss of consciousness. While signs of a concussion are sometimes obvious (i.e. loss of consciousness, dizziness, and confusion), other times, symptoms can appear later.

How Does Concussion Affect Brain Function?

During an impact, the brain, although protected by fluid and membranes, is pushed against the skull and can be bruised. When the membrane is disrupted in a concussion, it creates dysfunction in the brain cell. Further, damage from a concussion can alter the balance of chemicals in the brain, which impairs nerve cell function and can result in a variety of cognitive issues.

When the membrane is not working, the glucose transporter system gets disrupted, which results in a lack of energy transport into the cell. This shifts energy, resulting in a cellular energy crisis, which causes a disruption in brain function.

Further, different parts of the brain can move at different speeds, and these shearing forces can produce nerve tissue damage due to stretching and tearing. More serious injuries can result in changes in cerebral blood flow.

What Can I Do as a Parent to Help My Child with Concussion?

Follow Dr. Roseann's **It's Gonna Be OK™** eight pillars of foundational health: daily self-care strategies, nutrition, nutrients and supplements, lifestyle support for genetic mutations, increased detoxification, improving sleep, using proven holistic therapies, and positive parenting. Focusing on the foundational pieces is so important for symptom reduction and reversal. For more information on the eight pillars, check out Dr. Roseann's **It's Gonna Be OK™** book and the parent course, **The Get Unstuck Program™: The Step by Step Way to Change Your Child's Mental Health**, here: www.childrensmentalhealth.com/courses.

If you think your child has a concussion, take him or her to a neurologist or concussion specialist to be evaluated. Concussions are easily missed—even more so, post-concussion syndrome. Coordination issues after a concussion may result in an increased probability of another fall or injury, which can cause secondary injuries or prolonged-concussion syndrome, so going to a trained specialist is important in getting the right diagnosis and to avoid prolonged issues.

Learning Disability Info Sheet

What Is a Learning Disability?

When someone has a learning disability, it means he or she learns differently than most people, and that learning itself is more difficult and labored. Common signs include: difficulty in remembering, following directions, learning concepts, learning sounds and letters, reading, comprehension, expressive and receptive language, math, writing, spelling, putting thoughts on a page, organization, sequencing, efficient processing, self-monitoring, and with tests and quizzes.

How Does a Learning Disability Affect Brain Function?

People with learning disabilities process information differently than those without one, as the way their brain structures work and communicate over cortical networks differ. Research has found that learning disabilities are often inherited, and thus run in families.

What Can I Do as a Parent to Help My Child with a Learning Disability?

Follow Dr. Roseann's **It's Gonna Be OK™** eight pillars of foundational health: daily self-care strategies, nutrition, nutrients and supplements, lifestyle support for genetic mutations, increased detoxification, improving sleep, using proven holistic therapies, and positive parenting. Focusing on the foundational pieces is so important for symptom reduction and reversal. For more information on the eight pillars, check out Dr. Roseann's **It's Gonna Be OK™** book and the parent course, **The Get Unstuck Program™: The Step by Step Way to Change Your Child's Mental Health**, here: www.childrensmentalhealth.com/courses.

Parenting a child with a learning disability can be overwhelming. Receiving therapeutic coaching can provide parents with the tools they need to better support their child. Children can also benefit from direct counseling or behavioral support to learn ways to self-regulate and self-advocate. It can also help ensure that their self-esteem and emotional needs are being met.

Dyslexia Info Sheet

What Is Dyslexia?

As a language-based learning disability, dyslexia mostly impacts one's phonics and reading skills. The International Association of Dyslexia definition of dyslexia states: *"Dyslexia is a specific learning disability that is neurobiological in origin. It is characterized by difficulties with accurate and/or fluent word recognition and by poor spelling and decoding abilities. These difficulties typically result from a deficit in the phonological component of language that is often unexpected in relation to other cognitive abilities and the provision of effective classroom instruction. Secondary consequences may include problems in reading comprehension and reduced reading experience that can impede growth of vocabulary and background knowledge."*

It is important to recognize that dyslexia aggregates a variety of symptoms into an overarching disability that leads to difficulties with both oral and written language. Children can present dyslexia with numbers, letters, phonics, and writing. Moreover, since dyslexia's impact can change over time, children who are not diagnosed early may learn inappropriate coping mechanisms or executive functioning difficulties that makes diagnosing it more difficult as they grow older.

How Does Dyslexia Affect Brain Function?

Research has found that learning disabilities are often inherited and run in families. People with dyslexia have structural and functional differences in the brain in the area related to language and phonological processing.

What Can I Do as a Parent to Help My Child with Dyslexia?

Follow Dr. Roseann's **It's Gonna Be OK™** eight pillars of foundational health: daily self-care strategies, nutrition, nutrients and supplements, lifestyle support for genetic mutations, increased detoxification, improving sleep, using proven holistic therapies, and positive parenting. Focusing on the foundational pieces is so important for symptom reduction and reversal. For more information on the eight pillars, check out Dr. Roseann's **It's Gonna Be OK™** book and the parent course, **The Get Unstuck Program™: The Step by Step Way to Change Your Child's Mental Health**, here: www.childrensmentalhealth.com/courses.

Getting a formal evaluation is the first step toward helping a child who struggles with reading, whether with phonics or comprehension. Moreover, early intervention is often the key to helping your child not just learn to read, but also protect his or her self-esteem.

REPS Protocol™ Info Sheet

What Is the REPS Protocol™?

The REPS Protocol™ teaches people how to break free from stress and anxiety with four steps:

- Respirate

- Envision

- Positivity

- Stress Management

With Respirate, we teach the importance of breathwork in calming the brain and body. Breathwork impacts the autonomic nervous system (ANS) which receives information from the environment and other parts of the body (often at a subconscious level) and regulates the activity of the organs. The ANS is composed of the parasympathetic and sympathetic systems, both of which have a direct impact on how we manage stress. The body's fight-or-flight response is controlled by the sympathetic nervous system. The other part is the parasympathetic nervous system, which works to relax and slow the body's response.

When you're stressed or anxious, your breathing can become irregular, and shallow breath affects our ANS. When we breathe deeply, it allows for more carbon dioxide to enter the blood, which quiets down parts of the brain like the emotional centers that handle your anxiety response: the limbic system and the amygdala. On the other hand, slow, deep breathing functionally resets the autonomic nervous system.

There are many types of breathing techniques, but Dr. Roseann's favorite is a 4-7-8 breath. It works in making your exhale a few counts longer than your inhale, which causes the vagus nerve (which goes from the neck down through the diaphragm) to send a signal to your brain to increase your parasympathetic nervous system and decrease your sympathetic nervous system, thereby leading to a calmer state.

With the next step, Envision, we teach the power of visualizing positive outcomes. Being mindful of our surroundings and using visualization to reduce stress has become an increasingly popular technique. The intentful practice of visualization is different from meditation. Visualization is a powerful way to not only get clarity on your goals, but to help manifest them. Successful people spend a lot of time visualizing what they want. First, they hone in on their authentic purpose, and then, they create goals around it. They "see" and "feel" what they want and spend time every day visualizing that outcome. They also pair it with action around the goals that moves them toward positive outcomes. They essentially put themselves where they want to be and incorporate a sensory component of smells, feelings, and touch. They also focus on what they can control in the moment and connect to that moment even though they are visualizing a positive future event. Whether you have a goal to better manage stress or address a specific issue, intentful visualization is a great way to create positive momentum by getting to the core of the issue and its resolution.

Step three involves embodying Positivity in your thinking and words. Is your glass half full or half empty? Research is very clear that those with a positive outlook are happier and live longer. While some are born with a positive disposition and others are not, you can develop a sunny outlook with intention and practice.

When it comes to your child, the goal is to flip his or her internal and external dialogue when you catch him/her being negative. Didn't get the color paper he wanted, and now he is upset? Try saying, *"This is great! They have the purple one. I can't wait to see your awesome creativity on this."* Your child may not stop the behavior immediately, but over time with your positive role modeling and reinforcement of positive behaviors, he will. Be patient. Those subtle changes in how you view things, and how your child views things, help you both to remain positive in any situation while absolutely building resilience and reducing stressful reactions.

The final step is making time every day for Stress Management. Calming the nervous system down allows one to literally think. When your stress is at maximum capacity, your frontal lobes go 'offline,' and it is almost impossible to have a rational thought let alone react rationally. An over-activated nervous system causes children to go into a flight, fight, freeze response which explains frequent "over-the-top" reactions to seemingly minor things. So, nurturing your nervous system is critical to being able to think and react in a calm manner, so one can control his or her anxious (and even panicked) feelings and behaviors.

The daily practice of breathwork, meditation, biofeedback, neurofeedback, and yoga are proven and natural techniques and therapies that children and adults can use to effectively calm their brain and body down, so they can restore their attention, mood, and thinking, and make positive strides in how they respond to stress.

What Can I Do as a Parent to Help My Child with the REPS Protocol™?

The best way parents can support their child's use of the **REPS Protocol™** is to use it themselves to role model stress management. Making time every day for you and your child to incorporate stress management techniques will help him or her today and in the future.

Improving Transitions
Parent Strategy:
Transition Theme Song

What Is It?

This is a strategy to help children with transitioning from one activity to another, one place to another, or to stop/end.

Instructions:

- Come up with/agree on a song that will cue your child that it's time to pick up/ finish/move on.

- Explain to your child that every time he or she hears that song, s/he will complete or put aside what s/he is doing and move onto something else.

- Reinforce attempts at transitioning and completing transitioning.

- Ignore undesirable behaviors.

Improving Transitions
Parent Strategy:
Transition Timer

What Is It?

This is a strategy to help children with transitioning from one activity to another, one place to another, or to stop/end.

Instructions:

- Set the timer for a 10-minute warning, then a two-minute, and then transition to the next activity.

- Reinforce attempts at transitioning and completing transitioning.

- Ignore undesirable behaviors.

Improving Transitions
Parent Strategy:
The Walk-Through

What Is It?

This is a visual strategy to help children with transitioning from one activity to another, one place to another, or to stop/end.

Instructions:

- Walk through each step of the activity, as if participating in a play: Scene 1, Scene 2 … ending.

- Use visual details, so the child can see him/herself there—this increases the likelihood of him/her taking action since s/he can "see" what needs to be done instead of relying on an adult.

- Say, *"We are going to do X."*

- For example, say, *"We are going to the park."*

- Scene 1: Dressed and ready with shoes on.

- Scene 2: In the car with seatbelt on.

- Scene 3: Holding mom's hand in the parking lot, walking from the car.

- Scene 4: Playtime at the park (may need to specify areas).

- Scene 5: Use of timer and 10- and two-minute warnings.

- Scene 6: Hold mom's hand, walk to car, put on seatbelt.

- Final scene: Arrive at home, go inside with mom, and wash hands.

- Reinforce attempts at transitioning and completing transitioning.

- Ignore undesirable behaviors.

Positive Behavioral Reinforcement
Parent Strategy:
Reinforcing the Behavior You Want to See Marble Jar

What Is It?

This strategy uses positive reinforcement to help children understand what they should be doing. When we punish children, we are actually only showing them what they are doing wrong, so they don't learn what they *should* be doing. Through positive reinforcement, we shape the behaviors we want them to develop.

Instructions:

- Draw a picture of a marble jar.

- Have your family choose an activity all your children would like to participate in to earn marbles.

- Every time you catch your children doing something good, reward them with a marble.

- Tell your children that you will reward marbles when you need their cooperation. Example: *"Sally, if you can get your shoes on and get in the car before I count to 30, I'll give you a marble."*

- Never take marbles away.

- The earning of the marbles is a reward in and of itself, but children can earn a big prize (time with mom and dad, a toy, etc.) when the jar is full. Then, you can restart the process.

- This is a system that works well because there's always another opportunity to earn marbles, and everyone is working toward the same goal, so it's never a competition.

Managing Feelings
Parent Strategy:

Feelings Observer

What Is It?

This is a strategy for helping children manage feelings. When children feel overwhelmed by their feelings—when they feel too big to manage—they often don't have the words or the awareness to verbalize it. This strategy gives them that understanding and the words. It also helps parents remain in a teaching mindset versus a frustrated one.

Instructions:

- Focus on getting your child to connect to his or her body sensations.

- Ask your child questions when you see the signs that an emotional reaction is coming:

- *"I see you clenching your fists; this tells me you're feeling mad."*

- *"I see your tears; they tell me you're sad."*

- *"I can see you are upset by your voice/tone."*

- *"I can see your feelings are getting big right now."*

- The use of scales: faces, numbers, and hand motions are great for gaging the size of the feelings your child is experiencing. It also helps your child get a better sense of the range of his/her own emotions and build stress tolerance.

Managing Feelings
Parent Strategy:
Feelings Metaphor

What Is It?

This is a strategy to help children manage big (often overwhelming) feelings. It is important to acknowledge, normalize, and/or make feelings less scary for them. When we teach children to connect to their feelings and body sensations, they learn to tolerate and manage stress better.

Instructions:

- Use feeling metaphors to help your child understand the range of feelings we all have.

- Model using metaphors when real world issues happen with friends, siblings, yourself, or the child.

- Samples and sayings:

    - The volcano was rumbling (comparing emotions to things in nature, like tornadoes and storms, as well as colors and temperatures).

    - He is a chicken.

    - Ride the wave.

    - The kids were monkeys on the jungle gym.

    - My brother is a couch potato.

    - She is a rollercoaster of emotions.

    - He has a broken heart.

    - Her angry words were bullets to him.

    - The thunder was a lion.

    - I am an empty hole.

    - I am boiling with anger.

    - I am a ticking time bomb.

    - He just erupted without warning.

    - I am steaming.

    - I'm torn apart.

    - I am a fish out of water

    - My heart is shattered glass.

    - I am blue.

    - This is the icing on the cake.

Managing Anger
Parent Strategy:
What to Say to an Angry Child

What Is It?

Phrases parents can use to help calm angry children.

Instructions:

- Try out the following phrases:

- I'm here for you.

- I love you.

- I want to help you.

- Let me know when you're ready.

- You are mad; I get it.

- I understand.

Neuroscience Basics: What the Brain Does

Understanding what the brain does helps us comprehend why we act the way we do.

Our behavior is affected by brain structures, neurotransmitter activity, and brainwave activity. Often, we know little about what the brain structures do and how they communicate with each other.

The brain has many different parts that work together. The spinal cord and nerves (known as the nervous system) is what connects the different parts of the brain. The spinal cord lets messages flow back and forth between the brain and body. More specifically, neurons connect with one another to send and receive messages in the brain and spinal cord. Many neurons work together in each structure and impact the brain's communication. They are responsible for every decision made, every emotion or sensation felt, and every action taken. When a person learns things, the messages travel from one neuron to another, over and over, and eventually, the brain creates connections or pathways between the neurons, so things become easier and more automatic. This repeated-learning process is how habits—good and bad—are formed. Therapy is really about both unlearning unhealthy habits and learning new habits.

Brain Structure and Function

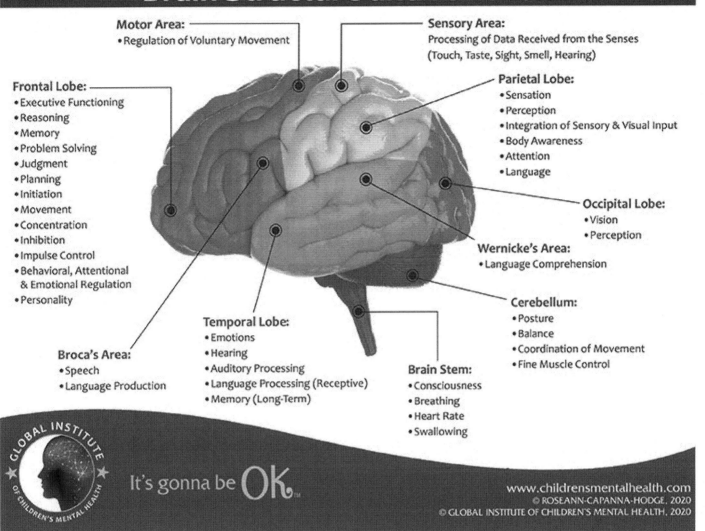

Motor Area:
• Regulation of Voluntary Movement

Sensory Area:
Processing of Data Received from the Senses
(Touch, Taste, Sight, Smell, Hearing)

Frontal Lobe:
• Executive Functioning
• Reasoning
• Memory
• Problem Solving
• Judgment
• Planning
• Initiation
• Movement
• Concentration
• Inhibition
• Impulse Control
• Behavioral, Attentional
  & Emotional Regulation
• Personality

Parietal Lobe:
• Sensation
• Perception
• Integration of Sensory & Visual Input
• Body Awareness
• Attention
• Language

Occipital Lobe:
• Vision
• Perception

Wernicke's Area:
• Language Comprehension

Broca's Area:
• Speech
• Language Production

Temporal Lobe:
• Emotions
• Hearing
• Auditory Processing
• Language Processing (Receptive)
• Memory (Long-Term)

Brain Stem:
• Consciousness
• Breathing
• Heart Rate
• Swallowing

Cerebellum:
• Posture
• Balance
• Coordination of Movement
• Fine Muscle Control

GLOBAL INSTITUTE OF CHILDREN'S MENTAL HEALTH

It's gonna be OK.™

www.childrensmentalhealth.com
© ROSEANN-CAPANNA-HODGE, 2020
© GLOBAL INSTITUTE OF CHILDREN'S MENTAL HEALTH, 2020

Positive Reinforcement
Parent Strategy:
'Catching' Children Being Good and Using Encouraging Phrases

What Is It?

This is a strategy to help children understand what they should be doing using positive reinforcement. When we punish children, we are actually only showing them what they are doing wrong, so they don't learn what they *should* be doing. Through positive reinforcement, we shape the behaviors we want our children to develop.

Instructions:

- When you 'catch' your child doing good things/behaving well, use reinforcing phrases to reward and encourage the behavior (example: *"I love how you're waiting your turn!"*).

- Reward behavioral attempts and when a task is completed.

- Give a high degree of positive reinforcement to encourage the behavior and break the habit of the less-desirable behavior.

- Ask questions that reaffirm the positive behavior and associated feeling (example: *"How good did you feel when you did that?"*).

Improving Family Communication
Parent Strategy:
Communication Strategies

Communication is the basis of all relationships. Good or bad, our children learn their communication skills through us. When we show them how to communicate and listen, we give them the tools they need for healthy relationships in all areas of their lives—friendships, family, love, work, and peers. It all starts with teaching them about listening and using kind, emotionally centered language.

Clear limits, use of emotion-centered language, and a good family community are key in establishing behaviors in children and teens.

Set Time for Communication Modeling.

Make sure you're eating together and having family meetings. If you don't practice regularly talking with your kids about the everyday stuff, they will be much less likely to come to you with the big stuff.

Listen.

Being mindful of what your children and teens are saying and/or what their body language is telling you is *so* important in the communication process. Don't make assumptions, and really hear your child out (even when you don't necessarily love what he or she is saying). This way, you're teaching him or her to do the same with others.

Have and Set Clear Expectations.

The lack of clear expectations is one of the biggest obstacles to communication. It is easy to get frustrated when you have expectations the child is unaware of.

Speak to Kids at Their Developmental Level.

If you child is young, don't blabber on and on, because it will go right over his or her head. Keep it clear and concise. Remember, teens have specific developmental needs for autonomy, to be viewed as competent, and for social connection, so keep that in mind when communicating with them. Again, be clear on your expectations, as well as prepared to really lean in and listen. Do not treat a teen like a baby/young child.

Use Positive Language.

A simple switch from a negatively framed statement to a positively framed one can really create dynamic change in a child or teen: *"I like how you apologized to your sister"* rather than, *"Why are you always apologizing?"* These two statements have very different impacts on a child. The latter criticizes, but the former reinforces the desired behavior. When we always point out what a child is doing wrong, we aren't teaching what s/he *should* do. Remember, discipline is about *teaching*, not punishment.

Empower Children and Teens with Choices.

When we give children and teens the power to make choices, it reduces their stress and anxiety. Start with easy things, such as having them come up with a list of chores they can do to earn media time.

Have Fun and Play Together.

So many good things happen when families have fun together: connection, social-emotional learning, learning in general, and communication. Children and teens connect through activities, so making time for fun activities is so critical not just for communication, but for connection.

Setting Limits
Parent Strategy:
Creating Healthy Boundaries

Children and teens feel insecure when they don't have clear limits, which can also lead to communication breakdowns and high stress for the family. It is important for parents to create and model healthy boundaries, as well as reinforce a child's or teen's positive behaviors.

Define the Boundaries.

Develop and define the boundaries, so there are no misunderstandings about your "non-negotiables." These are things like safety behaviors, aggressive behaviors and statements, and so on.

Involve Your Kids in Boundary Setting.

Have a family meeting so *everyone* is involved in setting the boundaries. When kids share ownership of the rules, they're more invested, and therefore more likely to follow them.

Set Clear Expectations.

The lack of clear expectations is one of the biggest obstacles to communication. It is easy to get frustrated when you have mismatched expectations because of a lack of clarity about each other's needs. Make a list of what you expect for yourself in relation to your kids and have your kids do the same. Next, discuss how you expect to manage these boundaries on both sides.

Be A Role Model.

If you are asking your child to change his or her behavior, then you need to model that process and behavior. It's simple: our children learn by watching what we do. Exemplify how you set boundaries in different areas of your life and how they help you. It is very important that parents practice self-care and model good stress management.

Be Consistent.

Whatever boundaries you set, *consistently* apply them with all your kids. Kids learn through consistency, so a lack thereof is confusing to them, and makes it much harder to learn the rules.

Reinforce Appropriate Behaviors.

When you 'catch' your child or teen "being good," reward him or her with positive reinforcement. This is a much more effective and powerful way to encourage behavioral change. When we criticize children, it actually reinforces the behavior we don't want, and fails to show them what they *should* be doing.

Allow for Mistakes.

Remember, your children and teens are constantly learning. Depending on their developmental level, it is perfectly normal to test boundaries. You may have to give your child a few reminders that his or her behavior will lead to a consequence he/she doesn't want.

Follow Through on the Consequences.

If your child is consistently crossing boundaries, it is time to follow through on the consequence. If you follow through in a positive manner with an emphasis on independent learning, he or she will eventually understand on a deeper level that it is important to respect the boundaries in order to better themselves while respecting others. When kids learn how to set good boundaries for themselves, they also learn the very important lesson of how to set boundaries with others.

Neuroscience Basics:
Signs of Chronic Stress

Chronic stress can derail any healing, therapy, or treatment. Our body is designed to deal with stress first and healing second. So, while you can try to outwit stress, your body will hold onto it and divert its resources to go after an unknown stress or potential "threat." You may think your child doesn't have a lot of stress in his or her life, but we *all* do. They are struggling, too, and that stress builds up in the body and can—and will—prevent him/her from reducing and reversing symptoms.

The good news is we can harness the power of neuroscience and use what we know to combat stress and get the body working, so your child can feel calm, focused, and happy while processing more easily.

Research has found that almost fifty percent of school children report and show signs of stress, and that children display their stress in a variety of ways including experiencing worry, accelerated heart rate, fear, chills, sadness, headache, and tiredness (Valizadeh, Farnam & Farshi, 2012). Chronic stress is also impacting our children's physical and mental health, as well as learning (Vogel & Schwabe, 2016).

Follow Dr. Roseann's **It's Gonna Be OK™** eight pillars of foundational health: daily self-care strategies, nutrition, nutrients and supplements, lifestyle support for genetic mutations, increased detoxification, improving sleep, using proven holistic therapies, and positive parenting. Focusing on the foundational pieces is so important for symptom reduction and reversal. For more information on the eight pillars, check out Dr. Roseann's **It's Gonna Be OK™** book and the parent course, **The Get Unstuck Program™: The Step by Step Way to Change Your Child's Mental Health**, here: www.childrensmentalhealth.com/courses.

Research Citations:

Valizadeh, L., Farnam, A., & Rahkar Farshi, M. (2012). Investigation of stress symptoms among primary school children. *Journal of Caring Sciences,* 1 (1), 25–30. https://doi.org/10.5681/jcs.2012.004

Vogel, S., & Schwabe, L. (2016). Learning and memory under stress: implications for the classroom. *NPJ Science of Learning,* 1, 16011. https://doi.org/10.1038/npjscilearn.2016.11

SIGNS OF
CHRONIC STRESS

Cognitive symptoms:
- Memory problems
- Focus and concentration difficulties
- Poor judgment
- Racing thoughts
- Constant worrying
- Obsessive compulsive thinking
- Negative thinking

Emotional symptoms:
- Unhappiness/Lack of pleasure
- Anxiety
- Agitation
- Emotional reactivity
- Moodiness, irritability, or anger
- Easily frustrated or overwhelmed
- Loneliness and isolation
- Problems with your memory
  or concentration

Physical symptoms:
- Aches and pains
- Chronic pain
- Diarrhea or constipation
- Stomach aches
- Nausea, dizziness
- Headaches
- Rapid heart rate or BP
- Chest pain
- Loss of sex drive
- Frequent illness or infection

Behavioral symptoms:
- Change in behavior
- Withdrawing from others or activities
- Procrastination
- Avodiant behaviors
- Impulsiveness
- Negative or inappropriate talk
- Use of substances for stress/coping
- Nervous or compulsive habits/behaviors
  (e.g. nail biting, handwashing)
- Over and under eating
- Sleeping too much or too little
- Sensory sensitivity

GLOBAL INSTITUTE OF CHILDREN'S MENTAL HEALTH

It's gonna be OK™

©ROSEANN-CAPANNA-HODGE
www.childrensmentalhealth.com

EFFECT OF STRESS
ON THE BRAIN

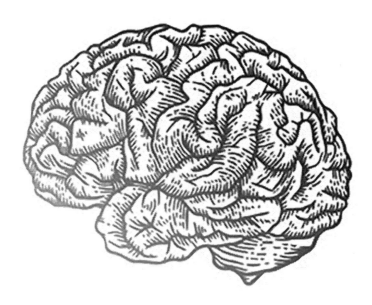

Cortisol levels spike
- Too much cortisol interferes
  with neurotransmitter function

Prefrontal cortex shrinks
- Impacts attention, learning & memory

Cellular changes
- Affects the hippocampus, which is part
  of the limbic system and is responsible for
  motivation, emotion, learning, and memory
- Autophagy of cells in hippocampus

Neurotransmitter changes
- Disrupts synaptic regulation
- Kills brain cells
- Reduces excitability of neurons
  and suppresses neuron regeneration

Amygdala
- Size increases and makes you more
  receptive to stress
- Activates Hypothalamic-pituitary-
  adrenocortical (HPA) axis
- Leads to constant activation
  of fight-flight-freeze response

GLOBAL INSTITUTE OF CHILDREN'S MENTAL HEALTH

It's gonna be OK™

©ROSEANN-CAPANNA-HODGE
www.childrensmentalhealth.com

EFFECT OF STRESS
ON THE BRAIN AND BODY

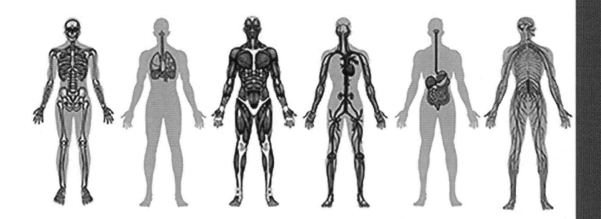

Musculoskeletal System
- Muscle tension
- Joint pain
- Changes blood flow to muscles in our arms and legs

Respiratory System
- Reduced oxygen to cell
- Shortness of breath and increased rapid breathing

Cardiovascular System
- Increased heart rate and BP
- Inflammation in the circulatory system
- Increased cholesterol levels

Endocrine System
- Impaired communication between the immune system and the HPA axis
- Increased steroid hormones production (glucocorticoids), which includes cortisol

Hormone & Reproductive Systems
- Can create hormone fluctuations
- Estrogen levels impacted
- Impact sperm production and maturation
- Conception and postpartum

Gastrointestinal System
- Increased gastrointestinal pain, bloating, nausea, & constipation
- Causes blood to flow away from the gut, slowing digestion and impacts what nutrients the intestines absorb

Nervous System
- The sympathetic nervous system (SNS) contributes to the "fight-or flight response" and signals the adrenal glands to release the hormones adrenaline and cortisol
- After the stress, the body returns to the unstressed state which is facilitated by the parasympathetic system (PNS).
- Continuous activation of the nervous system affects bodily symptoms

Immune System
- Suppressed immune function due to increased inflammation

It's gonna be OK™

©ROSEANN-CAPANNA-HODGE
www.childrensmentalhealth.com

Chapter 7 – Teletherapy Techniques for Rapport Building

It All Starts with Trust and Connection

Victoria, or Tori as she likes to be called, was one tough eleven-year-old. She had trouble getting along with others, and boy was it hard to get her to like anything! Even though I can get along with just about anyone, Tori will go down as the hardest client I've ever won over.

I started out with the classic rapport builders. You know … a therapy game or two, some Jenga, and incomplete sentences, but week after week, I felt like I'd have better luck getting a newborn to speak. She was making me sweat.

After consulting my therapist colleagues, I had a tactical plan. I had learned from her mom that she liked to knit, and guess what? So did I. So, I decided to try to connect with her through that. At our next session, I simply sat there knitting away while bringing up nonsense conversation: the weather, the latest music, etc. I thought to myself, "Ok, she is working me hard, but she isn't glaring at me with disgust anymore. Could this be working?!" This went on for the next few sessions, and slowly (and I do mean slowly), Tori started asking me questions and talking. She even smiled when I suggested she bring her knitting, which she did. I just about fell out of my chair when Tori's mom said, "I don't know what you are doing in there, but you're the first therapist Tori ever liked." Over time, we were able to dive into the many issues that impacted Tori, and whenever she faced a hurdle, she would ask to see me.

A good rapport is the basis of the therapeutic relationship, and as exemplified with my Tori story, it takes time to cultivate. As a therapist, we are the only ones who can understand how hard it can be to earn the kind of trust that creates change, and that is why building rapport is so critical. Kids need to feel safe and know they can trust you. They aren't just fun and games; they are carefully chosen techniques that build trust, so you can get to the real work of building healthy behaviors, feelings, and relationships.

This chapter contains rapport builders for both children and teens, so you can start your teletherapy sessions off right.

Technique Name:
Would You Rather?

What Is It?

An icebreaker to establish rapport with children and to get a sense of what is on their mind.

Materials:

Would You Rather Cards

Instructions:

- Using the Would You Rather Cards, ask child or teen the questions.

- Use them as a jumping-off point for dialogue.

Questions:

- What sensations did you notice?

Would You Rather Questions for Kids

Would You Rather...

Eat ice cream or pizza every day?

Would You Rather...

Be a tiger or a penguin?

Would You Rather...

Have a blue nose or purple fingers?

Would You Rather...

Live on a cloud or under the sea?

© Roseann-Capanna-Hodge, LLC 2020

Would You Rather...

Hang out with dinosaurs or dragons?

Would You Rather...

Wear your favorite shirt every day or never wear it again?

Would You Rather...

Be the President or the best athlete in the world?

Would You Rather...

Get sprayed by a skunk or stung by a bee?

Would You Rather...

Eat chips or cupcakes?

Would You Rather...

Have extra-long fingers or extra-long toes?

Would You Rather...

Be friends with a talking fish or with a talking monkey?

Would You Rather...

Be as small as an ant or as big as an elephant?

Would You Rather...

Live in a place where it is always warm or always cold?

Would You Rather...

Be the coolest person in the world or the smartest person in the world?

Would You Rather...

Meet your favorite superhero or meet your favorite cartoon character?

Would You Rather...

Be the main character in a movie or in a book?

Would You Rather...

Lick the bathroom floor or eat a caterpillar?

Would You Rather...

Eat candy or popcorn?

Would You Rather...

Skip or do jumping jacks whenever you see your friend?

Would You Rather...

Play in the snow or in the rain?

Would You Rather...

Be a talented painter or a talented singer?

Would You Rather...

Eat a cup of ketchup or a cup of mustard by itself?

Would You Rather...

Have an extra eye on your nose or a finger sticking out of your forehead?

Would You Rather...

Be a unicorn or fairy?

Would You Rather...

Have to whisper or sing your words when you talk?

Would You Rather...

Fly a kite or play catch?

Would You Rather...

Have butterfly wings or dragon wings?

Would You Rather...

Hang out with your favorite celebrity for a week or be him or her for one day?

Would You Rather...

Have a magic carpet or a flying bicycle?

Would You Rather...

Be able to fly or have super strength?

Would You Rather...

Live in space or on Earth?

Would You Rather...

Have an extra Halloween or an extra birthday per year?

Would You Rather...

Kiss a turtle or hug a bear?

Would You Rather...

Wear your pajamas everywhere or never have to brush your teeth?

Would You Rather...

Eat mac & cheese or a hot dog?

Would You Rather...

Cluck like a chicken or roar like a lion after you eat dinner?

Would You Rather...

Give up sugary or salty foods?

Would You Rather...

Find hidden treasure or rescue someone who needs help?

Would You Rather...

Clean the kitchen or your room?

Would You Rather...

Teach music or gym class?

Would You Rather...

Go to the park or the zoo?

Would You Rather...

Have a pet dog or a pet parrot?

Would You Rather...

Be a fireman or a police officer?

Would You Rather...

Wear a superman or batman suit?

Would You Rather...

Eat fruits or vegetables?

Would You Rather...

Go to the doctor or to school?

Would You Rather Questions for Teens

Would You Rather...

Live in a busy city or a quiet town?

Would You Rather...

Be a teacher or a business owner?

Would You Rather...

Win a million dollars and keep it all or win two million and share?

Would You Rather...

Read minds or have healing powers?

Would You Rather...

Discover aliens or build a time machine?

Would You Rather...

Live 100 years in the past or 100 years in the future?

Would You Rather...

Fight one giant duck or 100 small ducks at once?

Would You Rather...

Travel the world or relax at home?

Would You Rather...

Eat your favorite food for every meal or never eat it again?

Would You Rather...

Eat 15 crickets or 1 scorpion?

Would You Rather...

Be known for your kindness or your intelligence?

Would You Rather...

Live in a mansion by yourself or in a house with all of your extended family?

Would You Rather...

Have to eat one PB & J every day or a grilled cheese every day?

Would You Rather...

Be a researcher or a famous actor?

Would You Rather...

Speak every language or travel to every country?

Would You Rather...

Lick your phone or the floor of a gas station bathroom?

Would You Rather...

Sit out on the winning team or be the leader of the losing team?

Would You Rather...

Live in a rain forest or on a deserted island?

Would You Rather...

Be a pilot or the captain of a ship?

Would You Rather...

Be able to talk to animals or cure sickness?

Would You Rather...

Move around by running backwards or hopping on one foot?

Would You Rather...

Be a famous talk show host or a famous actor?

Would You Rather...

Go to a concert or to your favorite restaurant?

Would You Rather...

Have 10 siblings or 0 siblings?

Would You Rather...

Drink a cup of hot sauce or a cup of lemon juice?

Would You Rather...

Go tubing on a lake or on a snowy mountain?

Would You Rather...

Be the funniest person in the world or the most talented?

Would You Rather...

Be 10 years old or 30 years old for the rest of your life?

Would You Rather...

Design your own phone case or design your own app?

Would You Rather...

Eat moldy berries or drink spoiled milk?

Would You Rather...

Go bungee jumping or rock climbing?

Would You Rather...

Have magic but you can't use it or have wings but can't fly?

Would You Rather...

Be able to stop time or shrink and grow whenever you want?

Would You Rather...

Never have to get a haircut or never have to go to the dentist?

Would You Rather...

Smell like wet dog or sweat fruit punch?

Would You Rather...

Drive a convertible or a jeep?

Would You Rather...

It be hot and you have a cold drink or it be cold and you have a warm drink?

Would You Rather...

Visit France or Italy?

Would You Rather...

Have toilet paper stuck to your shoe or gum in your hair?

Would You Rather...

Play paint ball or dodgeball?

Would You Rather...

Get bitten by 5 spiders or take a bath with 100 worms?

Would You Rather...

Always be sunburned or always be shivering?

Would You Rather...

Play the drums or the violin?

Would You Rather...

Sit on the beach or swim in the water?

Would You Rather...

Have a pool or a bowling alley in your house?

Would You Rather...

Need a flashlight to see or never have sunglasses when you need them?

Technique Name:
Minecraft Questions

What Is It?

An icebreaker to establish rapport with children and help them connect to their body by paying attention to body sensations in order to learn to recognize the signs the body provides about how one feels.

Materials:

Body-Sensation Words (see pages 322-323)

Instructions—ask the following questions:

- Have you played Minecraft?

- What are you building right now?

- How do you build a nether portal?

- What is your favorite pig or creeper?

- Has anything ever happened on Minecraft that bothered you?

Technique Name:
Draw Your Family

What Is It?

An icebreaker to establish rapport.

Materials:

Paper, markers, crayons

Instructions:

- Have the child draw a picture of his or her family, including pets.

Questions:

- When was the last time something funny happened?

- What is everyone's favorite color/thing to eat?

- Do you have any family traditions?

- What do you like to do as a family?

Technique Name:
Magic Wand

What Is It?

An icebreaker to establish rapport with children and get a sense of what is on their mind.

Materials:

None

Instructions—ask the following questions:

- If you could have any three wishes, what would they be?

- Why did you choose each one?

- Use this as a jumping-off point for dialogue.

Questions:

- What sensations did you notice?

- Did any thoughts come up for you?

Technique Name: Superpowers

What Is It?

An icebreaker to establish rapport.

Materials:

None

Instructions—ask the following question:

- If you could have any three superpowers, what would they be and why?

- Use this as a jumping-off point for dialogue.

Questions:

- What sensations did you notice?

- What would you do with those superpowers?

- What is the favorite part about those superpowers?

- How would you help people with your superpowers?

Technique Name:
Earn a LEGO Questions

What Is It?

An icebreaker to establish rapport. Children can earn one LEGO, sticker, or bead every time they answer a question. They get a storage bag to put earnings in.

Materials:

Storage bag

Legos

Stickers or beads

Instructions:

- At the first session and at the beginning of each session, ask the child three questions that s/he can earn a reward for answering.

Questions to Ask:

- Ask questions that tap into feelings, problem-solving, and thinking.

- "How did you feel when you are doing your favorite thing? What is your favorite thing?"

- "When are you happiest? Sad? Irritated? Mad?"

- "What is the most frustrating thing for you at home (school or playground)?"

- "What stresses you out?"

- "How do you deal with stress?"

- "When do you feel most successful?"

- "What are three things I should know about you?"

- "Who was the last person to make you laugh? What did they do?"

- "Who was the last person to make you cry? What did s/he do?"

- "Who was the last person to make you mad? What did s/he do?"

- "When was the last time someone did something kind for you?"

- "What is something kind you did for another person?"

Technique Name:
Conversation Ice Breaker

What Is It?

An icebreaker to establish rapport.

Materials:

Conversation Ice Breaker Cube Handout

Instructions:

- At the first session, have the child toss the cube in the air and take turns asking each other questions.

Questions:

- What sensations did you notice?

- Did it make you think of anything?

Conversation Ice Breaker

This-or-That?

⭐ Ice cream -or- candy?

⭐ The beach -or- the pool?

⭐ Iced tea -or- lemonade?

⭐ Movie -or- play outside?

Basics

☀ Age?

☀ Birthday?

☀ My family?

☀ Activities?

Conversation Ice Breaker

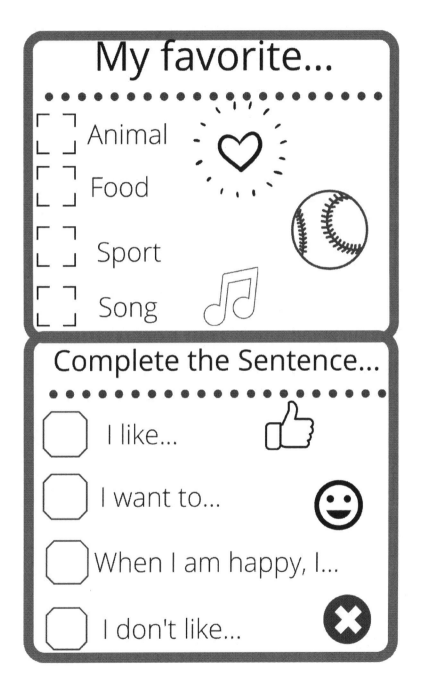

© Roseann-Capanna-Hodge, 2020
© Global Institute of Children's Mental Health, 2020

Technique Name:
I Spy

What Is It?

An icebreaker to establish rapport.

Materials:

None

Instructions:

- The child and clinician each take turns searching for objects. Each person keeps the object a surprise but gives clues to the other so he or she can guess what it is.

- Make a rule that it has to be visible in the room you are in.

- Say, "I spy with my little eye something X (color, texture)."

- Use it as a jumping-off point for dialogue.

Questions:

- What sensations did you notice?

- Did it make you think of something or remind you of a memory?

Technique Name:
Show-and-Tell

What Is It?

An icebreaker to establish rapport.

Materials:

None

Instructions:

- Tell the child you want to learn more about him or her, so you will be playing Show-and-Tell.

- Tell the child that s/he has one minute to find:

    1. One thing s/he loves.

    2. One thing that makes him/her laugh.

    3. One thing that makes him/her feel strong.

- Use this as a jumping-off point for dialogue.

Questions:

- What sensations did you notice?

Technique Name:
Simon Says

What Is It?

An icebreaker to establish rapport.

Materials:

None

Instructions:

- In this game, the leader is known as "Simon."

- He/she makes commands that others must listen to and follow until a mistake is made. When that happens, switch places.

- The child stands up and faces the screen.

- Simon begins calling out commands.

- If Simon begins the sentence with *"Simon says,"* everyone is required to do the action.

- If Simon does not begin with *"Simon says,"* the players should not complete the action.

Questions:

- What sensations did you notice?

Technique Name:
Name 10 Categories Game

What Is It?

An icebreaker to establish rapport with children/teens and to determine how they process information.

Materials:

Name 10 Categories Game Handout

Timer

Instructions:

- In this game, have the child or teen list 10 things in a specific category in a one-minute timeframe.

Questions:

- What sensations did you notice?

Name 10 Categories Game Handout

• Things you eat	• Towns
• Animals	• Countries
• Sports	• Musical Instruments
• Movie titles	• Cartoon characters
• Clothing	• Things that are square
• Games	• Heroes
• School supplies	• Breakfast foods
• Colors	• Hobbies
• Fruits	• Parts of the body
• Flowers	• School subjects
• Ice cream flavors	• Things in the sky
• Kinds of candy	• Pizza toppings

Technique Name:
Two Truths and One Lie

What Is It?

An icebreaker to establish rapport.

Materials:

None

Instructions:

- In this game, take turns offering three statements about yourself.

- Two of these statements must be facts, or "truths," and one must be a lie.

- You each try to guess which statement is the lie.

Questions:

- What sensations did notice?

- What clues did you pick up?

- What did you like or didn't like about this?

Technique Name:
Ice Breaker Questions

What Is It?

An icebreaker to establish rapport.

Materials:

Ice Breaker Questions Handout

Instructions:

- Select questions from the Ice Breaker Questions Handout to ask.

- Take turns asking each other questions until the dialogue begins to flow.

Questions:

- What sensations did you notice?

Ice Breaker Questions

- Do you love learning from home, or would you rather be in school?
- What's the hardest part about working virtually for you? The easiest?
- Do you have a dedicated learning space at home?
- Show us your learning space!
- Where do you work most frequently? At home? Your office? Your kitchen table? The backyard? Your bed?
- Be honest; how often do you study in bed?
- What did you eat for breakfast?
- What does your morning routine look like when working from home?
- What's your number one tip for combating distractions when working from home?
- How do you stay productive and motivated working virtually?
- What does your typical learning-from-home "uniform" look like?
- What do you drink each morning?
- Are you an early bird or night owl?
- What about showers? Do you prefer morning or night?
- What's one thing we could do to improve our virtual meetings?
- What's your favorite flower or plant?

- What's the best piece of advice you've ever been given?
- What do you want to be remembered for?
- What is your favorite item you've bought this year?
- What would be the most surprising scientific discovery imaginable?
- What is your absolute dream job?
- What would your talent be if you were Miss or Mister World?
- What would the title of your autobiography be?
- Say you're independently wealthy and don't have to work; what would you do with your time?
- If you had to delete all but three apps from your smartphone, which ones would you keep?
- What is your favorite magical or mythological animal?
- What does your favorite shirt look like?
- Who is your favorite Disney hero or heroine? Would you trade places with him or her?
- What would your dream house be like?
- If you could add anyone to Mount Rushmore, who would it be; why?
- You're going to sail around the world; what's the name of your boat?

Ice Breaker Questions

General

- What Netflix show did you like to watch?
- If you had to delete three apps from your phone, which would they be?
- If you could have a superpower, what would it be?
- Which Disney character is most like you? Why?
- What was your favorite cartoon character growing up?
- Which musical artist do you wish you could see in concert?
- Have you ever been told you looked like someone famous? If so, who?
- What emoji do you like to use the most?
- What game is your favorite to play?
- What's the best show on TV right now?
- If someone took a candid picture of you, what would they find you doing in it?
- What's the best piece of advice you've ever heard?
- What's your go-to song?
- How would you best describe yourself in three words?
- Who's the smartest person you know?
- If you could go on a dream vacation, where would you go?

Would You Rather

- Would you rather travel back in time or forward into the future?
- Would you rather go to school more hours over less days, or less hours over more days?
- Would you rather have a rewind or a pause button for your life?
- If you could invite one person (living or dead) to dinner, who would you?
- Would you rather have powers of invisibility or able to fly?
- Would you rather only be able to use the internet for one hour a week – or only be able to go outdoors for one hour a week?
- Would you rather always know when someone is lying, or always get away with lying?
- Would you rather be able to speak with animals or be able to speak all foreign languages in the world?
- If you could replace the actor in any film, who would you replace and with who?
- If you were stranded on a desert Island – what three things and three people would you take?
- What is your biggest pet peeve?

Technique Name:
20 Questions

What Is It?

An icebreaker to establish rapport.

Materials:

None

Instructions:

- In this game, you choose a subject (object), but do not reveal it.

- All other players are "questioners." You take turns asking the person who chose the subject questions about it which can be answered with a simple "Yes" or "No."

- Questions continue up to a total of 20 to guess the subject.

Questions:

- What sensations did you notice?

Technique Name:
What's Your Astrological Sign?

What Is It?

An icebreaker to establish rapport.

Materials:

12 Astrology Signs Handout

Instructions:

- Teach teens about astrology and use information about their astrological sign to better understand themselves.

- Explore if they feel that astrological signs help to understand personality features of themselves or others in their lives.

Questions:

- What sensations did you notice?

12 Astrology Signs Handout

Aries
(March 21-April 19)

Aries love to be number one. Bold and ambitious, Aries dive headfirst into even the most challenging situations. Aries are very energetic and constantly have to keep busy.

Taurus
(April 20-May 20)

Taurus are faithful and patient. They enjoy relaxing in the serene. Taurus place a high value on stability and security.

Gemini
(May 21-June 20)

Gemini is the most versatile and vibrant sign. They are often mentally gifted and well-informed. They try to gather as much information as they can, which helps them to easily adapt to any situation.

Cancer
(June 21-July 22)

Cancerians are very intuitive, and can be both shy and outgoing. They are very protective of their loved ones. They are strong-willed and like to get things done in their own way.

Leo
(July 23-August 22)

Leos are one of the most creative and ambitious signs. They are represented by the lion and are vivacious and passionate.

Virgo
(August 23-September 22)

Virgos are delicate and sensitive; however, they can be picky. Virgos are practical and logical in their approach to life, which contributes to their success and independence.

© Roseann-Capanna-Hodge, 2020
© Global Institute of Children's Mental Health, 2020

12 Astrology Signs Handout

Libra
(September 23–October 22)

Libras strive to create equilibrium in all aspects of life. They are elegant and charming and know how to appreciate the simple pleasures of life.

Scorpio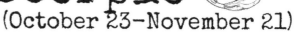
(October 23–November 21)

Scorpios have a very intense emotional energy, which makes them stand out. Scorpios know what they want and they are not afraid to work hard.

Sagittarius
(November 22–December 21)

Sagittarius people have a deep love for exploration, and they are open to anything new. They are perfectionists, and their positive attitude helps to keep them going. They rarely give up.

Capricorn
(December 22–January 19)

Capricorns love structure and order, and they are very determined. Sometimes, they need to relax and let go of their worries as they need to learn that not everything is under their control.

Aquarius
(January 20–February 18)

Aquarius has a very dominant and strong personality. Aquarians are independent and tolerant to every point of view. They can also be extroverts, which enables them to make friends effortlessly.

Pisces
(February 19–March 20)

Pisceans are able to adapt emotionally to any environment they encounter. They can be kind, compassionate and understanding. Pisces are existential and very deep thinkers.

Chapter 8 – Teletherapy Techniques:
General or Multi-purpose

Every Therapist Needs a Toolkit

When I got my first job as a therapist, I burst onto the scene ready to start making everyone "better." I learned a technique or two in graduate school, but like most programs, it was theory-heavy and technique-light. I bought every book I could get my hands on and picked the brain of my more experienced colleagues.

Therapy isn't just chit chat; it's using therapeutic techniques to help others create change. I knew you couldn't just play Connect Four all the time, but where were those techniques? It seemed like we all just had "a little of this and a little of that." I craved something more organized and useful.

After earning my second master's degree, I decided I was definitely a solution-focused therapist—not only because I worked in a school, but also because this style of counseling was chock-full of strategies. Oh, I just loved all my solution-focused counseling books! They included all kinds of useful worksheets I could use with my teenage clients, and they were well-received and effective.

By the time the 2000's rolled around, the Internet opened up a whole new world of accessible information. It became easier to find information, which was a godsend, because therapeutic book styles had changed, too. To my total geeky excitement, I could now get entire books on therapeutic strategies, even in specific subject areas.

The pandemic has thrust teletherapy out to the masses, and therapists of all ages and settings have quickly learned how to share their screen and use a virtual whiteboard like a 17-year-old. Now, this Teletherapy Toolkit™—the first teletherapy therapeutic activity book of its kind—will broaden your repertoire of techniques and tools, so you can help even more children, teens, and families.

Technique Name:
Self-Esteem Sentence Completion

What Is It?

A technique that helps children—especially those who tend to think the worst or are self-critical—to focus on things they are good at.

Materials:

The Sentence-Completion Worksheet

Instructions:

- Fill it out with the teen or have him/her fill it out independently.

- Review answers together.

Questions:

- How did achieving X on the worksheet feel?

Sentence-Completion Worksheet:

- My friends think I'm awesome because …

- My classmates say I'm great at …

- I feel very happy when I …

- Something I'm really proud of is …

- I make my family happy when I …

- One unique thing about me is …

- I like who I am because …

- I'm super at …

- I feel good about my …

- My friends think I have an awesome …

- Somewhere I feel happy is …

- I mean a lot to …

- Others think I'm great at …

- I think I'm pretty good at …

- Something I really enjoy is …

- I really admire myself for …

- My future goals are …

- I know I can achieve them, because I'm …

- I'm naturally gifted at …

- Others often praise my …

Technique Name:
Double Self-Portrait

What Is It?

An art therapy technique that helps children see themselves and how others see them through the process of making two self-portraits. Good for children with low self-esteem, social anxiety, social difficulties, impulsiveness, or any neurodevelopmental disorder.

Materials:

Two Self-Portrait Templates

Instructions:

- Instruct the child: *"You are making two portraits: one according to how you see yourself, and the other according to how you believe others see you."*

- *"Start with how you see yourself."* (Alternatively, you can ask the child which one he or she would like to start with—especially if s/he needs to have control.)

Questions:

- What is the big difference you see between the two drawings? Then, process the response together.

- What did you think about this activity?

- Were you surprised by something?

- Did you learn something new?

- Was there anything that made you feel comfortable or uncomfortable?

- Did any thoughts, feelings, or memories come up?

- Did your body feel different when you were doing one portrait from the other?

- What positive sensations did you notice?

Self-Portrait

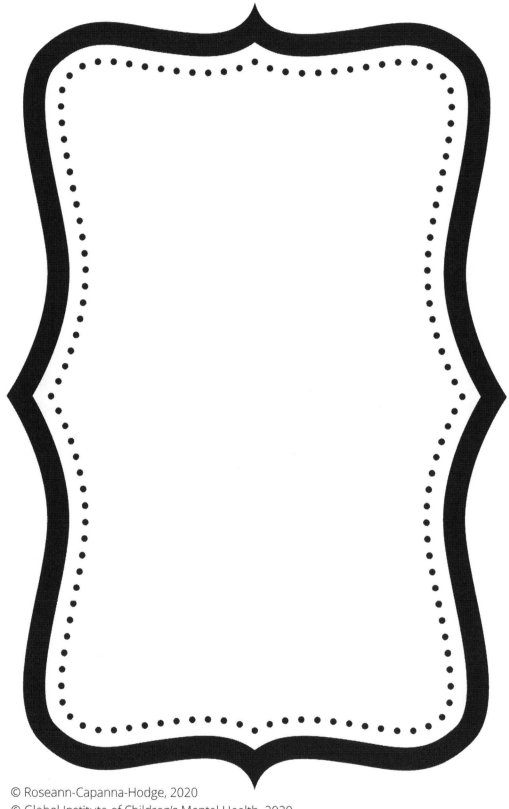

Self-Portrait

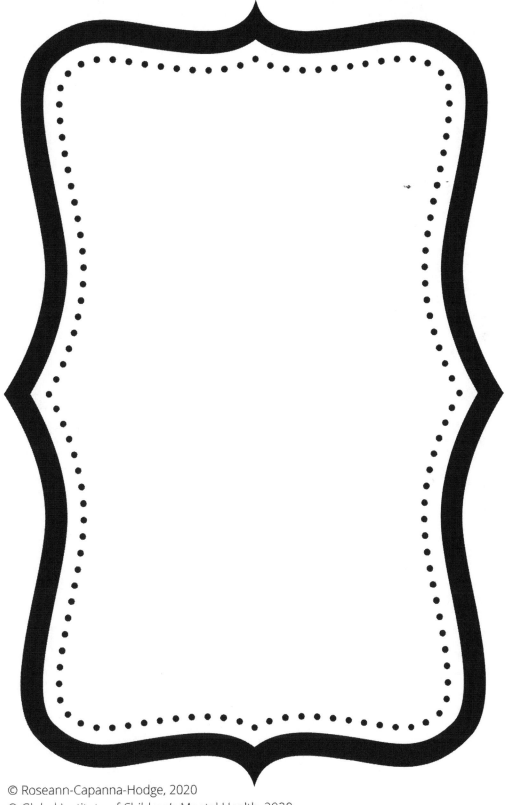

Technique Name:
Strategy Review

What Is It?

Use the whiteboard on a virtual platform or a literal whiteboard to draw or write stress tool words. This will reinforce what children can use to control uncomfortable feelings and body sensations.

Materials:

Whiteboard

Dry erase markers

Instructions:

- On the whiteboard, interactively write the names or draw pictures of the child's stress toolkit items.

- Dialogue about what works and doesn't, how the child is using them, and how often.

- Take a screenshot when finished for review during a future session and/or to share with parents.

- Pull out and review anytime a child hits an obstacle or is stuck.

Questions:

- What sensations do you feel when you use X tool?

- Which tools do you use the most?

Technique Name:
Cognitive Distortions

What Is It?

A therapeutic way to address false beliefs about self. Pair this technique with the Common Cognitive Distortions Handout and Worksheet for maximum effectiveness. This is a great psychoeducation tool, because teens love to better understand the "whys" of their behavior.

Materials:

Cognitive Distortions Handout and Worksheet

Instructions:

- Ask the teen what distortions s/he thinks s/he has.

- Review the handout together.

- Fill out the worksheet together or have the teen do it on his/her own.

- Review.

- Use the worksheet to flush out the distortions and alternatives.

Questions:

- What sensations in your body did you notice when you realized you have X cognitive distortion?

- When are you most likely to get caught up in a negative thinking pattern?

- What is an alternative to that cognitive distortion?

Common Cognitive Distortions

Filtering
When an individual focuses on the negative despite positive details. The positive details are filtered out, leaving only the negative, which become the focus points for the individual and are often magnified.

Polarized Thinking
Seeing things as very "black or white." Thinking in extremes.

Overgeneralization
Generalizations of the future based on a single event or piece of information.

Jumping to Conclusions
Making assumptions about other people's thoughts/ feelings or the future without knowing the true details.

Shoulds

Statements involving "should" or "shouldn't" directed toward the self or others illustrate a set of standards to guide behavior. When these standards are not met, individuals with this cognitive distortion become angry and/or guilty.

Emotional Reasoning

Emotions and feelings are viewed as the truth and override logic and fact. In this cognitive distortion, emotional experience is reality.

Fallacy of Change

Individuals push others to change to fit their own ideals and create happiness.

Global Labeling

Labeling yourself or an individual generally based on a singular event or piece of information. This is a more severe version of overgeneralization.

Always Being Right

Being right is the main focus of individuals with this cognitive distortion. They will go to great lengths to "win" and prove that they are right.

Heaven's Reward Fallacy

Believing that personal sacrifice will be worth it in the long run.

Catastrophizing

Viewing situations as vastly exaggerated or understated compared to their actual size. This can be seen as magnifying or minimizing situations.

Personalization

Seeing external events as personal. This is often seen as taking blame or responsibility for events outside of individual control.

Control Fallacies

Consisting of external control or internal control. External control involves an individual who believes that outside influences are responsible for the way in which his or her life unfolds. Internal control involves an individual who believes that he or she is responsible for the feelings of those around him or her.

Fallacy of Fairness

Individuals judge events based on fairness and are under the impression that others will not agree with their assessments of fairness.

Blaming

Placing responsibility on others for personal pain or placing responsibility on the self for external events.

Cognitive Distortions Worksheet

Sensation	Anxiety Rating	Automatic Thought	Behavior	Identify Distortions	Challenge Distortion	Anxiety Rating

Technique Name:
Coping Statements

What Is It?

A list of encouraging and positive statements that are used to replace negative and inaccurate thoughts. Therapists, teachers, and parents can use these coping statements to encourage children or teens to cope with and learn to tolerate stress and uncomfortable emotions and sensations. Use in a session to help a child or teen shift from negative to positive thinking, and/or assign as homework for the child/teen and his/her parent to practice.

Materials:

Coping Statements Handout

Coping Strategies Worksheet

Instructions:

- Review the statements together.

Questions:

- What happens to your thoughts when you shift your language from negative to positive?

- What happens to your body when you shift your language from negative to positive?

- Which statements do you use the most?

- When are you most likely to get caught up in a negative thinking pattern?

Coping Statements Handout

General Coping Statements:

- Stop, and breathe; I can do this.

- This will pass.

- This feeling will go away.

- I can be anxious/angry/sad and still deal with this.

- I have done this before, and I can do it again.

- This feels bad; it is a normal body reaction. It will pass.

- This feels bad, and feelings are very often wrong.

- These are just feelings; they will go away.

- This won't last forever.

- I can feel bad and still choose to take a new and healthy direction.

- I don't need to rush; I can take things slowly.

- I have survived before; I will survive now.

- I feel this way because of my past experiences, but I am safe right now.

- Things are not as bad as I am making them out to be.

- I'm stronger than I think.

- It's okay to feel this way; it's a normal reaction.

- Right now, I am not in danger. Right now, I`m safe.

- My mind is not always my friend.

- Thoughts are just thoughts. They are not necessarily true or factual.

- I will learn from this experience, even if it seems hard to understand right now.

- I choose to see this challenge as an opportunity.

- I can use my coping skills and get through this.

- I can learn from this, and it will be easier next time.

- Keep calm and carry on.

- Concentrate on what I have to do.

- I know I am going to be OK.

- The feelings always pass.

- Relax and think positively.

- One step at a time.

- I coped with that.

- I achieved that; I am getting better.

- I handled that; it should be easier next time.

- I can be pleased with the progress I'm making.

- I did that well.

- If I keep this up, I'm going to get really good at this.

Coping Statements for Anger:

- Don't sweat the small stuff.

- It's not worth getting mad about.

- Things are not as bad as I am making them out to be.

- I won't take this personally.

- I am going to close my eyes, breathe, and take a moment to think this through.

- I can breathe through this.

- I ignored this problem or person before and got through it.

- I am in charge, not my anger.

- Getting angry isn't going to help.

- I can handle this and stay in control.

- I can only control myself—not anyone or anything else.

Coping Statements for Anxiety:

- Keep calm and carry on.

- Relax and think positively.

- This worried feeling isn't comfortable, but I can handle it.

- Anxiety won't hurt me.

- Anxious feelings are unpleasant, but not harmful or dangerous.

- I can feel anxious and still deal with this situation.

- This is not a real emergency. Take a breath, slow down, and think about what I need to do.

- Focus on right now—where my body feels ok—and my anxiety will decrease.

- Fighting this doesn't help, so take a breath and let it float away.

- These are just thoughts; they aren't real.

- I can break this worry cycle by breathing and staying present.

- Listen to what my body is telling me, and focus on a part of my body that feels good.

- Feeling uncomfortable or having muscle tension is natural. It cues me to use my coping strategies.

- Focus on the positive.

- I have gotten through this worry before.

- I will use my positive affirmations.

Coping Statements for Fear:

- I'll just do the best I can.

- I can only do my best.

- I know I can do each one of these tasks.

- I can do this; I'm doing it now.

- It's easier once I get started.

- I will take it step by step; I won't rush.

- I've done this before, so I can do it again.

- I'll jump in and be alright.

- Fear doesn't rule me.

- If I don't think about fear, I won't be afraid.

- I can breathe through my fear.

- By facing my fears, I can overcome them.

- I won't let negative thoughts creep in.

- I can learn to face my fears.

- Worry doesn't help.

- I can handle whatever happens.

- I can only do my best.

- It's OK to make mistakes.

- I've succeeded with this before.

- Tomorrow, I'll be through it.

- There's an end to this.

- I am only afraid because I decided to be, so I can decide not to be.

Coping Statements for Overwhelm:

- I can breathe through this.

- What is my body telling me?

- What do I need to do right now?

- Take one step at a time.

- It will soon be over.

- Just do one thing.

- Take a breath, and take one action.

- Keep my mind on right now and on the task at hand.

Coping Statements for Pain Management:

- I can focus on where I have no pain in my body.

- I can control the pain by breathing through it.

- Stay present, focus on one area of sensation, and breathe through it.

- I need to stay focused on the positives.

- It will be over soon.

- This isn't as bad as I thought.

- No matter how bad it gets, I can get to the other side.

- I can feel bad and still choose to take a new and healthy direction.

- This is difficult and uncomfortable, but it is only temporary.

Coping Statements for Panic:

- This is my body's way of telling me to count from 10 to 1.

- This is difficult and uncomfortable, but it is only temporary.

- I won't be harmed.

- Nothing serious is going to happen.

- This is unpleasant, but I can get through it.

- I will just let my body pass through this, and breathe.

- Panic attacks happen. I can breathe through it.

- I have survived panic attacks before, and I will survive this as well.

Coping Statements for Phobias:

- I can control my worry.

- These feeling aren't real, and I am in control of my thoughts.

- I am safe.

- I can't be harmed by worry.

- Breathe deeply and work through this.

- This feeling is just my racing mind and adrenaline pumping—it will pass in a couple of minutes.

Technique Name:
Tell a Story

What Is It?

A therapeutic method for revealing children's fears and hopes, among other things. Can also be used as points of discussion.

Materials:

Story Mover Questions

Instructions:

- Ask the client to tell a story, starting with *"Once upon a time ..."*

- Use the story movers to move the story along.

Questions:

- What body sensations do you notice?

- What came up that you were surprised about?

Story Mover Questions:

- What do you see?

- What do you hear?

- What do you smell?

- Who else is there?

- What does the room/space look like?

- How do you feel?

- Where did you go?

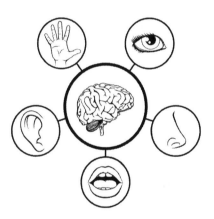

Technique Name:
Feel-Good Statements

What Is It?

A technique that helps children—especially those who tend to think the worst or are self-critical—to focus on things they are good at.

Materials:

I Am Good at Statements Handout

Instructions:

- Tell the child you are going to play a game where s/he has to finish sentences.

- Read the sentences aloud, listen to the child's additions, and dialogue about the answers.

Questions:

- How did your body feel when you were doing this activity?

- Did any thoughts, memories, or sensations come up for you?

I Am Good at Statements Handout

I AM GOOD AT …

- My friends think I'm awesome because …
- My classmates say I'm great at …
- I feel very happy when I …
- Something I'm really proud of is …
- I make my family happy when I …
- One unique thing about me is …
- I like who I am because …
- I'm super at …
- I feel good about my …
- My friends think I have an awesome …
- Somewhere I feel happy is …
- I mean a lot to …
- Others think I'm great because …
- I think I'm pretty good at …
- Something I really enjoy is …
- I really admire myself for …
- My future goals are …
- I know I can achieve them, because I'm …
- I'm naturally gifted at …
- Others often praise my …

Technique Name:
SUDS

What Is It?

A way for both the child and therapist to assess and monitor a child's level of distress. This helps the child to see his/her stress levels and get out of his/her "own head." It also helps the child and clinician see the progress they are making in therapy.

Subjective distress is defined as the discomfort, pain, and general uncomfortable feelings a person is experiencing. Subjective means that it comes from the perspective of the child experiencing it. Discomfort can result from real or perceived threats/experiences and is unique to each person.

SUDS is a numbered scale (1-10, 1-100) that measures the level at which an experience is disturbing or distressing to an individual. SUDS is very helpful for clients who are stuck, negative thinkers, or are experiencing any level of anxiety, panic, depression, or OCD, and can be used as a check-in at every session.

Materials:

SUDS Graph

Instructions:

- Explain what SUDS (subjective units of distress) means: a way for you to see how your mind and body is reacting to stressors.

- Explain how SUDS will help the child see how much progress s/he is making in therapy.

Questions:

- What sensations did you notice this week as you were monitoring your SUDS?

- Now that you are monitoring your triggers, what situations made your SUDS increase? And decrease?

- Which tools lowered your SUDS?

DR. ROSEANN AND ASSOCIATES

Subjective Units of Distress Scale (SUDS)

0- COMPLETELY RELAXED/ NO STRESS

1- COMFORTABLY ALERT

2- MINIMUM ANXIETY/ STRESS

3- MILD STRESS

4- MILD TO MODERATE STRESS

5-MODERATE STRESS

6- MODERATE TO HIGH STRESS

7- QUITE ANXIOUS/ STRESSED

8- VERY STRESSED

9- EXTREMELY STRESSED

10- THE MOST ANXIOUS/ STRESSED YOU HAVE BEEN

© Roseann-Capanna-Hodge, 2020© Global Institute of Children's Mental Health, 2020

Technique Name:
Socratic Questions Handout

What Is It?

A therapeutic way to help teens identify their own thoughts, better understand their challenges, and really try to get a handle on negative belief patterns that are not helping them, as well as devise their own more healthy ways of dealing with their challenges.

These questions are designed to inspire "lightbulb" moments of their own, instead of having adults always telling them what they should do. This is a therapeutic tool for those who have begun to regulate their nervous system and have some access to rational thoughts without being overwhelmed by their own thoughts. Use in sessions to help teens better understand their thinking and how the body gives us clues about our reactions and feelings.

Materials:

Socratic Questions Handout

Instructions:

- Use the Socratic Questions Handout as a conversation starter, and then dialogue.

Questions:

- What sensations in your body did you notice?

- What tools do you think you can use when you feel distressed or your SUDS (subjective unit of distress) level increasing?

Socratic Questions Handout

Behavior and Consequence Problems:

- What did you know at the time?

- What were you thinking at the time?

- Help me understand; why did you do [the action/behavior]?

- Did you know [X] would happen? And how did you know?

- What evidence did you have that [X] wouldn't happen?

- At the time, what did you think would happen?

- What did you want to happen?

- Had [X] ever happened before?

- Then what happens?

- Had [the same behavior] ever resulted in [X outcome] before?

- At the time, what evidence was there that [X behavior] was safe or unlikely to result in [X outcome]?

- How does [X] affect [X]?

- How could [X] be used to [X]?

- How does [X outcome] fit with what you learned before?

- Why is [X behavior or outcome] important?

Assumption Problems:

- What else can we assume?

- Why did you choose that assumption?

- What evidence do you have to support that assumption is true?

- You seem to be assuming X. How can you verify or disprove that assumption?

- Could the opposite of X be truer?

- How helpful, or unhelpful, is it to hold this particular assumption?

- Please explain the why and how of your decision to X.

Belief Problems:

- How helpful, or unhelpful, is it to hold this particular belief?

- What good, if any, comes of holding this belief?

- What is the downside of seeing things this way?

- If you see the world this way, how do you feel? How do others react?

Rationale, Reasons, and Evidence Problems:

- Why is this happening?

- Why do you think you had this outcome?

- I'm just wondering; do you have any experience of this not being the case?

- Is there anything that doesn't seem to fit with that thought?

- How might someone else view the situation?

- Is that so all of the time, or are there occasions when things are different?

- I wonder what seems so bad about that?

- In your view, what does that mean?

- What does that say about you?

- What would that mean about your life/your future?

- How might someone else view this situation?

- How would you label that?

- Can you describe the worst thing that could happen? What is so bad about that?

- And if that were true, then what?

- What supports this?

- How can I be sure of what you are saying?

- Are these reasons good enough?

- What contradicts these conclusions?

- How might it be refuted?

- What might you advise someone else in this situation?

- What evidence is there to support alternatives?

- What cognitive distortions can you identify?

- How does my thinking help or hinder my achieving goals?

- What effect would believing an alternative have?

- How would you cope if your worst-case scenario occurred?

- Can the problem situation be changed?

- What can you do differently?

- How can you check your options out?

- How do you know this?

- Can you give me an example of that?

- What do you think causes X?

Conceptual Clarification Problems:

- Tell me more about X.

- Why are you saying that?

- What makes you think that?

- What exactly does this mean?

- How does this relate to what we have been talking about?

- What is the nature of X?

- Help me to understand X.

- What do we already know about this?

- Can you give me an example?

- Are you saying X or X?

- Can you rephrase that, please?

Viewpoints and Perspectives Problems:

- What is another way of looking at this [X behavior or outcome]?

- Why is [X behavior or outcome] necessary?

- Who benefits from this?

- What is the difference between X and X?

- Why is X better than X?

- What are the strengths and weaknesses of X?

- How are X and X similar?

- What would [person] say about it?

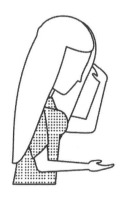

- How could you look at this another way?

Self-Blame Problems:

- Why was it your fault?

- What exactly do you think you should have done differently?

- What do you mean when you say that?

- What is your evidence for that?

Technique Name:
Things I Can and Cannot Control

What Is It?

A way for children to better understand the reality that there are things we can control and others we cannot. When children feel overwhelmed, they lose sight of what they can control. This activity helps them lessen their anxiety and empowers them with a sense of control.

Materials:

Things I Can and Cannot Control Handout

Markers, crayons, or pencil

Instructions:

- Explain that we all have things that are outside of our control and things we can control.

- When things get stressful, we may not see what we can control.

- Fill out the Things I Can and Cannot Control Handout or use a digital white board. A younger child can draw—an older child can write.

- Dialogue about what things he or she can control and what s/he cannot.

Questions:

- What did you think about this activity?

- Were you surprised by something? Did you learn something new?

- What sensations did you notice?

- Was there a time when you felt overwhelmed? What happened? How did you feel? How did you figure out a way to manage it?

- What do you do when you feel like things are out of control?

Dr. Roseann-Capanna-Hodge

Things I Can and Cannot Control

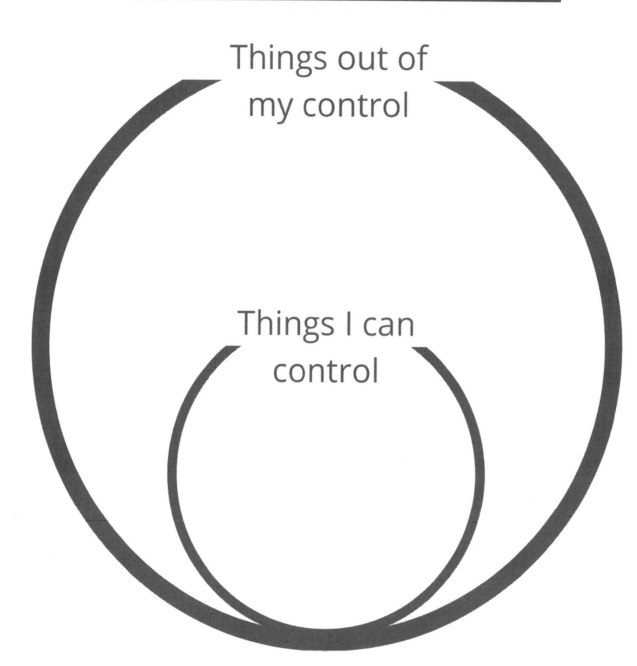

Things out of
my control

Things I can
control

© Roseann-Capanna-Hodge, 2020
© Global Institute of Children's Mental Health, 2020

154

Technique Name:
My Cheerleader

What Is It?

A way for children to see all the people in their life who support them and are there to "cheer" for them. This is helpful for children who feel worried, depressed, misunderstood, or lonely.

Materials:

My Cheerleader Handout

Markers, crayons, or pencil

Instructions:

- Explain that sometimes we feel like no one understands us, which can feel frustrating and lonely.

- Fill out the My Cheerleader Handout. A younger child can draw—an older child can write.

- Review how each person helps him or her, and what s/he has learned.

Questions:

- What did you think about this activity?

- Were you surprised by something?

- Did you learn something new?

- What sensations did you notice?

- Was there a time when you felt overwhelmed? What happened? How did you feel? How did you figure out a way to manage it?

- What do you do when you feel sad, mad, worried, or scared?

My Cheerleader Handout

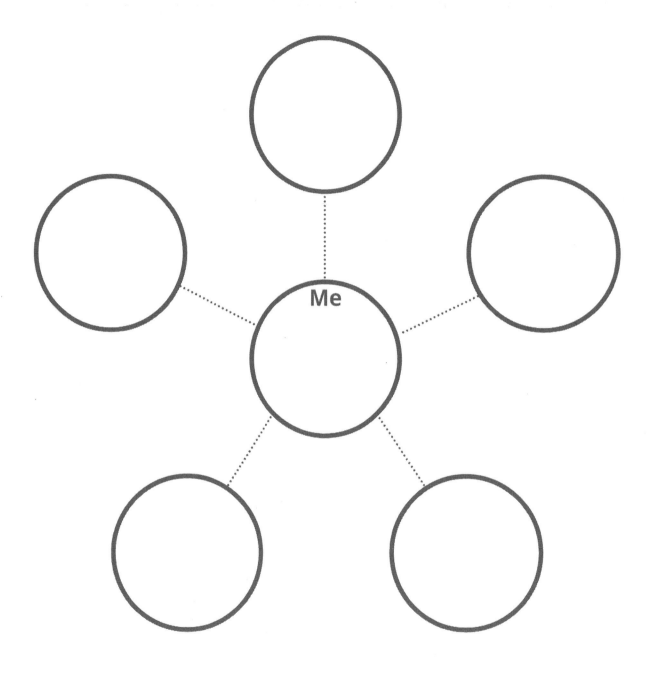

Technique Name: Problem Ranking

What Is It?

A way for children to understand that there are different types of problems, and not every problem is a BIG one—so they don't have to catastrophize everything. Categorizing problems helps to see them more clearly.

Materials:

Problem Ranking Handout

Markers, crayons, or pencil

Instructions:

- Explain that we all have problems, but that not every problem is the same.

- When things get stressful, we see a problem like a giant mountain that we can't get over, but really, it is just our reaction to the problem that is actually the problem.

- Fill out the Problem Ranking Handout. A younger child can draw—an older child can write.

Questions:

- What did you think about this activity?

- Were you surprised by something?

- Did you learn something new?

- What sensations did you notice?

- Was there a time when you felt overwhelmed? What happened? How did you feel? How did you figure out a way to manage it?

- What do you do when you feel like things are out of control?

PROBLEM RANKING

Big Problem

Medium Problem

Small Problem

Technique Name:
Old Habits/New Habits

What Is It?

A way for children to understand that habits can be changed by looking at habits they have successfully changed before.

Materials:

Old Habits/New Habits Handout

Markers, crayons, or pencil

Instructions:

- Explain that we all have changed certain habits before.

- Share an example of a habit you have changed: stopped biting nails, drinking more water, exercising, etc.

- Fill out the Old Habits/New Habits Handout. A younger child can draw—an older child can write.

Questions:

- What did you think about this activity?

- Were you surprised by something?

- Did you learn something new?

- What sensations did you notice?

Old Habits/ New Habits

Old Habits	New Habits

Technique Name:
Scavenger Hunt

What Is It?

This is a great icebreaker and way to get kids moving. It also teaches how to follow directions, problem-solve, and manage stress.

Materials:

Scavenger Hunt Lists

Instructions:

- Choose one of the scavenger hunt lists and have the child find items on it.

- Talk about how to problem-solve, manage frustration and stress, as well as about memory and listening.

Questions:

- What sensations do you feel?

- What was the hardest part of this? And how did you manage it?

- What was hard to remember?

- What was your strategy?

- What would you do differently next time?

Indoor Scavenger Hunt

○ Find a brush

○ Find something green

○ Find toothpaste

○ Find two things with circles

○ Find a sharpened pencil

○ Find a hat

○ Find something that makes noise

○ Find the most comfortable pillow

○ Find a toy that needs to be put away

○ Find a snack that is red

○ Find an eraser

○ Find a water bottle

Backyard Scavenger Hunt

O Find a bird that is singing

O Find two flowers

O Find a worm

O Find three rocks

O Find two leaves that are different colors

O Find something grey

O Find a bug that flies

O Find a shape in the clouds

O Find something orange

O Collect sticks and use them to spell your name

O Find a new plant

O Find something that feels rough

Book Scavenger Hunt

○ Find a book that has grass on the cover

○ Find a book with a character you would like to be friends with

○ Find a pet in a book

○ Find a book in which the main character goes to school

○ Find a book with the word "laugh" in it

○ Find your favorite book. What is the best part?

○ Find a book in which the character learns a lesson. What did he or she learn?

○ Find a hat in a book

○ Find a snack that looks delicious in a book

○ Find a book that has the letter "m" in the title

○ Find a book in which the character does his or her homework or chores

○ Find a flower in a book

Nature Scavenger Hunt

○ Find a frog

○ Find a spider (bonus if it is in its web!)

○ Find a fallen tree

○ Find a bird (bonus if you can find its nest!)

○ Find four different kinds of leaves

○ Find three different plants

○ Find a walking stick

○ Find two interesting rocks

○ Find a stream or body of water

○ Find two bugs: one that flies and one on the ground

○ Find two acorns

○ Find a bird feather

Inventor Scavenger Hunt

- ○ Find something stretchy

- ○ Invent a new use for a bowl

- ○ Draw a toy you would like to make

- ○ Find something made out of wood

- ○ Find two things that are square

- ○ Build a house out of pillows

- ○ Make a paper airplane that is great at flying

- ○ Find something that is plastic

- ○ Find something you can see through

- ○ Find something that is cold

- ○ Find something that doesn't make sound

- ○ Make a string out of paper clips

Math Scavenger Hunt

- Find three pencils and one marker. How many items do you have?

- Find three books. Put one back. How many are left?

- Find two toys. Find 2 more. How many do you have?

- Find two pairs of shoes. Put one pair away. How many do you have left?

- Find four forks. Put three away. How many do you have left?

- Grab your pillow. Find one more. How many do you have?

- Count the number of apples in the kitchen. How many are there?

- You buy four cupcakes. Then, you buy two more for your family. How many do you have?

- You grab four crayons and put two away. How many do you have?

- You grab two snacks and put one away. How many do you have?

- You have six hours before bedtime. You use two hours watching your favorite show. How many hours do you have left?

- You have five yellow M & Ms, and your friend has three. How many yellow M & Ms do you have together?

Senses Scavenger Hunt

○ Find a sound you hear inside

○ Find a sound you hear outside

○ Find something that smells good

○ Find something that feels soft

○ Find something that sparkles or shines

○ Find a snack that tastes sweet

○ Find something that is your favorite color

○ Find something that feels warm

○ Find something that smells calming

○ Find something that tastes bitter

○ Find something that is comfortable to wear

○ Find something that makes a quiet sound

Rainbow Scavenger Hunt

○ Find something that has more than one color

○ Find something yellow

○ Find two items that together make the color green (hint: find one blue item and one yellow item)

○ Find something that is purple

○ Find something that is your favorite color

○ Name a food that is blue

○ Find something that is your least favorite color

○ Find something light green and dark green

○ Find something you use every day

○ Find the coolest leaf that you can

○ Find something that is red

○ Find markers or crayons for all the colors of the rainbow and draw a rainbow

© Roseann-Capanna-Hodge, 2020 © Global Institute of Children's Mental Health, 2020

Technique Name:
Feelings Check-In Slide

What Is It?

A way to check-in with children at every session (including during a session) about how they are feeling. This slide has different pictures representing different feelings, so children can express how they are feeling non-verbally. Particularly useful for stressed children who naturally want to disconnect from their emotions and body sensations.

Materials:

SUDS Scale Handout

Feelings Slide

Instructions:

- Ask the child to point to the picture of the emotions he or she is feeling or felt during an event.

- Help a child connect emotions to his/her body sensations by asking him/her to first identify the emotion and then the body sensation experienced during the event.

Questions:

- Describe one POSITIVE experience you had this week. Show me the feeling you had during that experience. What sensations did you notice? What was your SUDS level before and after this task?

- Describe one NEGATIVE experience you had this week. Show me the feeling you had during that experience. What sensations did you notice? What was your SUDS level before and after this task?

Feelings Check-In

Technique Name:
Bibliotherapy

What Is It?

Bibliotherapy is a therapeutic approach that uses literature to support good mental health. There are many books readily available on a variety of mental health topics for children and teens.

Materials:

SUDS Scale Handout

Book on a mental health issue related to the client's issue

Bibliotherapy Book List

Instructions:

- Pick out a specific book on a mental health issue related to the child's issue.

- Either read it to the child, have the parents purchase it (that means sending the link), or get from the local library. Make sure you do this ahead of time, and plan at least a week to complete.

Questions:

- How can you relate to X character?

- What sensations did you notice?

- Did this make you think of anything?

- What was your SUDS level before and after this task?

Bibliotherapy Book List

- **ADHD**
  - **Cory Stories: A Kid's Book About Living With ADHD by Jeanne Kraus, and illustrated by Whitney Martin**
  - **I Can't Sit Still! Living With ADHD by Pam Pollack and Meg Belviso, illustrated by Marta Fabrega**
  - **Why Can't Jimmy Sit Still? by Sandra L. Tunis, PhD, illustrated by Maeve Kelly**
  - **Eagle Eyes: A Child's Guide to Paying Attention by Jeanne Gehret (Ages 6-11)**
  - **Jumpin' Johnny Get Back to Work! A Child's Guide to ADHD/Hyperactivity by Michael Gordon (Ages 5-9)**
  - **My Brother's A World-Class Pain: A Sibling's Guide to ADHD/Hyperactivity by Michael Gordon (Ages 5-9)**
  - **Sit Still! by Nancy Carlson (Ages 3-8)**
  - **Playing Tyler by T.L. Costa**
  - **Club Meds by Katherine Hall Page**
  - **Motorcycles, Sushi and One Strange Book by Nancy Rue**

- **Anger**
  - **Alexander and the Terrible, Horrible, No Good, Very Bad Day by Judith Viorst (Ages 4-8)**
  - **Andrew's Angry Words by Dorothea Lackner (Ages 4-8)**
  - **Bootsie Barker Bites by Barbara Bottner (Ages 4-8)**
  - **The Chocolate Covered Cookie Tantrum by Deborah Blementhal (Ages 5-8)**
  - **Don't Rant and Rave on Wednesdays! by Adolph Moser (Ages 4-9)**
  - **Goldie is Mad by Margie Palatini (Ages 3-7)**
  - **How I Feel Frustrated by Marcia Leonard (Ages 3-8)**
  - **How I Feel Angry by Marcia Leonard (Ages 2-6)**
  - **Let's Talk About Feeling Angry by Joy Berry (Ages 3-8)**
  - **Llama Llama Mad at Mama by Anna Dewdney (Ages 2-5)**
  - **Sometimes I'm Bombaloo by Rachel Vail (Ages 3-8)**
  - **That Makes Me Mad! by Steven Kroll (Ages 4-8)**
  - **The Rain Came Down by David Shannon (Ages 4-8)**

Bibliotherapy Book List

- **Anger Continued**
  - The Temper Tantrum Book by Edna Mitchell Preston (Ages 3-6)
  - When I'm Angry by Jane Aaron (Ages 3-7)
  - When I'm Feeling Angry by Trace Moroney (Ages 2-5)
  - When I Feel Angry by Cornelia Maude Spelman (Ages 5-7)
  - When Sophie Gets Angry – Really, Really Angry by Molly Garrett (Ages 3-7)
  - Lily's Purple Plastic Purse by Kevin Henkes. (Ages 4-8)

- **Anxiety/Worry**
  - Don't Feed the WorryBug Written and illustrated by Andi Green
  - The Fix-It Friends: Have No Fear! Written by Nicole C. Kear, illustrated by Tracy Dockray
  - Hector's Favorite Place Written and illustrated by Jo Rooks
  - How Big Are Your Worries Little Bear? by Jayneen Sanders, illustrated by Stephanie Fizer Coleman
  - Pilar's Worries Written by Victoria M. Sanchez, illustrated by Jess Golden
  - What to Do When You Worry Too Much: A Kid's Guide to Overcoming Anxiety Written by Dawn Huebner, illustrated by Bonnie Matthews
  - Creepy Things are Scaring Me by Jerome and Jarrett Pumphrey (Ages 4-8)
  - Don't Pop Your Cork on Mondays! by Adolph Moser (Ages 4-9)
  - Franklin in The Dark by Paulette Bourgeois & Brenda Clark (Ages 5-8)
  - How I Feel Scared by Marcia Leonard (Ages 2-6)
  - I Am Not Going to School Today by Robie H. Harris (Ages 4-8)
  - No Such Thing by Jackie French Koller (Ages 5-8)
  - Sam's First Day by David Mills & Lizzie Finlay (Ages 3-7)
  - Sheila Rae, the Brave by Kevin Henkes (Ages 5-8)
  - Wemberly Worried by Kevin Henkes (Ages 5-8)
  - When I'm Feeling Scared by Trace Moroney (Ages 2-5)
  - When I Feel Scared by Cornelia Maude Spelman (Ages 5-7)
  - How to Relax by Thich Nhat Hanh
  - War and Peace by Leo Tolstoy (Briggs translation)

Bibliotherapy Book List

- **Anxiety/Worry Continued**
  - Enchanted Forest: An Inky Quest and Coloring book by Johanna Basford
  - Zen: The Art of Simple Living by Shunmyō Masuno
  - The Enchanted April by Elizabeth von Arnim
  - Collected Poems by Edward Thomas
  - Haikus of Basho
  - Notes on a Nervous Planet by Matt Haig
  - City of Girls by Elizabeth Gilbert
  - Cutting for Stone by Abraham Verghese
  - Wabi Sabi by Beth Kempton
  - Swallows and Amazons by Arthur Ransome
  - The Things You Can See Only When You Slow Down by Haemin Sunim
  - The Hobbit: Illustrated Edition by J. R. R. Tolkien
  - Radical Compassion by Tara Brach
  - Silence: In the Age of Noise by Erling Kagge
  - Captain Corelli's Mandolin by Louis de Bernières
  - Gratitude by Oliver Sacks
  - A Walk in the Woods: Rediscovering America on the Appalachian Trail by Bill Bryson
  - Poem: The Lake Isle of Innisfree by W. B. Yeats
  - Collected Poems by William Wordsworth
  - Healing Without Freud or Prozac: Natural Approaches to Curing Stress, Anxiety and Depression by Dr Servan-Schreiber
  - The Nature of Jade by Deb Caletti
  - Anything but Typical by Nora Raleigh Baskin
  - Waiting for You by Susane Colasanti
  - Stupid Fast by Geoff Herbach
  - Dr. Bird's Advice for Sad Poets by Evan Roskos
  - I Don't Want to Be Crazy by Samantha Schutz

Bibliotherapy Book List

- Autism
  - Armond Goes to a Party: A Book About Asperger's and Friendship Written by Nancy Carlson and Armond Isaak, illustrated by Nancy Carlson
  - A Boy Called Bat Written by Elana K. Arnold, illustrated by Charles Santoso
  - A Whole New Ballgame: A Rip and Red Book Written by Phil Bildner, illustrated by Tim Probert
  - Ian's Walk: A Story About Autism by Laurie Lears (Ages 4-8)
  - Al Capone Does My Shirts by Gennifer Choldenko
  - Mockingbird by Kathryn Erskine
  - The Half-Life of Planets by Emily Franklin and Brendan Halpin
  - The Curious Incident of the Dog in the Night-Time by Mark Haddon
  - Screaming Quietly by Evan Jacobs
  - Harmonic Feedback by Tara Kelly
  - Rogue by Lyn Miller-Lachmann
  - Colin Fischer by Ashley Edward Miller
  - Mindblind by Jennifer Roy
  - Marcelo in the Real World by Francisco X Stork

- Bullying
  - Am I a Bully? by Hope Gilchrist, illustrated by Zoe Jordon
  - Chrysanthemum by Kevin Henkes
  - Tease Monster: A Book About Teasing vs. Bullying by Julia Cook, illustrated by Anita DuFalla
  - Warp Speed by Lisa Yee
  - Wonder by R.J. Palacio
  - A Children's Book About Being Bullied by Joy Berry (Ages 3-8)
  - A Children's Book About Teasing by Joy Berry (Ages 3-8)
  - A Weekend with Wendell by Kevin Henkes (Ages 4-8)
  - The Berenstain Bears and the Bully by Stan and Jan Berenstain (Ages 4-7)
  - Big Bad Bruce by Bill Peet (Ages 4-8)

Bibliotherapy Book List

- **Bullying Continued**
  - Chester's Way by Kevin Henkes (Ages 5-7)
  - Coyote Raid in Cactus Canyon by Jim Arnosky (Ages 4-8)
  - Don't Be a Menace on Sundays! by Adolph Moser (Ages 4-9)
  - Gobbles! by Ezra Jack Kets (Ages 4-8)
  - Hats by Kevin Luthardt (Ages 3-6)
  - Hooway for Wodney Wat! by Helen Lester (Ages 5-8)
  - Hugo and the Bully Frogs by Francesca Simon (Ages 3-7)
  - Trevor Trevor by Diane Cullen (Ages 3-8)
  - The Ant Bully by J. Nickle (Ages 3-8)
  - Bully Trouble by J. Cole (Ages 7-9)
  - Who's Afraid of the Big, Bad Bully? by T. Slater (Ages 7-9)
  - King of the Playground by P. Reynolds Naylor (Ages 7-9)
  - Push and Shove: Bully and Victim Activity by J. Boulden (Ages 9-11)
  - My Name is Not Dummy by E. Crary (Ages 9-11)
  - Simon's Hook: A Story About Teases and Put-Downs by K. Gedig Burnett (Ages 9-11)
  - Pinky Rex and the Bully by J. Howe (Ages 9-11)
  - Bully on the Bus by C.W. Bosch (Ages 10-14)
  - How to Handle Bullies, Teasers, and Other Meanies by K. Cohen-Posey (Ages 10-14)
- **Depression/Sadness**
  - Can I Catch It Like a Cold? Coping With a Parent's Depression by the Centre for Addiction and Mental Health, illustrated by Joe Weissmann
  - My Family Divided: One Girl's Journey of Home, Loss, and Hope by Diane Guerrero with Erica Moroz
  - The Little Prince by Antoine de Saint-Exupéry
  - Pride and Prejudice by Jane Austen
  - I Capture the Castle by Dodie Smith
  - The Secret Garden by Frances Hodgson Burnett

Bibliotherapy Book List

- **Depression/Sadness Continued**
  - **The Guernsey Literary and Potato Peel Pie Society by Mary Ann Shaffer**
  - **The Unlikely Pilgrimage of Harold Fry (Harold Fry, #1) by Rachel Joyce**
  - **Woody Notes, and Heat Sneaking up Fast by Danny Winter**
  - **7 Powerful Questions to Discover Your Dream Life by Ngan H. Nguyen**
  - **Hope for Garbage by Alex Tully**
  - **Notes from a Small Island by Bill Bryson**
  - **The Problem of Pain by C.S. Lewis**
  - **All Creatures Great and Small by James Herriot**
  - **Gunpowder Soup by Karl Wiggins**
  - **Overcoming Depression by Paul A. Gilbert**
  - **The Pursuit of Love (Radlett & Montdore, #1) by Nancy Mitford**
  - **A Street Cat Named Bob: How One Man and His Cat Found Hope on the Streets by James Bowen**
  - **The Secret Diary of Adrian Mole, Aged 13 3/4 (Adrian Mole, #1) by Sue Townsend**
  - **The Help by Kathryn Stockett**
  - **Chocolat (Chocolat, #1) by Joanne Harris**
  - **The Last Runaway by Tracy Chevalier**
  - **The Idle Traveller: The Art of Slow Travel by Dan Kieran**
  - **Steppenwolf by Hermann Hesse**
  - **To the Survivors: One Man's Journey as a Rape Crisis Counselor with True Stories of Sexual Violence by Robert Uttaro**
  - **The Other Side of Burnout: Solutions for Healthcare Professionals by Melissa Wolf**
  - **Be Happier, Healthier, and More Productive; 365 Inspiring Ideas by Leslyn Kantner**
  - **I Thirst (The Veritas Chronicles #1) by Gina Marinello-Sweeney**
  - **Anxiety by Danny Winter**
  - **The Perks of Being a Wallflower by Stephen Chbosky**
  - **Siddhartha by Hermann Hesse**
  - **Man's Eternal Quest (Collected Talks & Essays 1) by Paramahansa Yogananda**

Bibliotherapy Book List

- **Depression/Sadness Continued**
  - **Change Your Thinking: Overcome Stress, Anxiety, and Depression, and Improve Your Life with CBT by Sarah Edelman**
  - **Healing from Depression: 12 Weeks to a Better Mood : A Body, Mind, and Spirit Recovery Program by Douglas Bloch**
  - **Bournemouth Boys and Boscombe Girls by Danny Winter**
  - **Shit my History Teacher DID NOT tell me! by Karl Wiggins**
  - **Jack: A Life of C. S. Lewis by George Sayer**
  - **Dogshit Saved My Life by Karl Wiggins**
  - **Three Men in a Boat (Three Men, #1) by Jerome K. Jerome**
  - **The Dalai Lama's Cat (The Dalai Lama's Cat, #1) by David Michie**
  - **You Really Are Full of Shit, Aren't You? by Karl Wiggins**
  - **Pnin by Vladimir Nabokov**
  - **The Art of Purring (The Dalai Lama's Cat, #2) by David Michie**
  - **Calico Jack in your Garden by Karl Wiggins**
  - **The Dalai Lama's Cat and the Power of Meow (The Dalai Lama's Cat, #3) by David Michie**
  - **A Day No Pigs Would Die by Robert Newton Peck**
  - **Nobody Asked Me, But …. by Karl Wiggins**
  - **A Parrot in the Pepper Tree by Chris Stewart**
  - **The Dog Who Rescues Cats: True Story of Ginny by Philip González**
  - **Wrong Planet - Searching for your Tribe by Karl Wiggins**
  - **The Enchanted April by Elizabeth von Arnim**
  - **Really Important Stuff My Dog Has Taught Me by Cynthia L. Copeland**
  - **Let's Talk About Feeling Sad by Joy Berry (Ages 3-5)**
  - **Franklin's Bad Day by Paulette Bourgeois & Brenda Clark (Ages 5-8)**
  - **How I Feel Sad by Marcia Leonard (Ages 2-6)**
  - **Hurty Feelings by Helen Lester (Ages 5-8)**
  - **Knuffle Bunny by Mo Willems (Ages 3-6)**

Bibliotherapy Book List

- **Depression/Sadness Continued**
  - Sometimes I Feel Awful by Joan Singleton Prestine (Ages 5-8)
  - The Very Lonely Firefly by Eric Carle (Ages 4-7)
  - When I'm Feeling Sad by Trace Moroney (Ages 2-5)
  - When I Feel Sad by Cornelia Maude Spelman (Ages 5-7)
  - Reasons to Stay Alive by Matt Haig
  - Brave Enough: A Mini Instruction Manual for the Soul by Cheryl Strayed
  - The Uncommon Reader by Alan Bennett
  - The Lion, the Witch and the Wardrobe (The Chronicles of Narnia) by C.S. Lewis
  - Collected Poems by Edward Thomas
  - Three Men in a Boat: To Say Nothing of the Dog by Jerome K. Jerome
  - The Hundred-Year-Old Man Who Climbed out of the Window and Disappeared by Jonas Jonasson
  - All Creatures Great and Small: The classic memoirs of a Yorkshire country vet by James Herriot
  - The No. 1 Ladies' Detective Agency by Alexander McCall Smith
  - The BFG by Roald Dahl
  - Harry Potter and the Deathly Hallows by J.K. Rowling
  - A Guide to the Good Life: The Ancient Art of Stoic Joy by William B. Irvine
  - Captain Corelli's Mandolin by Louis de Bernières
  - The Jeeves Omnibus – Vol 1 by P.G. Wodehouse
  - Tennsyon's Collected Poems
  - Healing Without Freud or Prozac
  - Thirteen Reasons Why by Jay Asher
  - The Chance You Won't Return by Annie Cardi
  - Hazlewood High Trilogy by Sharon M Draper
  - Suicide Notes by Michael Thomas Ford
  - Will Grayson, Will Grayson by John Green and David Levithan
  - Get Well Soon by Julie Halpern
  - Try Not to Breathe by Jennifer R Hubbard

Bibliotherapy Book List

- **Depression/Sadness Continued**
  - **Damage by A.M Jenkins**
  - **Silhouetted by the Blue by Traci L Jones**
  - **Lovely, Dark and Deep by Amy McNamara**
  - **Sorta Like a Rock Star by Matthew Quick**
  - **This Song Will Save Your Life by Leila Sales**
  - **Black Box by Julie Schumacher**
  - **It's Kind of a Funny Story by Ned Vizzini**
  - **Belzhar by Meg Wolitzer**

- **Divorce**
  - **Fred Stays with Me! by Nancy Coffelt**
  - **Stranded in Boringsville by Catherine Bateson**
  - **We're Having a Tuesday by D. K. Simoneau**
  - **Step by Wicked Step by Anne Fine**
  - **Forever Amber Brown by Paula Danziger**

- **Dyslexia**
  - **Back to Front and Upside Down! by Claire Alexander**
  - **Fish in a Tree Written by Lynda Mullaly Hunt**

- **Grief**
  - **Art With Heart Presents: Draw It Out by Steffanie Lorig and Rosalie Frankel**
  - **I Miss You: A First Look at Death by Pat Thomas, illustrated by Lesley Harker**
  - **The Invisible String by Patrice Karst, illustrated by Joanne Lew-Vriethoff**
  - **One Wave at a Time: A Story About Grief and Healing by Holly Thompson, illustrated by Ashley Crowley**
  - **When Dinosaurs Die: A Guide to Understanding Death by Laurie Krasny Brown and Marc Brown**
  - **Don't Despair on Thursdays! by Adolph Moser (Ages 4-9)**
  - **The Fall of Freddie the Leaf by Leo Buscaglia (Ages 5-adult)**

Bibliotherapy Book List

- **Grief Continued**
  - **Goodbye Mousie by Robert Harris (Ages 3-8)**
  - **I Miss You by Pat Thomas (Ages 4-8)**
  - **The Next Place by Warren Hanson (Ages 5-adult)**
  - **Sad Isn't Bad: Grief Guidebook for Kids Dealing with Loss Series by Michaelene Mundy (Ages 5-8)**
  - **When Dinosaurs Die: A Guide To Understanding Death by Laurie Krasny Brown and Marc Brown (Ages 3-9)**
  - **Scat by A. Dobrin (Ages 5-9)**
  - **A Season for Mangoes by R. Hanson (Ages 5-9)**
  - **Nana Upstairs and Nana Downstairs by T. DePaola (Ages 5-13)**
  - **Bluebird Summer by D. Hopkinson (Ages 6-11)**
  - **Annie and the Old One by M. Miles (Ages 6-12)**
  - **Felita by N. Mohr (Ages 7-11)**
  - **Grandma's Scrapbook by J. Nobisso (Ages 7-12)**

- **Lyme**
  - **Little Bite, BIG Trouble: A Bird's-Eye View of Chronic Lyme Disease by Sarah Schlichte Sanchez**
  - **In Limbo Over Lyme Disease by Melanie S. Weiss**

- **Moving**
  - **Stranded in Boringsville by Catherine Bateson**
  - **Moving Day by Meg Cabot**
  - **The Purim Surprise by Lesley Simpson**
  - **TTFN (Ta-Ta for Now) by Lauren Myracle**
  - **Eagle Song by Joseph Bruchac**

Bibliotherapy Book List

- OCD
  - Finding Perfect by Elly Swartz
  - Mr. Worry: A Story About OCD by Holly L. Niner, illustrated by Greg Swearingen
  - OCDaniel by Wesley King
  - Up and Down the Worry Hill: A Children's Book About Obsessive-Compulsive Disorder and Its Treatment by Aureen Pinto Wagner, PhD, illustrated by Paul A. Jutton
  - Compulsion by Heidi Ayarbe
  - Total Constant Order by Crissa-Jean Chappell
  - Not as Crazy as I Seem by George Harrar
  - OCD Love Story by Corey Ann Haydu
  - Fallout by Ellen Hopkins
  - Lexapros and Cons by Aaron Karo
  - Say What You Will by Cammie McGovern
  - OCD, the Dude, and Me by Lauren Roedy Vaughn
  - Don't Touch by Rachel Wilson

- PANS/PANDAS
  - In A Pickle Over PANDAS by Melanie S. Weiss
  - My Story About PANS/PANDAS by Owen Ross

- Racism
  - Roll of Thunder, Hear My Cry by Mildred D. Taylor
  - Ruth and the Green Book by Calvin Alexander Ramsey; Floyd Cooper (Illustrator); Gwen Strauss
  - Amazing Grace by Mary Hoffman; Caroline Binch (Illustrator)
  - Separate Is Never Equal by Duncan Tonatiuh
  - Sit-In by Andrea Davis Pinkney; Brian Pinkney (Artist)

Bibliotherapy Book List

- Selective Mutism
  - Lola's Words Disappeared by Elaheh Bos
  - Speak by Laurie Halse Anderson
  - Louder Than Words by Laura Jarratt
  - A Quiet Kind of Thunder by Sara Barnard
  - Being Miss Nobody by Tamsin Winter
  - Persona Medusa: A Tale of Selective Mutism & Social Anxiety by D.J. Sharry
  - What I Couldn't Tell You by Faye Bird
- Social Skills/Friendship
  - A Rainbow of Friends by P.K. Hallinan (Ages 4-8)
  - Be Polite and Kind by Cheri Meiners (Ages 4-7)
  - Best Friends by Charlotte Labaronne (Ages 3-5)
  - Can You Be a Friend? by Nita Everly (Ages 3-6)
  - Can You Talk to Your Friends? by Nita Everly (Ages 3-6)
  - Care Bears: Caring Contest by Nancy Parent (Ages 3-6)
  - Care Bears: The Day Nobody Shared by Nancy Parent (Ages3-6)
  - Communication by Aliki (Ages 3-8)
  - Friendship Values to Live By by Sharon Lee Roberts (Ages 3-6)
  - Fox Makes Friends by Adam Relf (Ages 3-5)
  - Gigi and Lulu's Gigantic Fight by Pamela Edwards (Ages 3-7)
  - Heartprints by P.K. Hallinan (Ages 3-6)
  - How Do Dinosaurs Play with Their Friends by Jane Yolen and Mark Teague (Ages 3-5)
  - How Do I Feel About Making Friends by Sarah Levete (Ages 4-9)
  - How to be a Friend by Laurie Krasny Brown and Marc Brown (Ages 4-8)
  - How to Deal With Friends: A Child's Practical Guide by Richard Powell (Ages 3-7)
  - How to Lose All Your Friends by Nancy Carlson (Ages 4-9)
  - Hunter's Best Friend at School by Laura Malone Elliot (Ages 4-7)
  - I'm a Good Friend! by David Parker (Ages 3-5)
  - I Can Share by Karen Katz (Ages infant-5)

Bibliotherapy Book List

- **Social Skills/Friendship**
  - **I Can Cooperate! by David Parker (Ages 3-5)**
  - **I am Generous! by David Parker (Ages 2-5)**
  - **I'm Sorry by Sam McBratney (Ages 4-7)**
  - **It's Hard to Share My Teacher by Joan Singleton Prestine (Ages 5-6)**
  - **Jamberry by Bruce Degan (Ages 2-5)**
  - **Join In and Play by Cheri Meiners (Ages 3-6)**
  - **The Little Mouse, The Red Ripe Strawberry, and The Big Hungry Bear by Don and Audry Wood (Ages 2-5)**
  - **Making Friends by Fred Rogers (Ages 3-5)**
  - **Making Friends by Janine Amos (Ages 4-8)**
  - **Matthew and Tilly by Rebecca C. Jones (Ages 4-8)**
  - **Mine! Mine! Mine! by Shelly Becker (Ages 3-5)**
  - **Mine! A Backpack Baby Story by Miriam Cohen (Ages infant-2)**
  - **My Friend Bear by Jez Alborough (Ages 3-8)**
  - **My Friend and I by Lisa John-Clough (Ages 4-8)**
  - **One Lonely Sea Horse by Saxton Freymann & Joost Elffers (Ages 4-8)**
  - **Big Dog...Little Dog by P.D. Eastman (Ages 4-8)**
  - **The Rainbow Fish by Marcus Pfister (Ages 3-8)**
  - **Share and Take Turns by Cheri Meiners (Ages 5-8)**
  - **Sharing How Kindness Grows by Fran Shaw (Ages 3-5)**
  - **The Selfish Crocodile by Faustin Charles and Michael Terry (Ages 4-7)**
  - **Simon and Molly Plus Hester by Lisa Jahn-Clough (Ages 5-8)**
  - **Sometimes I Share by Carol Nicklaus (Ages 4-6)**
  - **Strawberry Shortcake and the Friendship Party by Monique Z. Sephens (Ages 2-5)**
  - **Sunshine & Storm by Elisabeth Jones (Ages 3-5)**
  - **Talk and Work it Out by Cheri Meiners (Ages 3-6)**
  - **That's What a Friend Is by P.K. Hallinan (Ages 3-8)**
  - **We Are Best Friends by Aliki (Ages 4-7)**

Bibliotherapy Book List

- **Stress**
  - **100 Small Ways to Manage Time by Oliver Luke Delorie**
  - **100 Small Ways to Quit Worrying by Oliver Luke Delorie**
  - **The Little Book of Stress Relief by David Posen**
  - **Why Zebras Don't Get Ulcers by Robert M. Sapolsky**

List compiled from the following resources
https://childmind.org/article/best-childrens-books-about-mental-health/
https://www.goodreads.com/list/tag/bibliotherapy
https://clearlakechildrenscenter.com/helpful-articles/bibliotherapy/
https://www.tolstoytherapy.com/bibliotherapy-recommendations/
https://www.slj.com/?detailStory=bibliotherapy-for-teens-helpful-tips-and-recommended-fiction
https://guides.auraria.edu/bibliotherapy/divorce
https://guides.auraria.edu/bibliotherapy/moving
https://library.ivytech.edu/c.php?g=231275&p=7584041
http://www.fmrq.qc.ca/anxietystress
https://minds.wisconsin.edu/bitstream/handle/1793/41811/2005schochn.pdf?sequence=1&isAllowed=y
https://thisandthat404.wordpress.com/2017/10/26/selective-mutism-in-fiction/

Technique Name:
Sentence Completion for Children

What Is It?

A therapeutic technique that helps to facilitate communication about feelings and issues.

Materials:

SUDS Scale Handout

Sentence Completion Sheet

Instructions:

- Explain to the child that you will be saying some sentences that are incomplete, so s/he can finish the with the first thing that pops into his/her head.

- Pick out sentences to read to the child and write them down.

- Use these responses as a jumping-off point for discussion.

Questions:

- Tell me more?

- What happened next?

- What sensations did you notice?

- What was your SUDS level before and after this task?

SENTENCE COMPLETION FOR CHILDREN

Name_____Age_____Gender_____Grade_____

1. The thing that really makes me mad is _____.

2. People say I am _____.

3. I feel bad when _____.

4. I get in trouble because _____.

5. My mom is _____.

6. I am usually _____.

7. The person I like best is _____.

8. I am really happy when _____.

9. My teacher wants me to _____.

10. I can't _____.

11. At lunch time _____.

12. At report card time I feel _____.

13. My parents worry that I _____.

14. School is _____.

15. I could do better if _____.

16. I think my classmates should _____

17. I get scared and worried when _____.

18. I would like my teacher to _____.

19. I would like to _____.

20. My favorite animal is _____.

21. My best school work is _____.

22. I could help my classmates if I _____.

23. I would like my mom or dad to _____.

24. The person who bothers me most is _____.

25. I wish _____.

26. When I grow up, I want to _____.

27. Girls are _____.

28. Boys are _____.

29. After school, I _____.

30. At night, I _____.

31. I usually dream about _____.

32. In the summer _____.

33. My dad _____.

34. Next year I will _____.

35. Homework is _____.

Technique Name:
Sentence Completion for Teens

What Is It?

A therapeutic technique that helps to facilitate communication about feelings and issues.

Materials:

SUDS Scale Handout

Sentence Completion Sheet

Instructions:

- Explain to the teen that you will be saying some sentences that are incomplete, so s/he can finish them with the first thing that pops into his/her head.

- Pick out sentences to read to the teen and write them down—or have the teen read and complete them.

- Use these responses as a jumping-off point for discussion.

Questions:

- Tell me more?

- What happened next?

- What sensations did you notice?

- What was your SUDS level before and after this task?

SENTENCE COMPLETION FOR TEENS

I am a person who ...

1. likes _____.

2. hates _____.

3. can _____.

4. cannot _____

5. would never _____.

6. would rather _____.

7. loves to _____.

8. wants to learn how to _____.

9. used to be afraid of _____.

10. would be better off _____.

11. is really good at _____.

12. gets really angry when _____.

13. "bugs" other people when _____.

14. has the good habit of _____.

Technique Name:
Teen Thinking Questions

What Is It?

Conversation starters for teens who have an inability or unwillingness to participate in a discussion of their issues.

Materials:

Teen Thinking Questions Handout

Instructions:

- In this game, you take turns sharing three statements about yourself.

- Two of these statements must be facts, or "truths," and one must be a lie.

- You each try to guess which statement is the lie.

- Use the Teen Thinking Questions Handout for ideas.

TEEN THINKING QUESTIONS

- Think of the worst thing that's happened to you. What did it teach you?
- What's the best invention you've seen, and what do you like about it?
- How do you think the world will eventually end? How many years from now do you think that will be?
- When someone is feeling stressed, what are 3 suggestions you'd share on how to feel less stressed?
- Do you think your family has enough money?
- What's your greatest strength and your greatest weakness?
- What are 3 things you did in the last two days to help someone you care about?
- What is your favorite show or book?
- How can you make someone smile today?
- Imagine you're the teacher tomorrow at school. What are 3 things you'd teach that everyone needs to know in life?
- What are 3 things that would make you truly happy?
- If you were a billionaire and did not have to work, what would you do with your time?
- Describe yourself in 5 words or less.
- If you could set one rule for the family that everyone has to follow, what would it be?
- If you had more money, what would you spend it on?
- If you could change anything in the world, what would it be?
- What are 3 small victories that you've experienced in the last few days that you're proud of?
- Which of your friends do you think your parents like the most? Why?
- Have you passed up on any opportunities that you now regret? What were they?
- What do you do and think when you see a homeless person?
- What could your parents do to help you feel more supported?
- If you were told you would live forever, what would you do differently with your life?
- What's a hobby that you wish you knew how to do? What's holding you back from starting?
- How would you change the world if you had one wish? How can you help reach that goal now?
- What is the best and worst food to eat for dinner?
- Who has had the greatest impact on your life and why?
- What product would you buy a ton of if you found out it wasn't going to be sold anymore?
- If your family lost everything they owned today but could keep 3 things, what would you keep and why?
- Would you rather be the boss or employee and why?
- Are you satisfied with the number of friends that you have? What makes your friendship with your best friend amazing?
- How would you explain the word love to someone without using the word "love"?
- Do you think it's better to have one skill you're amazing at or many skills you're okay at? Why?
- What is one important lesson that you have learned and what situation taught you that?

Technique Name:
Feelings Memory Match Game

What Is It?

A game in which children match feelings cards from memory. This helps children who lack awareness about the emotions of others or who may be disconnected from their own feelings due to grief, trauma, impulsivity, or neurological issues.

Materials:

Feelings Memory Match Handout

Instructions:

- Print out two sets of the cards: one for the child and one for the therapist.

- Place cards face down on the table or floor.

- One person at a time flips two cards over to try to find a match.

- When a match is identified, the person who finds the feelings pair is given the opportunity to share a time when he or she experienced that feeling.

- The therapist also gives specific examples related to the child's issues as a third person or as him/herself as an example.

- If the child cannot identify a time when he/she experienced the feeling, s/he can share anytime s/he has seen someone else experience that feeling.

- With younger children, you may want to use fewer pairs.

Questions:

- What clues does your body give that you might be feeling a certain way?

- What feeling is hardest for you to "see" in others? Why?

- What surprised you during this activity?

Feelings Memory Match Game

Excited

Excited

Bored

Bored

Unhappy

Unhappy

Feelings Memory Match Game

 Confused

 Confused

 Upset

 Upset

 Worried

 Worried

Feelings Memory Match Game

 Happy

 Happy

 Sad

 Sad

 Frustrated Frustrated

Feelings Memory Match Game

Surprised   Surprised

Chapter 9 –
Teletherapy Techniques for Anger and Frustration

Oh, What Do We Do with the Eruptor?

We have all had that angry kid walk into our office, right? You know, the one who sets off like a firecracker the moment things don't go his way?

For me, that boy with a hair-trigger temper was Marcus. He was a small child, but boy, could he blow up if the wind blew the wrong way! As his mother put it, "He came out ready for a rumble." When Marcus didn't get his way, he was mad. If he wasn't first in line, he had a fit. If you asked him to get off his device, well, I can't swear in this book … but it was basically a volcanic eruption!

When Marcus came to me, his parents were broken down and scared. Things had gotten so bad, school administrators wanted to send him to school for kids with significant behavioral problems. He was only eight, but his parents (and school administrators) already felt hopeless. No one knew what to do.

But I did. Marcus couldn't regulate. He never could. Right from birth, he had colic. Then, he couldn't sleep, and he had loads of sensory issues. We needed to get Marcus's brain and body to regulate, so he could transition and tolerate—heck, to even do well with—change.

At my center, we worked with Marcus intensively. We got him comfortable in his own body using biofeedback and somatic experiencing techniques and worked with his parents on how to cue and reinforce his behaviors. We then moved to sensory play and art therapy techniques to push the boundaries of what Marcus could tolerate. He learned to create a window of tolerance for uncomfortable feelings, which was a brand-new ability for him. The next layer of our work taught him tools he could use when he needed a resource to deal with whatever life threw at him.

Marcus will go down as one of my all-time favorite kids for many reasons. He really is the biggest softie and laughs like crazy at my funny jokes. Gosh, to see him thrive is why I do what I do!

And really, that's why we all do what we do, isn't it? We want to see kids, teens, and families grow and develop in beautiful ways.

In this chapter, you will find teletherapy resources to help all the Marcuses in the world move past their anger and toward learning healthy behaviors.

Technique Name:
Volcano

What Is It?

An activity that helps children better understand their anger in a hands-on manner.

Materials:

Play-dough, model magic, or air-drying clay

1/2 cup water

1/4 cup vinegar

1/4 cup dish detergent

Red or orange food coloring

2 tablespoons baking soda

Tissue

Clear tub

Instructions:

- Discuss how anger is like a volcano, and connect this simile to his/her meltdown or episodes of anger.

- Make the volcano.

- Add ingredients to the container. This includes water, vinegar, dish detergent and food coloring. Do not add baking soda at this stage.

- Add the baking soda when ready for an eruption. Wrap the baking soda in a tissue and drop into the volcano. The baking soda will react with the vinegar and cause the eruption.

- Repeat as many times as the child is interested.

Questions:

- How do you feel when you explode?

- What can you do before you explode?

- When was the last time you exploded?

- Where did you feel it in your body when you exploded?

Technique Name:
Anger Thermometer

What Is It?

A technique that helps children visualize their anger and what they can do to control it. It makes the anger more relatable—something they can better understand and address.

Materials:

Anger Thermometer Handout

Instructions:

- Have the child rate his or her anger on a scale from one to five.

- Discuss how anger can go up and down and "bubble."

- Discuss how it feels.

- Discuss what s/he can do when feeling anger bubbling.

Questions:

- How do you feel when you explode?

- What can you do before you explode?

- When was the last time you exploded?

- Where did you feel it in your body when your thermometer was bubbling?

- How does your body feel when you are at one?

- How does your body feel when you are at five?

- What sort of things get you to a three or four?

Anger Thermometer Handout

5- In the RED: Loss of control of my thoughts or actions, feelings of rage

4- Body tense, angry, last chance for putting on the brakes

3- Intensified feelings and body sensations, still can put the brakes on

2- Something made me feel uncomfortable, angry, or agitated thoughts

1- Calm

Technique Name:
Understanding Anger

What Is It?

Helps children visualize their anger and better understand their triggers, how they are managing their anger, and what they can do to control it. It makes the anger more relatable—something they can better understand and address.

Materials:

Understanding Anger Worksheet

Anger Thermometer Handout

Pencil, crayons, or markers

Instructions:

- First, find out what number the child is on the anger thermometer.

- Then, complete the worksheet together whether in words or pictures.

Questions:

- How does your body feel when you are at one?

- How does your body feel when you are at five?

- What sort of things get you to a three or four?

Understanding Anger Worksheet

What Makes Me Feel Angry?	Where am I Feeling the Anger?	How I Handle Anger:	How Else Could I Handle Anger?

Technique Name:
I Get Mad When ...

What Is It?

A way for children to recognize times they get mad and are unable to put the brakes on or act without thinking. Also illuminates alternatives to getting angry.

Materials:

I Get Mad When … Worksheet

Pencil, crayons, or markers

Instructions:

- Go through the worksheet with the child and have him or her draw or describe:
- Times s/he gets mad.
- Where s/he often gets mad.
- How s/he stops from exploding or getting mad.
- Discuss strategies.
- Give positive reinforcement.
- Address any shame or worries that surface.

Questions:

- How did your body feel when you were mad?
- How did your body feel when you were happy?
- What was easy?
- What was hard?

I Get Mad When...

Times when I get mad:

Places that I get mad:

How I stay happy and not let things bother me:

Technique Name:
Go with the Flow

What Is It?

A way for children to better understand and practice how to be more flexible when there is a change of plans or something unexpected happens.

Materials:

Go with the Flow Worksheet

Markers, crayons, or pencil

Instructions:

- During the session, explain that sometimes we have a hard time when there is a change of plans or something unexpected happens. These changes can make us feel uncomfortable, angry, sad, or worried.

- Ask the child about the last time s/he had to *go with the flow* or change plans suddenly, and what happened.

- *"How did it make you feel?"*

- *"What happened to your body?"*

- *"What did you do?"*

- Fill out the Go with the Flow Worksheet together. A younger child can draw—an older child can write.

Questions:

- What did you think about this activity?

- Were you surprised by something?

- Did you learn something new?

- What sensations did you notice?

Go With the Flow Worksheet

Draw or describe a time when you had to change your plans.

What was hard for you?

How could you have adjusted or changed your plan?

Technique Name:
How to Compromise

What Is It?

A way for children to visualize what a friend is along with qualities of a good friend. This technique also helps children learn how to compromise to reduce frustrations.

Materials:

How to Compromise Worksheet

Markers, crayons, or pencil

Instructions:

- During the session, explain that you will be discussing ways to compromise with others.

- Review a time when the child wanted something, but someone else wanted something else, and how s/he compromised.

- Fill out the How to Compromise Worksheet by drawing or writing.

- Discuss ways to cope when stressed.

Questions:

- What did you think about this activity?

- Were you surprised by something?

- Did you learn something new?

- What sensations did you notice?

How to Compromise Worksheet

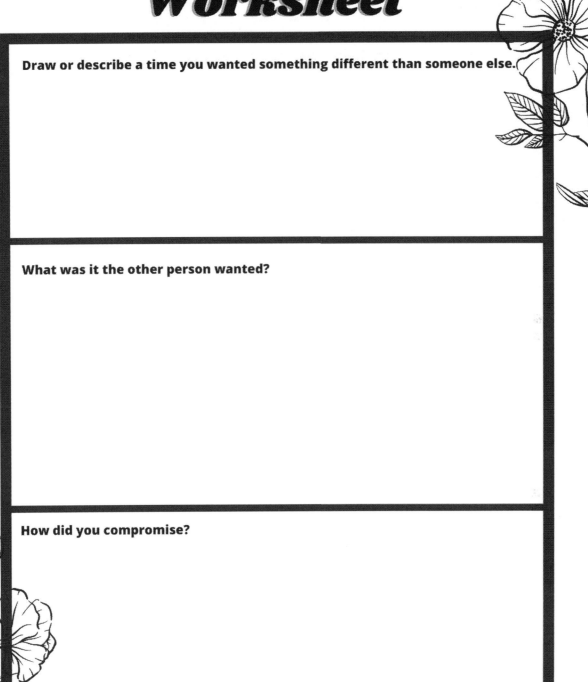

Draw or describe a time you wanted something different than someone else.

What was it the other person wanted?

How did you compromise?

Technique Name:
How to Be a Good Sport

What Is It?

A way for children to visualize what it takes to be a good sport and how to handle the frustration of not winning.

Materials:

How to Be a Good Sport Worksheet

Markers, crayons, or pencil

Instructions:

- During the session, explain that you will be talking about how to be a good sport and manage the frustrations that come with losing.

- Review a time when the child lost a game or some activity, and how s/he handled it.

- Fill out the How to Be a Good Sport Worksheet by drawing or writing.

- Discuss ways to cope when stressed.

Questions:

- What did you think about this activity?

- Were you surprised by something?

- Did you learn something new?

- What sensations did you notice?

- How can you handle not winning?

- How can you show you are a good sport to others?

How to Be a Good Sport Worksheet

Billy didn't get to be in the front of the line.

Amy didn't get the birthday present she wanted.

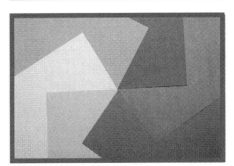

George got the last piece of blue paper that Jack wanted.

Carly lost the game by two points.

Technique Name:
Ways to Be Thoughtful

What Is It?

A way for children to better understand what thoughtfulness is and how it makes others feel.

Materials:

Ways to Be Thoughtful Worksheet

Markers, crayons, or pencil

Instructions:

- During the session, explain that you will be talking about thoughtfulness and how it makes others feel.

- Review a time when the child was thoughtful and how it felt when the person appreciated it.

- Fill out the Ways to Be Thoughtful Worksheet by drawing or writing.

Questions:

- What did you think about this activity?

- Were you surprised by something?

- Did you learn something new?

- What sensations did you notice?

- When was a time when someone was thoughtful to you? How did you feel?

- What are some ways we can show thoughtfulness to others?

- Who is the most thoughtful person you know? What makes him or her so thoughtful?

Ways to Be Thoughtful Worksheet

In each of these examples, what might someone say to show he or she is thoughtful or cares?

| Joe just lost a game. |  |

| Freddy broke his leg. |  |

| Marcy was riding her bike with the neighborhood kids, but got a flat tire. |  |

| Nick is new to the class. |  |

© Roseann-Capanna-Hodge, 2020
© Global Institute of Children's Mental Health, 2020

Ways to Be Thoughtful Worksheet

In each of these examples, what might someone say to show he or she is thoughtful or cares?

Your mom just dropped dinner on the floor.

Your sister failed a test.

Your teacher has her hands full of things.

Technique Name:
Anger Iceberg

What Is It?

A therapeutic technique that helps children see that their anger is only the "tip of the iceberg," and that there are many things that act as triggers to them. Once they identify the triggers that irritate them, they can learn to manage their irritations and not be so angry.

Materials:

Tip of the Iceberg Worksheet

Markers, crayons, or pencil

Instructions:

- During the session, fill out the Tip of the Iceberg Worksheet.

- Identify the child's irritations—things that get him or her mad.

- Identify other feelings present.

- Explore common anger triggers:

  - Being told "no."

  - Getting teased.

  - Being interrupted.

  - Not being listened to.

  - Noises.

  - When something is unfair.

  - Losing a game.

  - Getting ready for school in the morning.

  - The bus.

  - Hunger.

  - Someone taking something that belongs to me.

  - Turning off video games.

  - When someone hurts me.

- Playing with siblings or other kids.

Questions:

- When are you most irritated?

- What feelings other than mad do you have?

- Were you surprised by something?

- Did you learn something new?

- What sensations did you notice?

Anger Iceberg Worksheet

Anger

Technique Name:
Where Is My Anger?

What Is It?

A technique that helps children visualize their irritation and anger, understand where those feelings are in their body, their triggers, how they are managing them, and what they can do to control those feelings. It makes the anger more relatable—something they can better understand and address.

Materials

Where Is My Anger? Worksheet

Pencil, crayons, or markers

Instructions:

- Walk the child or teen through the worksheet.

- Help him or her recognize and connect to his/her body sensations.

- Explain what it means to develop a window of tolerance.

Questions:

- What about this activity surprised you?

- Did you recognize where the anger was in your body?

- How can you use those body sensations in the future?

- What tools do you have to manage your anger?

- What do you see yourself doing in a month (or whatever appropriate time)? How do you see yourself getting there?

WHERE IS MY ANGER WORKSHEET

Where am I feeling anger in my body?

How/When did it start?

What is this anger telling me?

What tools can I use to get through this anger?

Chapter 10 – Teletherapy Techniques for Anxiety and Worry

So Much Anxiety and Worry

In today's world, it is pretty rare for me to see a child or teen who doesn't have some level of worry or anxiety.

Thirty years ago, I would see children with some anxiety, do some cognitive behavioral or play therapy work with them, and combined with parenting support, the anxiety would normalize. Over time, though, issues have become more and more layered and complex.

The truth is, anxiety is an epidemic, and kids are in crisis. Parents are stressed and anxious, too.

Nicky was so stressed out; you could practically smell his cortisol burning. With shoulders up to his ears, constant sweating, and darting eyes, he always had some long-winded statement that he would repeat over and over until you reassured him in some way. Nicky was in a constant state of angst, which made it hard for other kids to relate to him. His body was so uncomfortable to him that he avoided it at all costs. Traditional talk therapy only worsened things for him, because he was already overthinking things.

Nicky was caught in that constant looping thought cycle—like a rollercoaster you can't get off.

Using a combination of neurofeedback, somatic experiencing, and EFT/Tapping, we got Nicky to connect to his body and learn to quiet down all the worried thoughts. He learned how to be in his body without his mind moving from catastrophe to catastrophe. Next, we addressed his cognitive distortions and worked on how to connect with others. It was a slow process of learning new ways to cope and how to be present enough to enjoy the moment.

Nicky is now an adult, and I still see him every once in a while. He is a vastly different human being: calm, engaged, and happy. He has adopted a healthy lifestyle and makes sure to prioritize his health needs every day, so he doesn't fall back into old habits.

Without a doubt, anxiety will be the biggest issue you face with the children, teens, and parents you work with. That's why this Teletherapy Toolkit™ not only provides you with activities to help your clients deal with stress and anxiety, but also with literature and psychoeducation for parents.

Technique Name:
Worry Thermometer

What Is It?

A technique that helps children visualize their worry and what they can do to control it. It makes the stress and worry more relatable—something they can better understand and address.

Materials:

Worry Thermometer Handout

Instructions:

- Have the child rate his or her worry on a scale from one to five.

- Discuss how worry can go up and down and how it can "bubble."

- Discuss how it feels.

- Discuss what s/he can do when s/he feels worry bubbling.

Questions:

- How do you feel when you're worried?

- What can you do before you feel really worried?

- When was the last time you worried about something? What was it?

- Where did you feel it in your body when your thermometer was bubbling?

- How does your body feel when you are at one?

- How does your body feel when you are at five?

- What sort of things get you to a three or four?

Worry
Thermometer
Handout

5- In the RED: Loss of control of my thoughts or actions, feeling like I can't think

4- Body tense, worried, last chance for putting on the brakes

3- Intensified feelings and body sensations, still can put the brakes on

2- Something made me feel uncomfortable, agitated, or worried thoughts

1- Calm

Technique Name:
Understanding Worry

What Is It?

Helps children to visualize worry, identify triggers and how they manage worry, and what they can do to control it. It makes the worry more relatable—something they can better understand and address.

Materials:

Worry Thermometer Handout

Understanding Worry Worksheet

Pencil, crayons, or markers

Instructions:

- Fill out the Worry Thermometer Handout first.

- Then, complete the worksheet together in words or pictures.

Questions:

- How does your body feel when you are at one?

- How does your body feel when you are at five?

- What sort of things get you to a three or four?

Understanding Worry Worksheet

What makes me feel worried?	Where am I feeling the worry?	How I handle worry?	How else could I handle worry?

Technique Name:
Palm of My Hand

What Is It?

Visualizing and remembering what it felt like to be happy makes those positive feelings accessible when children need to reframe or bring calm to their nervous system.

Materials:

Palm of My Hand Worksheet

Pencil, crayons, or markers

Instructions:

- Have the child visualize a happy memory in the palm of his/her hand and then draw it on the worksheet.

- Help him/her remember it in sensory memory by visualizing that happy time and describing how his/her body felt, smells, sensations, and sounds.

- Draw a picture of the happy memory on the worksheet.

- Spend time discussing why the memory felt good.

- Walk the child through how to access the memory when s/he feels stressed or wants to feel good.

Questions:

- What smells do you remember?

- What sounds do you remember?

- What made that a happy memory for you?

- How do you feel during X?

- How can you use that happy memory to improve your mood?

Dr. Roseann-Capanna-Hodge

Palm of My Hand Worksheet

Technique Name:
Butterflies in My Belly

What Is It?

Helps children connect to the physical sensations they are feeling due to stress, worry, sadness, frustration, etc.

Materials:

Pictures of butterflies and butterfly net

Plain white paper

Scissors

Crayons and/or markers

Instructions:

- Have the child cut out and color the butterflies.

- Talk to the child about the physical sensations felt in the body when s/he feels worried, such as butterflies in the belly.

- Ask the child to write down, draw, or talk about different things that stress him/her out or make him/her uncomfortable.

- Have the child arrange the butterflies and use the various sizes for big or little worries.

- Continue discussing big, medium, and little worries.

- End with a discussion about calm-down strategies to use when the "butterflies in the belly" show up, and write them down in the butterfly net to symbolize "catching the butterflies."

Questions:

- How does your body feel when you are at one?

- How does your body feel when you are at five?

- What sort of things get you to a three or four?

Technique Name:
5, 4, 3, 2, 1

What Is It?

A technique that helps stop or end a panic attack.

Materials:

None

Instructions:

- Start with conscious breathing. Breathe in for five seconds, hold the breath for five seconds, and breathe out for five seconds. Continue this pattern until you find your thoughts slowing down.

- Say five THINGS around you that you can SEE. However big or small, recognize five items you can see with your eyes. It could be a painting, a pencil, a pad of paper, etc.

- Say four THINGS around you that you can TOUCH. Recognize four items you can feel with your hands or body. It can be the chair you are sitting on, your legs or hair, a pillow, etc.

- Say three THINGS around you that you can HEAR. Name three things that are audible to you. Tune into the small sounds you hear, such as the tick of a clock, the buzzing of insects, birds chirping, etc.

- Say two THINGS around you that you can SMELL. Take in the smells around you. What do your clothes smell like, your pillow, etc.?

- Say one THING that you can TASTE. It can be real or imagined. You can remember a taste, or eat something.

- Take at least three deep breaths at the end.

Questions:

- How does your body feel?

- What came up for you?

- What positive sensations did you notice?

Technique Name:
Blowing Bubbles

What Is It?

Use breath and blowing bubbles to regulate breathing to calm the nervous system.

Materials:

Bubbles

Instructions:

- Have the child blow imaginary bubbles or practice with real bubbles.

- Then, have him/her practice blowing bubbles without real bubbles.

- Ask him/her to visualize the bubbles s/he is blowing.

- Focus on how s/he feels when blowing bubbles.

- Discuss how s/he can "blow bubbles" anytime s/he is feeling worried.

Questions:

- How does your body feel when you are blowing bubbles?

- In which situations do you feel worried and could "blow bubbles" to regulate your breathing?

Technique Name:
Worry Box

What Is It?

Children create a decorative box to put all their worries in. This activity gives children a sense of control over their worries.

Materials:

A small box

Container or jar

Glue and Glitter

Markers and Paint

Stickers

Old magazines

Paper

Ribbons and/or other decorative items

Instructions:

- Explain to the child that you are making a box to put his or her worries in.

- Explain that the box will be a place in which s/he keeps worries when s/he doesn't have time to think about them.

- Simply write the worry on a piece of paper and place it in a box to be addressed at a later time.

- Regularly check in with the child about the worries in the worry box.

- When the worry no longer needs addressing, the piece of paper can be ripped up and thrown in the garbage, which is a therapeutic activity in itself.

Questions:

- How do you feel now that your worries are put away?

- What sensations do you notice?

- What came up for you?

Technique Name:
Raise Your Body Temperature

What Is It?

A technique that teaches children to calm themselves down or reduce uncomfortable feelings anywhere they are.

Materials:

None

Instructions:

- Instruct the child to focus on his or her hand and intently try to raise his/her body temperature.

- Encourage the child to stay present and continue raising the hand's body temperature, and then, to envision his/her whole body's temperature raising.

- Explain that when you raise your body temperature, your brain goes into an alpha state, which is a calm and happy brain wave state.

Questions:

- How did your body feel?

- Where do you notice your body feeling most calm?

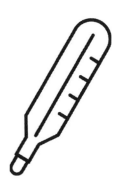

Technique Name:
Dance Party Tension Mover

What Is It?

A technique that removes tension from the body and increases endorphins. Especially useful when a child's endorphins are low, s/he is unfocused, or tension is building.

Materials:

Music

Disco ball (optional)

Instructions:

- Say, *"Hey, we need to move. Do you have a song you really like?"*

- Find the song on YouTube, and make sure it is the radio edited (clean) version.

- Dance together.

- Take at least three deep breaths at the end.

- At the end, share an observation; *"I like this move,"* or *"You look so happy right now."*

Questions:

- How does your body feel?

- How does your mood feel?

- What came up for you?

- What positive sensations did you notice?

Technique Name:
Over the Hurdle Story

What Is It?

Ask children to tell a story starting with a prompt. The story might reveal some of their fears and hopes around a particular issue or event, among other things, and can act as a point of discussion.

Materials:

Over the Hurdle Story Questions

Instructions:

- Explain to the child, *"You are going to create a story about a time you overcame a worry."*

- Explain how you'll successfully address a worry, and that s/he will be able to see him or herself doing it.

- Explain how, when we see ourselves doing something, we are more likely to achieve it.

- Start with the specific worry or fear the child has.

- Create a story in which the child overcomes the worry.

- Walk the child through successful management of the worry.

- Have the child visualize his/her success.

    Step 1: Identify the worry and what is preventing the child from taking action.

    Step 2: Create a story with the child in which s/he overcomes the worry.

    Step 3: Questions to ask the child to build the scene:

- Where are you when this is happening?

- Who else is there?

- How does your body feel?

    Step 4: Questions to ask the child to overcome the fear, worry, problem:

- What do you need to address this problem? (Prompt with physical item, person, song, mantra, etc.)

- How do you see yourself solving this problem?

Questions:

- How is your body feeling?

- What sensations, feelings, and/or memories are you noticing?

Over the Hurdle Story Questions:

- **What do you notice that is different?**

- **What do you miss?**

- **What are you enjoying that is different?**

- **What are the new things you are experiencing that you want to keep?**

- **What would you do differently?**

- **What feelings came up for you during the story?**

- **Is there anything in the story that is familiar to you?**

Technique Name:
Your Story – Quarantine

What Is It?

Children tell a story starting with a prompt. The story might reveal fears and hopes around a particular issue or event, among other things, and can also be a point of discussion.

Materials:

Story Questions

Instructions:

- Explain to the child that you are going to create a story about overcoming worry (or any problem) s/he feels or has had during the quarantine period.

- Explain how you will work on how to successfully address a worry, and that s/he will be able to see him or herself doing it.

- Explain how, when we see ourselves doing something, we are more likely to achieve it.

- Start with the specific worry or fear the child has.

- Create a story for the client in which the worry is overcome.

- Walk the child through successful management of the worry.

- Have the child visualize his or her success.

    Step 1: Identify the worry and what is preventing the child from taking action.

    Step 2: Create a story with the child in which s/he overcomes the worry.

    Step 3: Questions to ask the child to build the scene:

- Where are you when this is happening?

- Who else is there?

- How does your body feel?

    Step 4: Questions to ask the child to overcome the fear, worry, problem:

- What do you need to address this problem? (Can prompt with: physical item, person, song, mantra, etc.)

- How do you see yourself solving this problem?

Questions:

- How is your body feeling?

- What sensations, feelings, and/or memories are you noticing?

Story Questions:

- **What do you notice that is different?**

- **What do you miss during quarantine?**

- **What are you enjoying that is different?**

- **What are the new things you are experiencing that you want to keep?**

- **What feelings came up for you during quarantine?**

Technique Name:
I Get Worried When …

What Is It?

A way for children to see times and places that they get worried and how they can manage their worries.

Materials:

I Get Worried When … Worksheet

Crayons and markers

Instructions:

- Go through the worksheet with the child and have him or her draw:
  - Times s/he gets worried.
  - Where s/he often gets worried.
  - How s/he deals with or get through their worries.
- Discuss strategies.
- Give positive reinforcement.
- Address any shame, feeling, or worries that surface.

Questions:

- How does your body feel when you are worried?
- How does your body feel when you are happy?
- What was easy?
- What was hard?

I Get Worried When ...
Worksheet

Times when I get worried:

Places that I get worried:

How I stay happy and not let things bother me:

Chapter 11 – Teletherapy Techniques: OCD

Breaking the Habit of Obsessions and Compulsions

Morgan had such an intense fear of being contaminated by her brother's germs that she demanded her parents make him live at her grandparent's house. Like a dictator, Morgan would fly off the handle the moment her brother came within six feet of her. Her family did the best they could to deal with her germ-related worries, but her obsessive-compulsive disorder (OCD) was spiraling out of control. It impacted the family's daily life to the point of even having to hang plastic between the kids in the car, or Morgan wouldn't get in.

So how did this all this come to be? Morgan was a happy kid who was developing normally until the summer she was bitten by a tick. Several weeks later, she started having trouble sleeping, and was cranky here and there. School began again, and Morgan seemed to be back to herself for the most part. While her sleep wasn't great, she was happy to be at school. It wasn't until her teacher called and said Morgan was completely unfocused that her parents started to worry. At first, they thought maybe the fourth grade was just harder, but they weren't sure. So, they saw her pediatrician, who gave her a clean bill of health, and they thought all was okay.

As the year went on, Morgan started getting sinus infections. She always had seasonal allergies in the fall but never sinus infections. Her eating slowed, she had big circles under her eyes, and she wasn't as energetic. Then, just before Christmas, she got the flu, and within two weeks of that, her OCD started. At first, she asked a lot of questions. You know, those reassurance-type questions: *"Mom, you will never die, right?" "When will you be back?"* Within days of that, the germ-contamination fears sprang up. Back to the pediatrician they went, who said, *"There is nothing physically wrong with her. You need a psychiatrist."* Luckily, they asked a friend who sent them to our center.

After a QEEG brain map and a clinical intake, it was clear that Morgan had infection-induced mental health issues. It isn't typical to be developing normally and, without any life stressors, have a sudden onset of a mental health issue. Plus, her brain map showed clear signs of active inflammation and multiple patterns of infection. Combined with a sudden onset of OCD, we suspected PANS/PANDAS, which was confirmed by a physician.

Her treatment plan was an intense regime of biofeedback, PEMF, dietary changes, supplements, antimicrobials, and sauna. Once her obsessions and compulsions began to reduce and Morgan wasn't quite so agitated, we introduced Exposure and Response Prevention (ERP) therapy. With ERP, Morgan learned to talk back to her obsessions and compulsions instead of constantly avoiding the things that made her anxious. Her entire family participated, and they learned that with OCD, you can't give in to demands, because if you do, you're reinforcing the behavior (or "feeding the barking dog"). The more they accommodated Morgan's obsessions and compulsions, the more likely she would be to repeat her habits or behaviors. When her family stopped giving her reassurance and accommodating her contamination fears, Morgan's behavior changed.

Infectious disease is on the rise, and so are conditions like Lyme and tick-borne disease and PANS/PANDAS. OCD is one of the many conditions that can result from chronic disease states and inflammatory conditions. With OCD, it is imperative as therapists that we teach children, teens, and their families to not accommodate the obsessions and compulsions, as again, doing so only provides negative reinforcement.

In The Teletherapy Toolkit™, we provide you with some great OCD therapy techniques based on ERP foundational pieces. I highly suggest getting trained in ERP and joining the International Obsessive-Compulsive Disorder Foundation (IOCDF) to learn more about OCD and get further training.

Technique Name:
Trigger List

What Is It?

A way for children and therapists to assess and monitor triggers that contribute to obsessive thoughts and compulsive behaviors. This will create awareness around what triggers them, how much anxiety they have around each trigger, and their behaviors around and response to each trigger. This list is a critical part of ERP treatment, because from it, the client and therapist will determine which triggers need to be addressed first.

Materials:

Trigger List Graph

SUDS Level Handout

Instructions:

- During the session, explain that you are making a list of the child's worries, and how understanding triggers helps one break the worry and behavioral cycle of obsessions and compulsions.

- Next, ask the child about what triggers his or her anxiety.

- Explain that you will both be writing them down (therapist writes for younger child) and giving them a SUDS rating.

Questions:

- What did you think about this activity?

- Were you surprised by something?

- Did you learn something new?

- What sensations did you notice?

TRIGGER LIST

Ranking	Trigger	SUDS (0-10)	What I Do To Feel Better	Sensations I Notice

Technique Name:
Worry Script

What Is It?

A therapeutic technique that helps children manage excessive worries.

Materials:

Worry Script Worksheet

Instructions:

- Explain to the child that he or she will be writing about his/her worries as if it were a story someone can pick up and read.

- Explain how doing so makes him/her a 'detective' in figuring out what bothers him/her, so s/he can understand discomfort and what triggers it.

- For a younger child, s/he can dictate it as you write it, whereas an older child can write it with your help.

- If the child is very young or has a processing or learning issues, this activity can be completed verbally with puppets.

- Explain how you want them to include:

  - What the worry is.

  - What the trigger was.

  - How s/he handled or coped with the worry.

- Ask the child to include vivid and visual details and note how his or her body felt or thoughts that came up.

Questions:

- What did you think about this activity?

- Were you surprised by something?

- Did you learn something new?

- Was there something that made you feel comfortable or uncomfortable?

- What sensations did you notice?

Worry Script Worksheet

What is the thing or situation you are worrying about?

_____

_____

_____

_____

_____

_____

Describe when you worried, and paint the picture of what it looked like.

_____

_____

_____

_____

_____

_____

_____

Describe how you coped with or managed your worry.

_____

_____

_____

_____

_____

_____

Technique Name:
Negative Reinforcement Cycle

What Is It?

A therapeutic technique that provides the neuroscience explanation of how OCD is easily reinforced through a process of negative reinforcement. Once children understand that OCD behaviors get reinforced, they also will understand that this negative reinforcement cycle can be broken or unlearned.

Materials:

Worry Script Worksheet

Negative Reinforcement Cycle Handout

Virtual or real whiteboard

Instructions:

- Devote an entire session to this activity to explain what the Negative Reinforcement Cycle is and how the child can break it.

- Use The Negative Reinforcement Cycle Handout and the virtual whiteboard to interact with the child.

- Provide psychoeducation around what obsession, compulsion, and distress mean/are (use Worry Technique with accompanying script).

- Explain how the purpose of a compulsion is to relieve the distress (use Worry Technique with accompanying script).

- Review the whole Negative Reinforcement Cycle.

- Explain that any relief gained is temporary. Write on the whiteboard, "Temporary Relief," and then open up dialogue with parents about codependent and reassurance behaviors.

- Use this document again and again to review how obsessive thoughts and behaviors get reinforced and how the child and family can break them.

Questions:

- What did you think about this activity?

- Were you surprised by something?

- Did you learn something new?

- Was there something that made you feel comfortable or uncomfortable?

- What sensations did you notice?

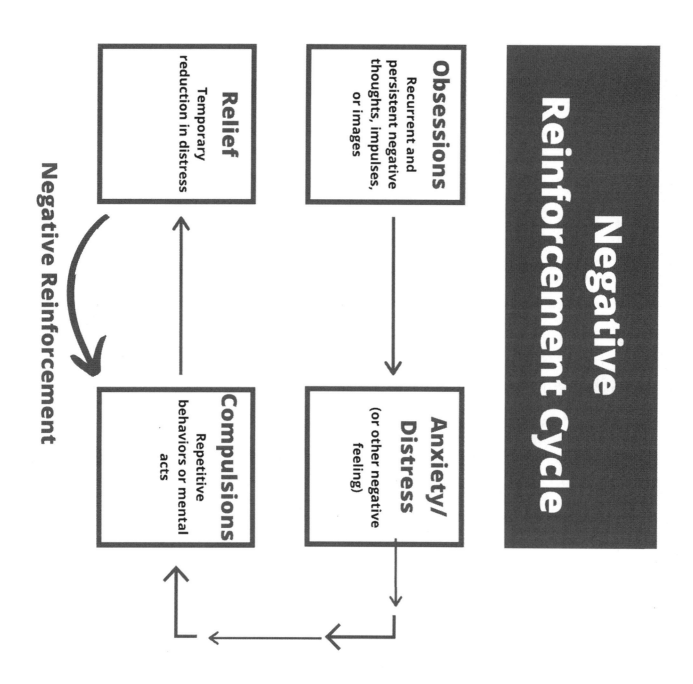

© Roseann-Capanna-Hodge, 2020
© Global Institute of Children's Mental Health, 2020

Technique Name:
OCD Thought-and-Behavior Keeper

What Is It?

A way to track obsessive or compulsive thoughts and behaviors to create awareness and mindfulness around them. Helps a clinician to assess if clients are taking ownership of their OCD piece. Are they saying, *"OCD is making me ... think"*? Or *"I keep thinking ..."*? Also assists clinician in determining when to differentiate between story content versus repetitive fears in order to focus on teaching clients to increase their tolerance to discomfort via treatment and exposures.

Materials:

Journal

Instructions:

- Explain to the child that he or she will be keeping track of obsessive thoughts that are intrusive or that keep coming back and repetitive compulsive thoughts and behaviors that are occurring in order to feel better/push down uncomfortable thoughts.

- Children should use a journal, so they can look back during a session in order to remember things (OCD/anxiety makes you forget things) as well as monitor and celebrate their progress over time.

- Children should include not just thoughts and behaviors, but strategies that work as well, so they can use them when stuck in and out of sessions.

- At the next appointment, explain that the first time they keep track of the thoughts and behaviors, that it is their first exposure. It is very important to build up confidence and success through reinforcement of their activity.

- At the next appointment, should re-explain the negative cycle (use handout) and the therapeutic process of talking back to OCD.

Questions:

- What did you think about this activity?

- Were you surprised by something?

- Did you learn something new?

- Was there something that made you feel comfortable or uncomfortable?

- What sensations did you notice?

Technique Name:
An OCD Character

What Is It?

A therapeutic technique that helps children separate themselves from their OCD thoughts. When children see their own thoughts on the page, it is much easier for them to recognize—and then learn to "talk back" to—their obsessions and compulsions. Those with OCD often get stuck in obsessive thinking, which doesn't accurately represent who they are as people. This activity gives them a visual to see who they really are. This is a very empowering technique for any person of any age to understand that the OCD isn't who they are, and that they can take control of those obsessions and compulsions and really build that confidence to talk back to their OCD.

Materials:

Coping Statements Worksheet

Negative Reinforcement Cycle Handout

OCD Character Thought-Bubble Worksheet

Markers or crayons

Instructions:

- Explain to the child that he or she will be drawing a character that represents his/her OCD.

- Say, *"When you visualize your OCD, that is what I want you to draw on this page."*

- Encourage the child to draw whatever s/he wants in any form—it can even be a stick figure. Everyone's drawing is unique.

- Say, *"We just need you to draw an image that your brain can relate to and will recognize. This is what your OCD looks like."*

- In the thought bubbles, ask the child to write what the OCD is saying—dictate and record the obsessive thoughts.

- This activity will have to be paced according to individual needs; you might want to complete each part of the activity over one to three sessions. Slow the process if the client appears overwhelmed. For example, Session 1: Drawing the character. Session 2: Filling in the thought bubbles. Session 3: Preparing the thought statements.

- Use the Coping Statements Worksheet as a supplement if needed for overwhelm.

- It is essential to provide support and build confidence without giving any reassurance to the child (use Negative Reinforcement Cycle Handout).

- *Note: This activity can be very emotional for children, because it may be the first time they have really looked at their obsessions and compulsions.

Questions:

- What did you think about this activity?

- Were you surprised by something?

- Did you learn something new?

- Was there something that made you feel comfortable or uncomfortable?

- What sensations did you notice?

OCD Character Thought-Bubble Worksheet

Technique Name:
SUDS - ERP OCD Therapy

What Is It?

A way for both children and therapist to assess and monitor children's levels of distress. This helps children to see their stress levels and get "out of their own head." It also helps track progress they are making in therapy.

Subjective distress is defined as *"the discomfort, pain, and general uncomfortable feelings a person is experiencing."* "Subjective" means that it comes from the perspective of the child experiencing it. Discomfort can result from real or perceived sources and is unique to each person.

SUDS is a numbered scale (1-10, 1-100) that measures the level at which an experience is disturbing or distressing to an individual. SUDS is very helpful for clients who are stuck, negative thinkers, or experiencing any level of anxiety, panic, depression, or OCD.

Materials:

SUDS Level Handout

Trigger Graph

Instructions:

- Explain what SUDS means: Subjective Units of Distress.

- Explain how it is a way for you to see how your mind and body is reacting to stressors.

- Explain how you will use SUDS to monitor how much anxiety the child is experiencing during an exposure and from triggers.

- Explain how using SUDS will help to know when to use tools if triggered.

- Explain how SUDS will help the child to see how much progress s/he is making in therapy.

- Can use it as a check-in at every session.

Questions:

- What sensations did you notice this week as you were monitoring your SUDS?

- What happened to your obsessions and compulsions when using SUDS?

- Now that you are monitoring your triggers, what situations made your SUDS increase? And decrease?

- What tools lowered your SUDS?

DR. ROSEANN AND ASSOCIATES

Subjective Units of Distress Scale (SUDS)

0- COMPLETELY RELAXED/ NO STRESS

1- COMFORTABLY ALERT

2- MINIMUM ANXIETY/ STRESS

3- MILD STRESS

4- MILD TO MODERATE STRESS

5-MODERATE STRESS

6- MODERATE TO HIGH STRESS

7- QUITE ANXIOUS/ STRESSED

8- VERY STRESSED

9- EXTREMELY STRESSED

10- THE MOST ANXIOUS/ STRESSED YOU HAVE BEEN

Technique Name:
I Get Obsessive or Compulsive When ...

What Is It?

A way for children to see times and places they get triggered and have obsessions or compulsions and how they can manage them.

Materials:

I Get Obsessive or Compulsive When ... Worksheet

Crayons and markers

Instructions:

- Go through the worksheet with the child and have him or her draw:
    - Times s/he has obsessions or compulsions.
    - Places s/he often has obsessions or compulsions.
    - How s/he deals with or gets through obsessions or compulsions.
- Discuss strategies.
- Give positive reinforcement.
- Address any shame, feeling, or worries that surface.

Questions:

- How did your body feel when you had obsessions or compulsions?
- How did your body feel when you were happy?
- What was easy?
- What was hard?

I Get Obsessions or Compulsions When ...

Times when I have obsessions or compulsions:

Places that I get obsessions or compulsions:

How I talk back to my obsessions or compulsions:

Technique Name:
Wait, Distract, and Evaluate

What Is It?

A way for children or teens to see how they can gain control of their obsessions or compulsions, evaluate options, and determine how they can manage their obsessions and compulsions.

Materials:

Wait, Distract, and Evaluate Worksheet

Pen, pencil, or markers

Instructions:

- Go through the worksheet with the child or teen and have him or her make a commitment to how long s/he can wait before (and let him/herself be distracted from) giving into obsessions and compulsions.

- Discuss strategies to distract from obsessions and compulsions.

- Evaluate the pros and cons of completing and not completing the thought or behavior.

- Give positive reinforcement.

- Address any shame, feeling, or worries that surface.

Questions:

- How did your body feel when you waited and distracted yourself from your obsessions or compulsions?

- What was easy?

- What was hard?

- How proud are you for distracting yourself?

Wait, Distract, Evaluate Worksheet

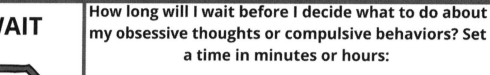

WAIT	How long will I wait before I decide what to do about my obsessive thoughts or compulsive behaviors? Set a time in minutes or hours:
DISTRACT 	Things I can do to occupy myself, talk back to, or distract me from my obsessive thoughts or compulsive behaviors:
EVALUATE 	Examine the pros and cons of this habit. Pros of doing this: Cons of doing this: Reasons I want to stop: The strategy that works the best for me:

Technique Name:
Coping Thoughts

What Is It?

A way for children or teens to cultivate encouraging and positive statements that are used to replace negative and inaccurate thoughts. This helps children/teens practice and learn to tolerate stress and uncomfortable emotions and sensations, as well as gain control of their obsessions or compulsions.

Materials:

Coping Strategies Worksheet

General Coping Statements Handout

Blank paper

Pen, pencil, or markers

Instructions:

- Go through the worksheet with the child or teen and have him or her write down a coping thought or positive statement for each triggering or distressing situation.

- Encourage him/her to write down something to tell him/herself to help get through.

- Encourage him/her to write them down on a piece of paper and carry it in a pocket or put it in a journal to help remind him/her to use them.

Questions:

- How did your body feel when you used these coping statements after talking back to your obsessions or compulsions?

- What was easy?

- What was hard?

COPING STRATEGIES WORKSHEET

Triggering or Distressing Situation	Coping Statement

General Coping Statements

"I know I am going to be okay."

"Feelings always pass."

"Relax and think positively."

"One step at a time."

"I have learned how to cope with that."

"I achieved that and I am getting better."

"I handled that and it should be easier next time."

"I can be pleased with the progress I'm making."

"I did that well."

© Roseann-Capanna-Hodge, 2020

© Global Institute of Children's Mental Health, 2020

General Coping Statements

"My mind is not always my friend."

"Thoughts are just thoughts. They are not necessarily true or factual."

"Keep calm and carry on."

"This is difficult and uncomfortable but it is only temporary."

"I choose to see this challenge as an opportunity."

"I can use my coping skills to help me get through this."

"I can learn from this and it will be easier next time."

"I will concentrate on what I have to do."

"I will learn from this experience, even if it seems hard to understand right now."

© Roseann-Capanna-Hodge, 2020
© Global Institute of Children's Mental Health, 2020

General Coping Statements

"Short term pain can lead to long term gain."

"I can feel bad and still choose to make a new and healthy decision."

"I don't need to rush. I can take things slowly."

"I have survived before and I will survive now."

"I feel this way because of my past experiences, but I am safe right now."

"Things are not as bad as I make them out to be."

"I'm stronger than I think."

"It's okay to feel this way as it is a normal reaction."

"Right now, I am not in danger. Right now, I am safe."

© Roseann-Capanna-Hodge, 2020
© Global Institute of Children's Mental Health, 2020

General Coping Statements

"I can breathe through this."

"Don't sweat the small stuff."

"It's not worth getting mad about."

"I won't take this personally."

"I will not ignore this problem or person. I will get through this."

"I am going to close my eyes, breathe, and take a moment to think this through."

© Roseann-Capanna-Hodge, 2020
© Global Institute of Children's Mental Health, 2020

General Coping Statements

"I can handle this and stay in control."

"Getting angry isn't going to help."

"I am in charge, not my anger."

"Things are not as bad as I am making them out to be."

"I can only control myself and not anyone or anything else."

© Roseann-Capanna-Hodge, 2020
© Global Institute of Children's Mental Health, 2020

General Coping Statements

"Keep calm."

"Relax and think positive thoughts."

"Anxiety won't hurt me."

"This worried feeling isn't comfortable, but I can handle it."

"Anxious feelings are unpleasant, but not harmful or dangerous."

"I can feel anxious and still deal with this situation."

"This is not an emergency. I will take a breath, slow down, and think about what I need to do."

"If I focus on the present moment, my anxiety may decrease."

"Fighting this won't help, so take a breath and let it float away."

© Roseann-Capanna-Hodge, 2020
© Global Institute of Children's Mental Health, 2020

General Coping Statements

"These are just thoughts and they are not real."

"Focus on pleasant things."

"I can break this worry-cycle by breathing and staying present."

"Feeling uncomfortable or having muscle tension is natural. These signs alert me to use my coping strategies."

"I have been through this worry before."

"I will use positive affirmations."

"I will listen to what my body is telling me and focus on a part of my body that feels calm."

© Roseann-Capanna-Hodge, 2020
© Global Institute of Children's Mental Health, 2020

General Coping Statements

"I will do the best I can."

"I can do one task at a time."

"I can do this and I'm doing it now."

"It will get easier once I get started."

"I will take it step by step and I will not rush."

"I will persevere."

"I will jump in and be alright."

"Fear doesn't rule me."

© Roseann-Capanna-Hodge, 2020
© Global Institute of Children's Mental Health, 2020

272

General Coping Statements

"I can breathe through my fear."

"Worry doesn't help."

"If I do not focus on fear, I will not be afraid."

"Facing my fears can help me overcome them."

"I won't let negative thoughts creep in."

"I can learn to face my fears."

© Roseann-Capanna-Hodge, 2020
© Global Institute of Children's Mental Health, 2020

General Coping Statements

"I can handle whatever happens."

"It is okay to make mistakes."

"All I have to do is try."

"I have succeeded before."

"There's an end to this difficult situation."

"I am only afraid because I decided to be. I can decide not to be."

"Tomorrow I will feel better."

© Roseann-Capanna-Hodge, 2020
© Global Institute of Children's Mental Health, 2020

General Coping Statements

"Inhale, exhale."

"What is my body telling me?"

"My distress will soon be over."

"Take one step at a time."

"What do I need to do right now?"

"Try to accept things as they are."

"Take a breath and take one action."

"I am only in control of my own thoughts and actions."

© Roseann-Capanna-Hodge, 2020
© Global Institute of Children's Mental Health, 2020

General Coping Statements

"Things will get better."

"I am in control of how I react to this situation."

"This isn't as bad as I thought."

"I can turn this situation around."

"Focus on one sensation at a time."

"No matter how bad things seem, I can can get to the other side."

"I can meditate through."

© Roseann-Capanna-Hodge, 2020

© Global Institute of Children's Mental Health, 2020

General Coping Statements

"Good things are going to happen."

"I won't be harmed."

"I am strong enough."

"This is my body's way of telling me to count down from 10 to 1."

"I will allow my body to experience this."

"Right now I can treat my body with love and kindness."

"I will heal from this."

"I have survived panic attacks before and I will survive this as well."

© Roseann-Capanna-Hodge, 2020
© Global Institute of Children's Mental Health, 2020

General Coping Statements

"I am very powerful."

"I am loved."

"I am not alone. There are others that share these experiences."

"I will calm my nervous system with big deep breaths."

"Everything will work itself out."

"This feeling is just my racing mind and adrenaline pumping. It will pass in a couple of minutes."

© Roseann-Capanna-Hodge, 2020
© Global Institute of Children's Mental Health, 2020

General Coping Statements

"Stop, and breathe. I can do this."

"This will pass."

"This feeling will go away."

"I can be anxious, angry, or sad and still deal with this."

"I have done this before and I can do it again."

"This feels unpleasant but it is my body's reaction to stress. It will pass."

"This does not feel pleasant, however feelings are often wrong."

"These are just feelings and they will go away."

"This won't last forever."

© Roseann-Capanna-Hodge, 2020
© Global Institute of Children's Mental Health, 2020

Chapter 12 – Teletherapy Techniques: Breathwork, Mindfulness, Progressive Relaxation, and Visualization

Slowing Down and Connecting to Your Brain and Body Is More Important Than Ever

Jordan was a little girl who worried *all the time*. She worried about herself, her parents, her teachers, and everyone in her life. Her constant worry affected her physically; she was constipated and had trouble settling for sleep. She was also prone to emotional outbursts. Her parents had tried traditional talk therapy, but it only seemed to make Jordan even more emotional.

Her parents noticed that Jordan was less worried and tense when she participated in a family yoga class, and knowing she had to get more comfortable in her own skin and decrease her tension, they thought a different approach to her anxiety—something other than traditional counseling—might be more effective.

(Did I forget to mention that Jordan wasn't some Wall Street floor trader, but a fourteen-year-old girl? And no, these weren't new behaviors; Jordan had always been tense.)

When I met with Jordan, it was obvious she was a rapid chest breather. Her body was so tense, she looked like a wooden doll when she sat. She hated connecting with her body, because she experienced everything from headaches to muscle aches. Her mind was always busy, and her body paid the price for it.

The first thing I did with Jordan was teach her the 4-7-8-second breathing exercise. She had to create a rhythm to her breathing and learn how to belly breathe, so she could pull her nervous system out of the stressed sympathetic dominant state and into a calmer parasympathetic state. Simple breathing was very hard for Jordan. She struggled to calm her mind and connect to the rhythm of her breath. Her level of stress was so intense, it was almost like working with someone who had nearly been run over crossing the street.

Once Jordan could maintain a regular breath, I helped her work through a progressive relaxation exercise where she tensed and relaxed her muscles. Her body began to relax, and her breath moved to her belly. Jordan welcomed (and needed) an entire session on just learning how to breathe and release tension from her muscles. I gave her homework, which was to practice 4-7-8 breathing at least three times a day and to take magnesium l-threonate at least one hour before bed. We worked on this for weeks, each time changing the balance of the session to include more and more cognitive behavioral therapy.

Over time, Jordan became more comfortable in her own skin, and the physical discomfort she felt from stress and worry subsided. She was no longer a prisoner to her thoughts, and she had the resources to stop that inner chatter and challenge cognitive distortions.

As therapists, we often feel like we have to just deal with the mind, even when a child's or teen's body is a stress bomb waiting to detonate. I have always operated on the belief that therapists should help a client connect mind, body, and spirit. We can't separate these interconnected parts, and instead should facilitate their integration to support mental health at a deeper level.

It truly fills my heart to see therapists embrace breathwork, mindfulness, progressive relaxation, and visualization. I have helped so many people with these techniques over 30 years, and now, The Teletherapy Toolkit™ gives you the tools to do the same with your virtual clients.

Technique Name:
4, 7, 8 Breath

What Is It?

This breathing technique shows children and teens how to regulate their breathing. Intentful breathing shifts your energy, connects you more deeply with your body, calms your nervous system, and decreases stress in your brain and body.

Materials:

None

Instructions:

- This is a great warm-up or ending exercise.

- Breathe in through the nose for four seconds.

- Hold your breath for seven seconds.

- Exhale from your mouth for eight seconds.

- Repeat at least three times.

Questions:

- Do you feel different than you did before we started?

- Tell me what's different about how your body feels now.

Technique Name:
Bubble Breath

What Is It?

This breathing technique shows children and teens how to regulate their breathing. Intentful breathing shifts your energy, connects you more deeply with your body, calms your nervous system, and decreases stress in your brain and body. This is a good exercise for a child who is stuck on a worry, upsetting thought, or incident.

Materials:

None

Instructions:

- This is a great warm-up or ending exercise.

- Explain that this exercise will help the child "blow out" worry bubbles, so s/he can feel more relaxed.

- Tell the child to imagine s/he has an imaginary bottle of bubbles.

- Tell the child to think about anything that upsets him/her.

- Next, have the child imagine blowing that concern into the bubble as he/she blows into the bubble wand.

- Tell him/her to picture the worry in the bubble as it drifts away.

- When it pops, explain that the worry has popped outside of him/her, and can no longer bother him/her. Have the child continue blowing bubbles until s/he is relaxed and calm.

Questions:

- Do you feel different than you did before we started?

- Tell me what's different about how your body feels now.

Technique Name:
Butterfly Breath

What Is It?

This breathing technique shows children and teens how to regulate their breathing. Intentful breathing shifts your energy, connects you more deeply with your body, calms your nervous system, and decreases stress in your brain and body. Great for children with sensory needs, focus issues, or any issues connecting to the body.

Materials:

None

Instructions:

- This is a great warm-up or ending exercise.

- Have the child stand up. Explain that s/he is going to pretend to be a butterfly.

- Ask the child to relax his/her shoulders.

- Instruct the child to imagine being a butterfly.

- Next, ask the child to breathe in and out, flexing his/her wings (expand arms way out).

- Then, instruct the child to breathe out as s/he brings arms in.

- Repeat at least five to 10 times.

Questions:

- Do you feel different than you did before we started?

- Tell me what's different about how your body feels now.

Technique Name:
Belly Bear Breathing

What Is It?

This breathing technique shows children and teens how to regulate their breathing. Intentful breathing shifts your energy, connects you more deeply with your body, calms your nervous system, and decreases stress in your brain and body.

Materials:

A stuffed bear or animal

Instructions:

- This is a great warm-up or ending exercise.

- Ask the child or teen to sit comfortably and place his/her hands on his/her belly (if using a stuffed animal, s/he can hold it on top of the belly).

- As you count to three, ask the child to inhale deeply through the nose.

- Ask the child to fill his/her belly with air with the inhale.

- Tell the child that his/her belly should feel like it is getting bigger as it fills with air.

- Focus on making the stuffed animal rise as the belly fills with air and fall with the exhale.

- Have the child exhale on a slow count of four.

- Repeat at least three times.

Questions:

- Do you feel different than you did before we started?

- Tell me what's different about how your body feels now.

Technique Name:
Star Breathing

What Is It?

This breathing technique shows children and teens how to regulate their breathing. Intentful breathing shifts your energy, connects you more deeply with your body, calms your nervous system, and decreases stress in your brain and body.

Materials:

Star Breathing Handout

Instructions:

- This is a great warm-up or ending exercise.
- Start at any "Breathe in" side on the star.
- Have the child trace his or her finger over the "Breathe in" side of the point.
- Have the child hold his/her breath when his/her finger gets to the tip of the point.
- Have the child breathe out as s/he traces a finger over the other side of the point.
- Keep going until s/he reaches where s/he started.
- Trace over and breathe until s/he has gone around the whole star.

Questions:

- Do you feel different than you did before we started?
- Tell me what's different about how your body feels now.

STAR BREATHING

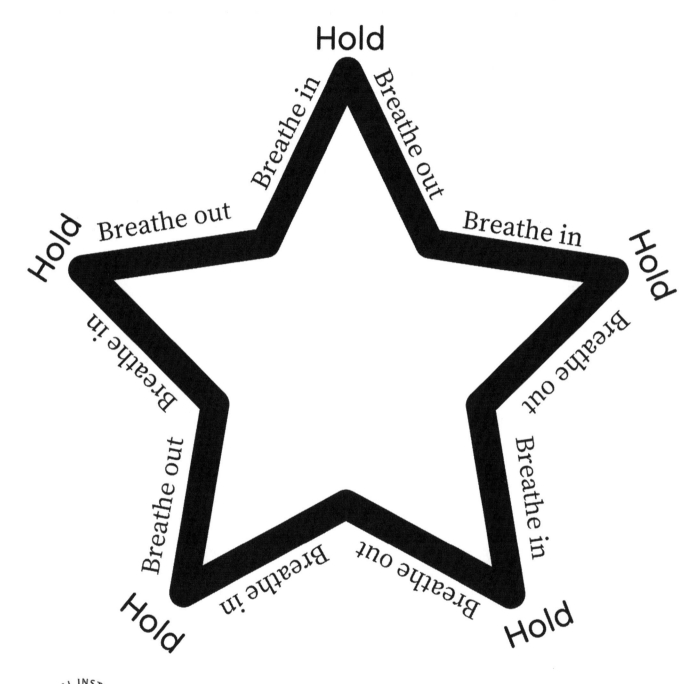

Hold

Breathe in

Breathe out

Breathe out

Breathe in

Hold

Hold

Breathe in

Breathe out

Breathe out

Breathe in

Hold

Breathe in

Breathe out

Hold

Technique Name:
Square Breathing

What Is It?

This breathing technique shows children and teens how to regulate their breathing. Intentful breathing shifts your energy, connects you more deeply with your body, calms your nervous system, and decreases stress in your brain and body.

Materials:

None

Instructions:

- This is a great warm-up or ending exercise.

- Have the child or teen sit comfortably in a chair, optimally with feet on the ground.

- Instruct the child to begin by slowly exhaling all air.

- Then, gently inhale through the nose on a slow count of four.

- Hold at the top of the breath for a count of four.

- Then, gently exhale through the mouth for a count of four.

- At the bottom of the breath, pause and hold for the count of four.

- Repeat at least three times.

Questions:

- Do you feel different than you did before we started?

- Tell me what's different about how your body feels now.

Technique Name:
Infinity Breathing

What Is It?

This breathing technique shows children and teens how to regulate their breathing. Intentful breathing shifts your energy, connects you more deeply with your body, calms your nervous system, and decreases stress in your brain and body.

Materials:

Infinity Breathing Handout

Instructions:

- This is a great warm-up or ending exercise.

- Start in the middle of the eight—or infinity—sign.

- Tell the child to go up to the left and trace the left part of the 8/infinity sign with his/her finger while s/he breathes in.

- When s/he gets to the middle of the eight/infinity sign, breathe out while s/he traces the right part of the 8/infinity sign with his/her finger.

- As the child or teen gets more comfortable with this breathing exercise, have him/her stand up and incorporate the infinity hand movements along with the breath.

- Do this exercise 10 times.

Questions:

- Do you feel different than you did before we started?

- Tell me what's different about how your body feels now.

Infinity Breathing

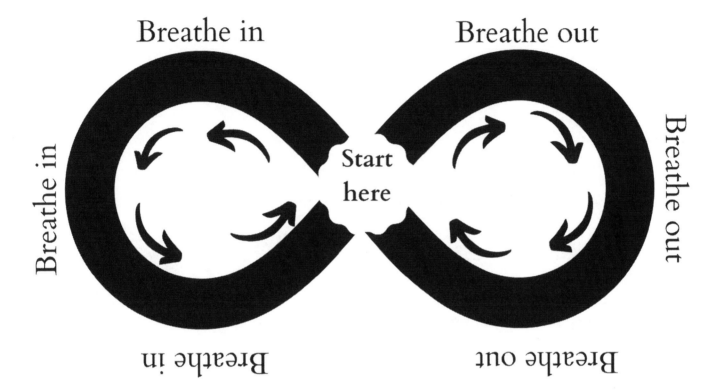

Technique Name:
Progressive Relaxation

What Is It?

A technique that shows children how they can release tension from their body, as well as differentiate between tense muscles and relaxed muscles. This is an easy and enjoyable way for children to learn how to release tension and ground themselves.

Materials:

This script

Instructions:

- Read through the script slowly, using a calming tone. Lengthen and shorten it based on the child's age.

- *"During this relaxation, I will ask you to tense different muscles throughout your body, like this."* (Demonstrate a tensing and releasing of a muscle and have the child practice with you.)

- *"Close your eyes and keep them closed until we've concluded all of the breathing and relaxation exercises."*

- *"We are going to breathe in through your nose and hold for a few seconds, then breathe out through your mouth. We will do this a few times. Let's get started."*

- *"Feel your tummy, and place one hand right above your belly button. Put your other hand on top of that hand, like this."* (Demonstrate.) *"Breathe in deeply, and let out the breath slowly. Notice how your tummy rises and falls."*

- Have the child breathe in deeply and let out the breath slowly, and repeat for five to 10 breaths.

- *"Next, let's relax the muscles in your body. Pretend you have an orange in your right hand and squeeze it as hard as you can."* (Hold the squeeze for about five seconds.) *"Pay attention to the tension in your muscles. Now, drop the orange and let your muscles relax."* Repeat with the left arm.

- *"Now, stretch your arms high above your head, like you are trying to touch the sky. Now, let your arms fall. Notice how your body feels. Now, reach for the ceiling."*

- *"Stretch higher. Higher! Go as high as you can. Then, pull back and hold for a few seconds. Now, let your arms drop to your side. Doesn't that feel good?"*

- *"Now, let's work on your jaw muscles. We're going to pretend you're chewing something really chewy in your mouth, and you're going to try as hard as you can to bite through it. Bite hard. Harder! Now, relax your jaw muscles. Let's try it again."*

- *"We're going to work on your face and nose now. Scrunch up your nose as tight as you can. Hold that scrunchy face. Now relax. Let's try it again; scrunch harder. Harder! Relax. Notice how relaxed your face feels."*

- *"We're moving to your tummy now. For this exercise, you're going to squeeze your belly as hard as you can, trying to pull your muscles tight. Now squeeze … squeeze … squeeze. Good. You can relax now. Let's do that again and hold it for five seconds. Squeeze."* (Slowly count to five.) *"Relax. Let's try it one more time. Squeeze as hard as you can."* (Count to five.) *"Relax. Now relax your entire body, and notice how good that feels."*

- "Now, pretend you're on a white, sandy beach. Feel the sun on your face and body. Squeeze your toes into the sand. Feel the wet sand squish between your toes, using the muscles in your legs to squeeze your toes into the sand as hard as you can. Relax the muscles in your legs. Feel the tension wash away into the ocean. Let's try it again, only this time, dig deeper into the sand, using your legs once again to help you grip with your toes. Relax your toes. Relax your legs. Now relax your entire body, and notice how good that feels."

- *"Now, let your whole body relax. Ahhh. Notice how good it feels to be relaxed. Now, just enjoy the feeling. I am going to slowly count to three. When I get to three, slowly open your eyes. One … two … three."*

- *"Now you know how to melt away the tightness in your body. Whenever you feel worried, stressed, or even sad, take a few minutes to tighten your muscles and then relax them."*

Questions:

- Do you feel different than you did before we started?

- Tell me what's different about how your body feels now.

- Were there parts that were easier to squeeze and release than others?

Technique Name:
Progressive Relaxation - Spaghetti Body

What Is It?

A technique that shows children how they can release tension from their body. This is an easy and enjoyable way for children to learn how to release tension and ground themselves.

Materials:

This script

Instructions:

- *"Sometimes, it is easy to get tense and not even realize it. This exercise will help us learn the difference between being tense and being relaxed. It will also show you an easy way to relax."*

- *"Have you seen wet spaghetti noodles? They are wiggly, not tight. You can make your body like spaghetti noodles."*

- *"To get your spaghetti body, first you have to make your body very tight all over. Let's practice. Scrunch your hands very tight, and then let go."*

- *"Now, we are ready. First, imagine that you are a piece of cooked spaghetti. Tighten both your fists and arms, squeeze your legs and stomach, and make your whole body as stiff as possible, so you can't bend. Keep your whole body tense until you count to five. Now relax. Pretend that you are now a piece of cooked spaghetti. Let your whole body become loose and floppy. Let go of all the tension in your body. Relax your shoulders and stomach, take a deep breath, and let your body be as loose and floppy as cooked spaghetti."*

- *"Which feels better, being cooked or uncooked spaghetti?"*

- *"Now, become raw spaghetti again. Squeeze all the muscles in your body until you are as stiff as raw spaghetti. Even make your face tense—squeeze all the muscles in your mouth and forehead. Squeeze your shoulders up to your ears. Make fists with your hands. Squeeze your eyes shut and push your feet into the floor. Hold your body stiff like raw spaghetti until the count of five. Now, relax your whole body. Go floppy like cooked spaghetti. Relax your face, your shoulders, your stomach, your arms, and your legs."*

- *"Now, which felt better, being cooked or uncooked spaghetti?"*

- *"Become the raw spaghetti one last time, and tense your whole body from head to toe. Make every part of your body as tense and stiff as you can until the count of five. Now, relax your body like cooked spaghetti. It takes a lot of work to be as tense as raw spaghetti, and it can make you feel tired to do this all day. When you notice that your body is feeling stiff or tense, don't forget that you can make yourself feel like cooked spaghetti by relaxing the muscles in your body."*

- *"You have to practice spaghetti body for it to really help your body get rid of all that tension. Can you practice every day?"*

Questions:

- Do you feel different than you did before we started?

- Tell me what's different about how your body feels now.

Technique Name:
Progressive Relaxation – Treehouse

What Is It?

A technique that shows children how they can release tension from their body. This is an easy and enjoyable way for children to learn how to release tension and ground themselves.

Materials:

This script

Instructions:

- *"Get your body comfortable, and gently close your eyes."*

- *"Slowly take three deep breaths in through your nose, and then out through your mouth."*

- *"Spend a moment or two relaxing your feet and legs, letting go of any tightness. Let them become heavy and relaxed."*

- *"Imagine a wave of blue light traveling up from the earth into your feet and legs, relaxing everything it touches."*

- *"Now, relax your tummy, chest, and shoulders. Imagine this wave of blue light sweeping through and relaxing this area for you."*

- *"Pay attention to your arms and fingers—allow the blue light to move through. Feel how relaxed you are."*

- *"Finally, bring the blue light to your head, and allow it to flow out of the top of your head and into the air around you. Beautifully done!"*

- *"Now, imagine you are standing in front of a massive tree. This tree has deep, deep roots and branches that reach out in every direction."*

- *"This tree is home to your very own treehouse. This is a treehouse of your own design. Picture how you would like your treehouse to look."*

- *"Take a minute and look around. See what your treehouse looks like. You can add anything you want to it. It can be whatever color you want. Does it have windows? Maybe a slide? A ladder? Is it high up or down low?"*

- *"Can you see it? Good. Now, go inside the treehouse."*

- *"Are you inside the treehouse? Good."*

- *"Inside the treehouse, take a look around. What does it look like inside? Is there a cozy chair? Which of your favorite items are there? Take a few minutes to think about what you want in there."*

- *"You feel really relaxed. This is a place to let go of all your thoughts, all your worries."*

- *"Take a deep breath. Notice how good you feel. Allow your body and mind to be relaxed inside your treehouse."*

- *"This is a place you can go any time you would like to feel calm. Know that your treehouse is available to you any time you would like. You can visit here whenever you would like."*

- *"Now, take a deep breath and imagine yourself walking down out of your treehouse. Gently bring your attention back to the room."*

- *"Rub your hands together to make them warm. Gently place them over your eyes."*

- *"You can open your eyes whenever you are ready."*

Questions:

- Do you feel different than you did before we started?

- Tell me what's different about how your body feels now.

Technique Name:
Nature Walk

What Is It?

Connecting with nature and movement helps a child be more present in the moment. The more mindful we become, the better we can identify our emotions and sensations. This is great for children of all ages, especially those who have a hard time verbally expressing themselves.

Materials:

Device with a cellular connection

Instructions:

- Set up with the parent and child in advance.

- Have the child walk and listen for:

  - Nature sounds.
  - Animals.
  - Other sounds.

  - Birds.
  - Wind sounds.

- Have the child walk and look for:

  - Types of birds.
  - Types of trees.

  - Types of insects.

- Have the child walk and collect various natural materials like:

  - Leaves.
  - Cones.

  - Rocks.

- Stop and put a hand over the child's heart. Practice 4-7-8 breathing, and ask him or her to notice any body sensations or thoughts that come up. Use this as a point of discussion.

Questions:

- Were you surprised by something?

- Did you learn something new?

- What sensations did you notice?

Technique Name:
Where's My Center?

What Is It?

A way to focus attention on grounding oneself and what that feels like. Grounding oneself helps to calm the nervous system, making one feel less overloaded and worried.

Materials:

Where's My Center? Handout

Paper

Pencil or markers

Instructions:

- Ask the child to draw him or herself the last time s/he felt centered and grounded, or use the body outline.

- Point to where your center is in the picture.

Questions:

- How did your body feel when you were centered?

- How did your mind feel when you were centered?

- Do you feel like that is your constant center, or does it move?

- How can you practice centering your body?

Where's My Center?

Technique Name:
Calm Mind Art Activity

What Is It?

A way for children to connect with what their brain feels like when they feel anxious, overwhelmed, or disconnected. Can help anyone who feels anxiety, stress, anger, depression, lack of focus, and/or overwhelm, or who isn't always connected or present.

Materials:

What's on My Brain? Handout

Paper

Pencils, markers, or crayons

Instructions:

- Have the child draw his or her brain, or use the What's on My Brain? Handout.

- Have him/her draw what it looks like now, and then draw another picture of what it looks like when s/he is calm.

Questions:

- Describe how your mind feels when you are thinking.

- Describe how your mind feels when you are quiet.

- Do any images or shapes come up?

- Show me what your mind looks like when things feel chaotic or "all over the place."

- Show me what your mind looks like when you feel calm.

- How can you practice having a calm brain?

What's On My Brain?
Worksheet

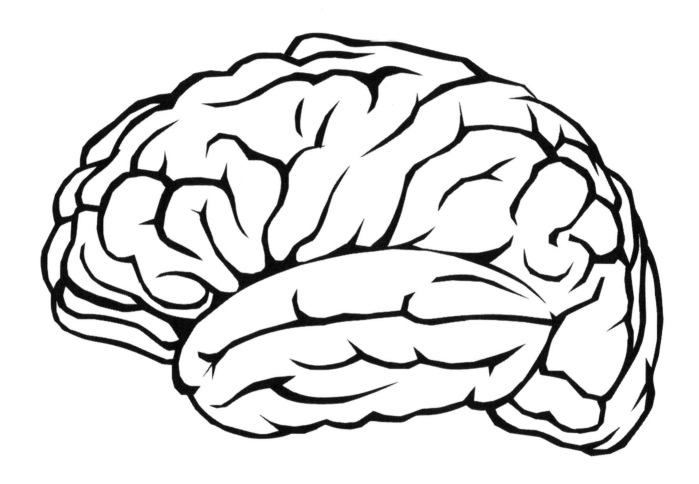

Technique Name:
Dot Art Activity

What Is It?

By making a piece of art using only dots, it forces children to slow down and be mindful of their thoughts and body. Can help anyone who is impulsive, feels anxious, stressed, angry, depressed, or who is unfocused, overwhelmed by issues, and/or not always connected or present.

Materials:

Paper

Pencils, markers, or crayons

Instructions:

- Have the child make a picture using only dots.

- If a child is unsure of what to do, have him or her look around the room or close his/her eyes and think of something that feels or smells good. Then, ask him/her to draw that using dots.

Questions:

- Did any images come up? (Explore them.)

- What made you pick the image?

- How did you organize your drawing?

Technique Name:
Be Kind

What Is It?

A therapeutic technique that helps children break negative thinking patterns and self-criticism.

Materials:

Be Kind Worksheet

Instructions:

- During the session, fill out the Be Kind Worksheet.

- Dialogue about how the child is kind to others.

- Dialogue about how this child is kind to him or herself.

Questions:

- What are small ways you can be kind to yourself?

- Is it hard to say nice things about yourself?

- What would others say about how you show kindness?

- Were you surprised by something?

- Did you learn something new?

- What sensations did you notice?

Be Kind Worksheet

In what ways are you kind to others?

In what ways are you kind to yourself?

© Roseann-Capanna-Hodge, 2020
© Global Institute of Children's Mental Health, 2020

Technique Name:
Gratitude Scavenger Hunt

What Is It?

A therapeutic technique that helps children break negative thinking patterns and focus on the many positive things around them by developing the practice of gratitude. Helps children develop a positive mindset and to look for the positives in every situation.

Materials:

Gratitude Scavenger Hunt Handout

Instructions:

- Dialogue about what the child found on the scavenger hunt.

- Dialogue about examples of when something was hard, but s/he learned or gained something.

- Try to use personal examples in the child's world, but if s/he can't connect, use a hero's journey story or some other example of learning from and overcoming hardship.

Questions:

- How does your body feel after doing this?

- Were you surprised by something?

- Did you learn something new?

- What sensations did you notice?

Kids Gratitude Scavenger Hunt

Find something outside you enjoy looking at.

Find something inside you enjoy looking at.

Find something your mom or dad enjoys looking at.

Find something that is useful for you.

Find something you could use to make a gift for someone you love.

Find something you know someone else will enjoy.

Find something that is your favorite color.

Find something that is your favorite texture.

Find something that makes you happy.

Find something that makes someone you love happy.

Find something that smells good.

Find something that tastes good.

Kids Gratitude Scavenger Hunt

☆ Find something that feels good.

☆ Find something that makes a sound that makes your body feel good.

☆ Find something new inside.

☆ Find something new outside.

☆ Find something that can be made into something else.

☆ Find something that someone gave you that you cherish.

☆ Find something that makes you feel safe.

☆ Find something that makes you feel calm.

☆ Find something that makes you feel alert.

☆ Find something that brings you comfort.

☆ Find something that is unique.

☆ Find something that makes you laugh.

Kids Gratitude Scavenger Hunt

☆ Find something that makes someone you love laugh.

☆ Find something that makes someone you love smile.

☆ Find something you enjoy in the night.

☆ Find something you enjoy in the morning.

☆ Find something that you enjoy doing outside with friends or family.

☆ Find something that reminds you of the people you love.

☆ Find someone you are grateful for.

☆ Find a pet that you love spending time with.

☆ Find a person that you love spending time with.

☆ Find a place that you love.

☆ Find your favorite place to spend alone time.

☆ Find your favorite place to spend time with others.

Technique Name:
Gratitude Wall

What Is It?

A therapeutic technique that helps children break negative thinking patterns and focus on the many positive things around them by developing the practice of gratitude. Helps children develop a positive mindset and to look for the positives in every situation.

Materials:

Gratitude Questions Handout

Big pieces of paper/paper roll

Chalkboard or whiteboard

Chalk or dry erase markers

Instructions:

- Start a gratitude word wall where the child can list things s/he is grateful for.

- Dialogue about gratitude and the benefits of it:

  - Improves physical health.

  - Improves mental health.

  - Calms the nervous system and makes a person less likely to react to stress.

  - Improves relationships.

  - Helps one feel—or have empathy—for others.

  - Reduces irritability and feelings of anger.

  - Helps one sleep better.

  - Improves how people feel about themselves and self-esteem.

- Try to use personal examples in the child's world, but if s/he can't connect, use a hero's journey story or some other example of learning from and overcoming hardship.

Questions:

- How does your body feel after doing this?

- Were you surprised by something?

- Did you learn something new?

- What sensations did you notice?

Gratitude Questions

- What was the best part of the day?

- When did I feel grateful today?

- What made me smile today?

- What made me laugh out loud today?

- Who helped me today?

- Who was kind to me today?

- What insight did I gain today?

- What did I learn today?

- How am I better today than I was yesterday?

- What did I read or listen to today that added value to my life?

- How did technology make my life easier today?

- What activity did I most enjoy today?

- What was the most delicious thing I ate today?

- What did I enjoy listening to today?

- What made me think, "That smells good!" today?

- What was pleasant to the touch today?

- What beauty did I see today?

- What was one small victory I had today?

Gratitude Questions

- What simple pleasure did I enjoy today?

- What act of kindness did I witness today?

- What did I create today?

- What skills did I use today?

- What strengths did I apply today?

- What weakness was I able to keep in check today?

- How was I able to help others today?

- How did I move an important goal forward today?

- How was my body an ally today?

- Who was I happy to meet with, chat with, or run into today?

- What compliment did I receive today?

- How did I feel appreciated today?

- Who showed me affection today?

- What positive emotions did I experience today?

- What negative thoughts, beliefs, or emotions was I able to release today?

- What opportunity presented itself today?

Technique Name:
It's All in Your Hand

What Is It?

Children visualize or draw positive, happy images in their hand to connect their body to happy thoughts.

Materials:

Paper

Pencil or markers

Old magazines

Instructions:

- Outline the child's hand on a paper, and then have him or her draw or collage images that make him/her happy.

- Have him/her connect to the images and stay present in the moment.

- Discuss the images chosen.

Questions:

- How do the images make you feel?

- Where in your body do you notice good sensations when you look at or visualize these images?

Technique Name:
Grounding Guided Visualization Exercise

What Is It?

A way for children to focus attention to how to ground themselves and what that feels like, so they can be more present in that moment and in their life. Can help anyone who feels out of their body, impulsive, disconnected, or is avoidant/ overwhelmed by their issues.

Materials:

None

Instructions:

- Have the child sit in a chair with feet firmly planted on the floor. Instruct child to close his/her eyes.

- Walk him or her through a progressive relaxation exercise from toe to head to help him/her release tension and be more present.

- Ask him/her to plant feet on the ground and visualize roots growing from his/her feet into the ground. Have the child stay present, and walk him/her through individual roots growing. If an uncomfortable emotion springs up, have the child visualize his/her calming color wash over his/her body.

Questions:

- Point to where you feel most grounded.

- What emotions came up for you?

- How did your body feel when you were grounded?

- How did your mind feel when you were grounded?

- How can you practice this grounding exercise?

Technique Name:
Calming Color Guided Visualization Exercise

What Is It?

A way for children to focus attention to how to ground themselves and what that feels like, so they can be more present in that moment and in their life. Can help anyone who feels anxious, stressed, or overwhelmed by issues, is impulsive, or isn't always connected or present.

Materials:

None

Instructions:

- Have the child get comfortable and close his or her eyes.

- Walk him/her through a progressive relaxation exercise from toe to head to help release tension and be more present.

- Have him/her pick a color that is calming, and then visualize it slowly pouring over his/her body.

- Talk the child through keeping that calming color in his/her mind's eye, as s/he works to calm the nervous system.

Questions:

- Point to where you feel most grounded.

- What emotions came up for you?

- How did your body feel when you were grounded?

- How did your mind feel when you were grounded?

- How can you practice this grounding exercise?

Technique Name:
Vision Board

What Is It?

A way for teens to see themselves successfully achieving a goal. It helps make achievement tangible while also helping them work toward something themselves without any negative associations.

Materials:

A large piece of hard stock paper

Old magazine

Scissors

Glue

Adornments or glitter

Instructions:

- During the session, explain how visualizing what we want can help us work toward our goals.

- Ask the teen the following questions:

    - *"Where do you see yourself in X months or years?"*

    - *"What would you like to be doing?"*

    - *"What does that look like? Sound like? Feel like?"*

- Begin making a vision board.

- Use the vision board to set goals and check in on them.

Questions:

- What did you think about this activity?

- Was it easy or hard for you to see what is next for you?

- What obstacles do you think could get in the way of this goal?

- How will you address these obstacles?

- Were you surprised by something?

- Did you learn something new?

- What sensations did you notice?

Chapter 13 – Teletherapy Techniques: Somatic

The Clues Our Body Gives Us

Jacob was just four years old when he witnessed a traumatic event that would affect the rest of his life.

His grandmother—Jacob's primary caregiver and buddy—tripped, fell, and hit her head right in front of him. She died a few days later, and the family was grief-stricken.

This tragedy was difficult for the family to process. Jacob's mom, Darcy, vacillated between full-on waterworks and feeling like a zombie. She did the best she could, getting medication to help her through and spending the next few years *"in a fog."*

Darcy couldn't believe how brave her son was. At the time, he barely shed a tear and seemed to adjust better than she even could.

It wasn't until several months later that the nightmares started. Then, regressive behaviors like bedwetting and temper tantrums, which concerned his mom. Darcy thought his transition into kindergarten was driving his behaviors. But as time went on, more and more behaviors surfaced. Jacob was pushing kids in school, was easily tearful, and called himself *"stupid."* When his teacher suggested they speak with a therapist, Darcy agreed.

Jacob marched into my office with his mother trailing behind. He started playing with toys as I spoke to them both. Out of the corner of my eye, I could see Jacob playing with the dollhouse. He quickly grabbed the dolls, choosing the grandmother doll and repeatedly banging her onto the floor. I let Jacob complete this process, as we know how trauma stays in the body when a process isn't complete. Eventually, he slowed down and began to, as his mom stated, *"recreate that day."* He played out the same scene multiple times as I quietly observed. My role in that moment was to simply be there, letting my physical proximity be his safety while building rapport.

Eventually, Jacob began to play with the dog figure. I asked him to put his hand over a part of his body where he felt something different. He put it over his heart. I asked him to sit there for a moment keeping his hand on his heart. I told him he could look down or close his eyes, and that we were going to breathe through his heart. We worked on diaphragmatic breathing for a few minutes until I watched Jacob connect with his mother.

At the next session, I put the dolls away and worked on sensation words with him, asking him to identify the sensations he was feeling before we played (I did the same after playing, too). Then, we pulled out the dolls, and off Jacob went to reenact the same scene over and over.

I had kids like Jacob before who were just sort of waiting for the opportunity to play out a trauma but had never seen one who could so easily go back to the moment. As he worked out what happened through play, I helped Jacob to connect to the somatic sensations as well as pay attention to the thoughts and emotions that he never got to process. By connecting to his bodily sensations and processing out through play, Jacob finally got to complete something that he hadn't yet: he got to say goodbye to his Nanna.

Outside of the session, Jacob began to developmentally progress and become more affectionate. Most importantly, his emotions matched his experiences. No more big reactions or complete lack of emotions. He felt safe again and moved through the grief and trauma as he reconnected to himself.

When trauma, chronic stress, or any distressing event happens, we instinctively disconnect from our body, so our bodies can prepare for "battle" if need be. Unfortunately, this is a primitive reflex of sorts designed to help us deal with stress. The problem is, we are *always* stressed. With so much stress and anxiety in the world, the last place an anxious or distressed child wants to be is in his or her own skin. Throughout The Teletherapy Toolkit™, you'll notice words and phrases that teach clinicians how to help children and teens connect to their body in a safe way.

The practice of Somatic Experiencing® is a form of therapy that should be in every clinician's toolkit. I highly recommend following Peter Levine's work and his Somatic Experiencing® Trauma Institute.

Technique Name:
Body-Sensation Words

What Is It?

This technique helps children develop a broader range of words to assist them in connecting to their body sensations.

Materials:

Body-Sensation Words Handout

Instructions:

- Review the body-sensation word list.

- These words are the primer for the other somatic experiencing techniques in this book and overall body-focused questioning.

Questions:

- When you think of body sensations, what words come to mind?

- Are there other words you can think of to describe body sensations that are not on this list? If so, what are they?

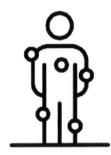

Dr. Roseann-Capanna-Hodge

Body-Sensation Words Handout
For Older Children and Adults

Achy
Bloated
Boiling
Breathless
Bruised
Burning
Bursting
Butterflies
Calm
Cold
Comfortable
Congested
Dark

Dehydrated
Disconnected
Dizzy
Dry-mouthed
Energetic
Exhausted
Flexible
Floaty
Floppy
Frozen
Full
Giddy
Goose-bumpy
Grounded
Heavy
Hollow
Hot
Hungry
Hurting
Itchy
Jittery
Jumpy
Light
Limp
Nauseous
Nervy
Numb
Open
Pressure
Prickly
Puffy

Pulsing
Queasy
Quivering
Radiating
Raw
Relaxed
Released
Rigid
Rolling
Saggy
Satisfied
Sensitive
Shaky
Shivery
Shuddering
Sick
Soft
Sore
Spacey
Squirmy
Squishy
Stabbing
Stinging
Stretchy
Stuffed
Suffocated
Sweaty
Tall
Teary
Tender
Tense

Throbbing
Tickly
Tight
Tingling
Tired
Trembly
Twitchy
Uncomfortable
Vibrating
Warm
Wet
Wobbly
Woozy

© Roseann-Capanna-Hodge, 2020
© Global Institute of Children's Mental Health, 2020

322

Body-Sensation Words Handout For Younger Children

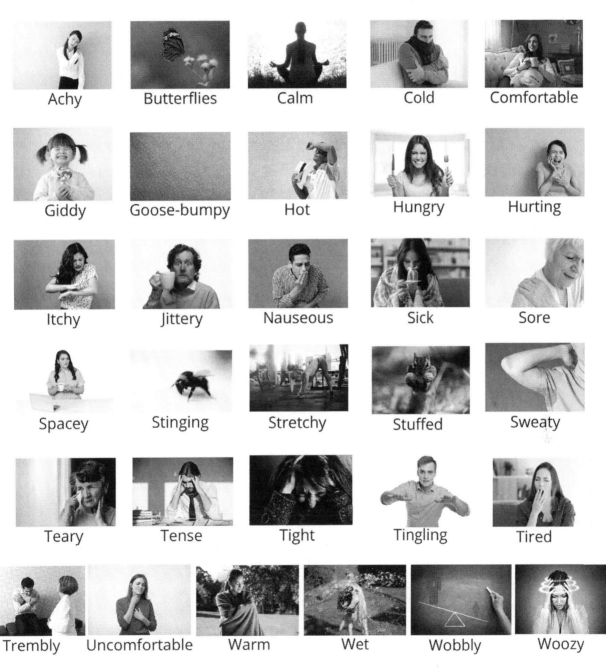

Achy	Butterflies	Calm	Cold	Comfortable
Giddy	Goose-bumpy	Hot	Hungry	Hurting
Itchy	Jittery	Nauseous	Sick	Sore
Spacey	Stinging	Stretchy	Stuffed	Sweaty
Teary	Tense	Tight	Tingling	Tired
Trembly	Uncomfortable	Warm	Wet	Wobbly	Woozy

© Roseann-Capanna-Hodge, 2020
© Global Institute of Children's Mental Health, 2020

Technique Name:
Body Scan

What Is It?

Helps children connect to their body and pay attention to body sensations, so they can recognize the signs their body is giving about how they feel. A technique that helps children identify where they don't feel stress, discomfort, or pain in the body. When they learn how to sit with and increase the amount of time they experience the stress or discomfort, they can build tolerance while simultaneously settling the activation. This builds their ability to feel their stress without being immobilized by it.

Materials:

Body-Sensation Words Handout

Body-Scan Exercise Handout

This script

Instructions:

- Introduce the concept of body scanning.

- Teach them to connect the words on the Body-Sensation Words Handout.

- Say: *"Now, I am going to have you pick a body part and do a body scan. This is like when you make a copy in a copier. We are going to do the same thing with our brain."*

- *"You are going to focus on one body part at a time, and I will help you stay focused on that part."*

- Have the child close his or her eyes and ask him/her to focus on one part of the body.

- For younger children, focus on hands, feet, heart, and stomach.

- For older kids, can add focus on the shoulder, eyes, legs, etc.

- Say: *"You will notice sensations in that part of the body."*

- After 30 seconds, ask the child which sensations s/he noticed.

- In regard to extremities, the child may want to move/wiggle around. In this case, you can say: *"I see that your hand (or leg, etc.) is moving. You can move it. What sensations do you notice in your hand now?"*

- If a child denies any sensation, then say: *"If you were to imagine there was a sensation in this part, what might it be?"*

- You can also have him or her squeeze his/her hand and then release the tension. Ask what sensations s/he notices.

Questions:

- What sensations did you notice in each part?

- Did you notice if there was any body part that wanted to move?

- Is there a body part that was easier to find sensation in?

- How can you practice paying attention to your body sensations?

Dr. Roseann and Associates
Body Scan Exercise

Technique Name:
Tracking the Body for Positive Sensations

What Is It?

A technique that helps children identify where in the body they feel good, shifting their awareness from the negative to positive through the use of imagery.

Materials:

Body-Sensation Words Handout

This script

Instructions:

- *"Identify a part of the body where you don't feel pain, discomfort, or tension, and stay focused on that part of your body for a few minutes."*

- *"Try to track the different sensations that come up as you simultaneously focus on the part of your body that actually feels good."*

- *"Hold for a minute."* (Gradually build to longer amounts of time.)

- *"When you focus on what feels good in your body, even if you are stressed or in pain, your brain alerts to those positive sensations and can transfer that good sensation to other parts of the body that may be holding stress or pain."*

- *"When you continue this process and stay present, the body will shift, and pain and discomfort will lessen."*

- Note: If the child can't identify where it feels good, say: *"If you were to imagine a part that feels good, where would it be?"*

Questions:

- What sensations do you feel?

- What happens to other parts of your body when you focus on this part?

- Was it difficult at any point to stay focused on this part?

Technique Name:
Window of Tolerance

What Is It?

"Window of tolerance" is a term used to describe a person's comfort zone or range in managing stressors and sensations. A person's "zone of arousal" is that in which a person is able to manage and process information and sensations in everyday life. Outside of this zone, or window of tolerance, a person is reactive and activated by stressors, sensory information, and struggles to integrate information. For those who don't have a window of tolerance, they are prone to frequent activations or hyper- and hypo-arousal states. Through psychoeducation, mindfulness techniques, and connection to sensations, a therapist helps children build a window of tolerance while adding to his or her resource toolkit.

Materials:

SUDS Level Handout

Whiteboard or virtual whiteboard

Instructions:

- Explain the difference between "above the window" and "below the window":

- Above the window is hyperarousal—our body's "fight-or-flight" response to stimuli.

- Below the window is our "freeze" response—how we dissociate or disconnect from our body.

- Have the child or teen identify where s/he thinks s/he goes when out of his/her window and what sensations s/he experiences.

- Identify whether or not s/he always goes in a certain direction, or cycles a certain way, or if s/he goes back and forth, so s/he can identify patterns and triggers.

- Dialogue about the things make his/her body feel good or uncomfortable.

- Dialogue about triggers or stressors that cause him/her to feel activated or stressed.

- Dialogue about the body sensations s/he notices when above and below the window of tolerance.

Questions:

- What sensations do you feel?

- What level were you before this activity (SUDS)? And after (SUDS)?

- What surprised you as a stressor?

- How do you manage stress and uncomfortable feelings or sensations?

- How do you see yourself managing X tomorrow (or X)?

DR. ROSEANN AND ASSOCIATES

Subjective Units of Distress Scale (SUDS)

0- COMPLETELY RELAXED/ NO STRESS

1- COMFORTABLY ALERT

2- MINIMUM ANXIETY/ STRESS

3- MILD STRESS

4- MILD TO MODERATE STRESS

5- MODERATE STRESS

6- MODERATE TO HIGH STRESS

7- QUITE ANXIOUS/ STRESSED

8- VERY STRESSED

9- EXTREMELY STRESSED

10- THE MOST ANXIOUS/ STRESSED YOU HAVE BEEN

© Roseann-Capanna-Hodge, 2020© Global Institute of Children's Mental Health, 2020

Chapter 14 –
Teletherapy Techniques: Sadness and Mood

A Glass Half Empty

James' parents described him as, *"always in a mood."* In fact, they couldn't recall a time when he saw things in a positive light. They had spent years *"walking on eggshells"* around him and were worried about what might happen in the future. As a teen, James wasn't too thrilled about coming to see me at school. I would send a hall pass down for him, because otherwise, he was certain to *"forget."*

James was a straight shooter kind of kid, and true to his nature, shortly after meeting me, he announced, *"I am not going to talk to you, because I am not crazy. And my mom is making me come here."*

Ah, here we go, I thought.

James was like so many I had worked with; he thought something was "wrong" with him and couldn't see all of his strengths and gifts.

From the time he was little, James saw things as from a "glass-half-empty" lens. Going with the flow wasn't in James' wheelhouse. Even the most mundane things stressed him out, and he was often angry and emotional. As a teenager, he frequently felt sad and hopeless, but didn't know why.

James wasn't hard to connect with. We both enjoyed sarcasm, and he had a great sense of humor. He also loved music, so I won a lot of points for being a regular concert goer, especially when I showed him all my concert pictures. Over time, James was able to understand what made him sad, build a window of tolerance, and feel confident. With therapeutic guidance, he was able to build a toolkit, as well as improve not just his ability to recognize his stressors, but also communicate about them appropriately … you know, without biting off someone's head!

Eventually, James began to think differently about himself, and his perceptions and behavior began to change, too. He went from a glass-half-empty to a glass-half-full perspective (at least some of the time!).

Children and teens with mood issues often don't perceive themselves, their interactions, or their future in a positive light, so changing that inner dialogue is an essential part of the therapeutic process.

This chapter of The Teletherapy Toolkit™ will not only give you activities, but literature for parents in an effort to provide psychoeducation.

Technique Name:
Sadness Thermometer

What Is It?

This technique helps children visualize their sadness and what they can do to control it. It makes the sadness more relatable—something they can better understand and address.

Materials:

Sadness Meter Worksheet

Pencil, crayons, or markers

Instructions:

- Have the child rate his or her sadness on a scale from one to five using the Sadness Meter Worksheet.

- Discuss how worry can go up and down and how it can bubble.

- Discuss how it feels.

- Discuss what s/he can do when s/he feels sadness bubbling.

Questions:

- How do you feel when you're sad?

- What can you do before you feel really sad?

- When was the last time you were sad about something? What was it? Was it a small thing or a big thing?

- Where did you feel it in your body when your thermometer was bubbling?

- How does your body feel when you are at one?

- How does your body feel when you are at five?

- What sort of things get you to a three or four?

Sadness Meter

5- In the RED: Loss of control of my thoughts or actions, feelings of sadness, mood up and down

4- Body tense, sad, last chance for putting on the brakes

3- Intensified feelings and body sensations, still can put the brakes on

2- Something made me feel uncomfortable, sad, rejected, lonely, hopeless, negative, stuck, stressed

1- Calm

Technique Name:
Understanding Sadness

What Is It?

A technique that helps children visualize their sadness, identify their triggers, and understand how they are managing it and what they can do to control it. It makes the sadness more relatable—something they can better understand and address.

Materials:

Sadness Meter Worksheet

Understanding Sadness Worksheet

Pencil, crayons, or markers

Instructions:

- Fill out the Sadness Meter Worksheet first.

- Fill out the Understanding Sadness Worksheet together using words or pictures.

Questions:

- How does your body feel when you are at one?

- How does your body feel when you are at five?

- What sort of things get you to a three or four?

Understanding Sadness Worksheet

What makes me feel sad?	Where am I feeling sadness?	How do I handle sadness?	How else could I handle sadness?

Technique Name:
I Get Sad When ...

What Is It?

A way for children to see times and places they get sad and how they can manage their own sadness.

Materials:

I Get Sad When ... Worksheet

Crayons or markers

Instructions:

- Go through the worksheet with the child and have him/her draw:

- Times s/he is sad.

- Places s/he is often sad.

- How s/he deals with or gets through sadness.

- Discuss strategies.

- Give positive reinforcement.

- Address any shame, feeling, or worries that surface.

Questions:

- How does your body feel when you are sad?

- How does your body feel when you are worried?

- How does your body feel when you are happy?

- What was easy?

- What was hard?

I Get Sad When ...
Worksheet

Times when I am sad:

Places I am sad:

How I deal with my sad feelings:

© Roseann-Capanna-Hodge, 2020
© Global Institute of Children's Mental Health, 2020

Technique Name:
Draw Your Safe Place

What Is It?

A therapeutic technique for those who are struggling with mood, anxiety, or trauma.

Materials:

Paper

Markers or crayons

Instructions:

- Have the child draw a picture of his/her safe place.

- Ask the child to close his/her eyes (or look down) and take a few minutes to think about a place (real or imaginary) where s/he feels very safe, calm, and happy.

- Talk to him/her about how s/he can go to this safe place anytime s/he wants by visualizing it and experiencing the sensations.

Questions:

- What can you see, hear, smell, and taste in your safe space?

- How did your body feel before and after this activity?

Technique Name:
Your Perfect Day

What Is It?

A therapeutic technique for teens who are depressed and having a hard time feeling hopeful about the future or who may be stuck emotionally and behaviorally.

Materials:

Paper

Pen or pencil

Instructions:

- Have the teen write a letter to him or herself one year in the future.

- Have him/her offer three pieces of advice.

- Have him/her describe what s/he will be doing on a single "perfect" day one year in the future.

Questions:

- What can you see, hear, smell, and taste on this "perfect" day?

- What one action can you take to get closer to this "perfect" day?

- How did your body feel before and after this activity?

Technique Name:
A Letter to Someone Who Hurt Me

What Is It?

A therapeutic technique for individuals who are sad after being hurt by someone. This is a cathartic activity—the letter does not have to be sent. The act of writing can be very therapeutic to those who may have a hard time speaking up, or if the other party is unwilling (or it is unsafe) to share feelings.

Materials:

Paper

Pen

Instructions:

- Have the teen write a letter to the person who hurt him/her.

- Using "I" statements, have the teen write how it felt when X happened.

- Discuss forgiveness and assess if s/he is ready for forgiveness.

Questions:

- Where can you feel this sadness in your body?

- What is the one thing you can do to get unstuck?

- How did your body feel before and after this activity?

Technique Name:
Where Is My Sadness?

What Is It?

A technique that helps children visualize their sadness, understand where it is in their body, what their triggers are, how they are managing it, and what they can do to control it. It makes the sadness more relatable—something they can better understand and address.

Materials

Where Is My Sadness? Worksheet

Pencils, crayons, or markers

Instructions:

- Walk the child or teen through the worksheet.

- Help him or her to recognize and connect to his/her body sensations.

- Teach him/her about developing a window of tolerance.

Questions:

- What about this activity surprised you?

- Did you recognize where the sadness was in your body?

- How can you use those body sensations in the future?

- What tools do you have to manage your sadness?

- What do you see yourself doing in a month (or whatever appropriate time)?

- How do you see yourself getting there?

WHERE IS MY SADNESS? WORKSHEET

Where am I feeling sadness in my body?

How/When did it start?

What is this sadness telling me?

What tools can I use to get through this sadness?

Technique Name:
Fortune Teller

What Is It?

Fortune-telling (or forecasting, negative predicting, jumping to conclusions) is a cognitive behavioral technique that challenges the common cognitive distortion of predicting that things or events will go badly. Those who fortune-tell are generally catastrophizers who think negatively and predict that a situation will turn out badly without fairly and objectively looking at all possible outcomes.

Materials:

Cognitive Distortions Handout, Fortune-Teller Worksheet

Instructions:

- Dialogue about the child's cognitive distortion.

- Ask questions to challenge this distortion:

  - *"What do you think will happen?"*

  - *"What evidence do you have that this will happen?"*

  - *"What is the evidence to suggest it might not happen?"*

  - *"Do you know for certain this will happen?"*

  - *"How good is your evidence, especially the evidence to support your negative prediction?"*

  - *"Would people you know agree with your prediction, given the facts?"*

  - *"What are five less-negative predictions you could make?"*

  - *"What is the best possible thing that could happen?"*

  - *"Are you maybe thinking this worst-case scenario has already happened, when it actually hasn't?"*

  - *"Would you be willing to experiment with your negative prediction by collecting more information or trying something else?"*

Questions:

- What has changed in your thinking about what happened?

- Were you surprised by something?

- Did you learn something new?

- What sensations did you notice?

Fortune Teller Worksheet

What do you think will happen?

 What's your evidence?

What are five less-negative things that can happen? ★

★ What is the best-case scenario?

When you tested this out, what happened?

© Roseann-Capanna-Hodge, 2020
© Global Institute of Children's Mental Health, 2020

Technique Name:
Memory Box

What Is It?

This therapeutic technique helps children move through the grief process. It also helps children/teens remember the person who died and the relationship they had.

Materials:

Box

Glue

Old magazines

Pictures of the person who passed (optional)

Markers, crayons

Scissors

Glitter, stickers, or other decorations

Instructions:

- Decorate a box with pictures, magazine images, and other items that remind the child or teen of the person who has passed.

- During this activity, dialogue about the memories the pictures and images represent.

Questions:

- What is your favorite memory?

- What will you miss most?

- What would this person say about you?

- What sensations did you notice?

Technique Name:
Memory Sculpture

What Is It?

This therapeutic technique helps children move through the grief process. It also helps children/teens remember the person who died and the relationship they had.

Materials:

Air-dry clay, play dough, or modeling clay

Instructions:

- Instruct the child or teen to make a sculpture of something that reminds him/her of something special that s/he used to enjoy doing with the person who died.

Questions:

- What is your favorite memory?

- Tell me what that favorite memory was about. What did you do?

- What will you miss most?

- What would this person say about you?

- What sensations did you notice?

Technique Name:
Inside and Outside Feelings

What Is It?

This therapeutic technique helps children move through the grief process. It also helps children/teens to identify their feelings, and which they are showing others versus holding in.

Materials:

Paper bag

Two boxes or containers

Paper, Tape

Pencil, pen, or marker

Instructions:

- Explain to the child or teen that we feel many emotions when someone in our life dies. Some of these feelings we choose to share with others, and some we choose to keep to ourselves. Sometimes, those feelings or sensations get stuck in our body. This activity is a way to move those feelings out.

- Ask the child or teen to write down or draw a picture of all the feelings s/he has felt since his or her loved one died.

- Ask him or her to think about which feelings s/he expresses to others. Explain that those are called "outside feelings."

- Have the child or teen sort his/her feelings into two piles: 1) Feelings s/he has kept inside (or hasn't talked to others about) and 2) Feelings s/he has shared with others.

- Ask the child or teen to write those feelings inside and outside on the boxes or paper bags.

- Alternatively, s/he can tape those "inside" and "outside" feelings onto the different boxes or paper bags.

- Ask the child or teen to share his/her inside and outside feelings.

- Feelings can be moved from inside to outside as they are discussed.

Questions:

- Did any of these feelings surprise you?

- What feeling makes your body feel most uncomfortable?

- How did it feel to move your feeling from inside to outside?

- What sensations did you notice?

Chapter 15 – Teletherapy Techniques: Attention and Executive Functioning

Attention AND Executive Functioning— a 'Unicorn' Combination?

I'll never forget the day I met Ethan. He came bolting through the door like a horse out of a stable, and literally bounced off the walls. His exhausted mother, Cynthia, came trailing in behind him with a newborn. Her first words were, "*And this is why we are here!*"

Cynthia wasn't the only person worn-out by Ethan and his constant hyper behaviors—so were his teacher, classmates, and the rest of his family. Even his dog, Biscuit, ran from him like he was the plague. Ethan had no brakes, no filter, and boundless energy. Listening was a foreign concept, and his body was in constant motion. He couldn't slow down long enough to respond to even simple requests, like "*Put your shoes away,*" or "*Don't touch the dog.*" Whether at school or home, someone had to be constantly present to help Ethan with even the most basic tasks typical six-year-olds could complete. With the new baby, his mother realized that Ethan needed help putting the brakes on.

The first thing I did with Ethan was to teach him how to get into his body. The only time he turned off his switch was when he was sleeping. The rest of the time, he was in overdrive. I needed to teach him how to regulate and move *between* "on and off" … within all the gray shades between.

Since Ethan was such a physical kid, I started with sensory techniques and games that had him practice how to put on the brakes so he could actually feel his body being regulated. With a child as young as Ethan, a lot of our time was spent teaching his parents how to practice and reinforce those techniques at home. That one-hour session was the "*miracle*" his parents needed to change how they were parenting him.

Ethan certainly didn't learn or hear in the same way other children do. He needed things to be physical. He was a kinesthetic learner who required a high level of positive reinforcement. As hyper as he was, he was young, so his brain had greater neuroplasticity. That meant Ethan could learn more quickly than an older child.

Little by little, Ethan's parents saw that he could regulate for increasing lengths of times, and they were motivated even more to be vigilant with their rewards. When Ethan got his first-ever birthday party invitation, Cynthia came into my office and burst into tears of happiness. For her, acceptance by other children was the most important thing. It meant that others loved Ethan as much as she did.

Many children have difficulties with executive functioning—organizing behavior as one works toward a goal. And while attentional and executive functioning issues can be standalone problems, they are often comorbid with other conditions such as anxiety, OCD, autism, and so forth.

Throughout The Teletherapy Toolkit™, you'll notice an emphasis on body sensations, self-regulation, and mindfulness, because they are all primers to good cognitive functioning.

Technique Name:
Simon Says

What Is It?

A game that helps children give and follow directions, sequence, pay attention, plan motor action, and learn turn-taking skills.

Materials:

None

Instructions:

- In this game, the leader is known as "Simon." He/she makes commands that others must listen to and follow until a mistake is made. When that happens, switch places.

- The child stands up and faces the screen.

- Simon begins calling out commands.

- If Simon begins the sentence with *"Simon says,"* then everyone is required to do the action.

- If Simon does not begin with *"Simon says,"* then the players should not complete the action.

- Take turns calling out, *"Simon says move your X."*

Questions:

- How did your body feel when you had to put the brakes on?

- What was easy?

- What was hard?

Technique Name:
Red Light/Green Light

What Is It?

A game that helps children give and follow directions, pay attention, gain impulse control, plan motor action, and learn turn-taking skills.

Materials:

None

Instructions:

- Describe/explain the Red Light/Green Light game and rules.

- Children walk or run forward whenever the leader says, *"Green Light!"* (or holds up a "go" sign) and freeze when they hear *"Red Light!"* (or see the "stop" sign).

- Take turns being the leader.

Questions:

- How did your body feel when you had to put the brakes on?

- What was easy?

- What was hard?

Technique Name:
Freeze Dance

What Is It?

A game that helps children give and follow directions, pay attention, gain impulse control, plan motor action, and learn turn-taking skills.

Materials:

Music

Instructions:

- Describe/explain the Freeze Dance game and rules.

- Children dance to an upbeat song until the leader pauses the music. Then, they must freeze in position until the music begins again.

- Take turns being the leader.

Questions:

- How did your body feel when you had to put the brakes on?

- What was easy?

- What was hard?

Technique Name:
Putting the Brakes On

What Is It?

A way for children to see times they don't put the brakes on—or act without thinking—and how they can apply the brakes.

Materials:

Putting the Brakes On Worksheet

Crayons and markers

Instructions:

- Go through the worksheet with the child and have him or her draw:
  - Times s/he doesn't put the brakes on.
  - Places s/he doesn't put the brakes on.
  - How s/he does put the brakes on.
- Discuss strategies.
- Give positive reinforcement.
- Address any shame or worries that surface.

Questions:

- How did your body feel when you couldn't put the brakes on?
- How did your body feel when you had to put the brakes on?
- What was easy?
- What was hard?

Putting the Brakes On Worksheet

Times when I don't put the brakes on:

Places that I don't put the brakes on:

How I put the brakes on:

© Roseann-Capanna-Hodge, 2020
© Global Institute of Children's Mental Health, 2020

Technique Name:
What Is a Good Leader?

What Is It?

A way for children to visualize what a good leader is and the qualities one has. The emphasis of this activity is to get kids to think about why being independent is a good thing.

Materials:

What Is a Good Leader? Worksheet

Markers, crayons, or pencil

Instructions:

- During the session, explain that you will be discussing qualities of a good leader.

- Ask the child about a person s/he knows who is a good leader. Why does s/he think so?

- Complete the What Is a Good Leader? Worksheet with words or pictures.

- Discuss ways the child does things without asking and how s/he feels when being independent.

Questions:

- What did you think about this activity?

- Were you surprised by something?

- Did you learn something new?

- What sensations did you notice?

- What ways can you do things without being asked?

- What would your parents think if you did helpful things without asking?

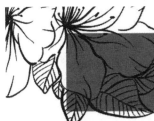

What Is a Good Leader? Worksheet

Who is someone in your life you think is a good leader?

Why is this person a good leader?

What helpful things can you do without asking?

© Roseann-Capanna-Hodge, 2020
© Global Institute of Children's Mental Health, 2020

Technique Name:
Obstacle Course

What is it?

A therapeutic technique that helps children regulate their behavior, improve listening skills, use planning skills, and manage frustration.

Materials:

Obstacle Course List

Instructions:

- During the session, have the child work through an obstacle course that the parent set up in advance or that you set up together.

- Give the child different commands and tasks:

  ▫ Jump to the third square.

  ▫ Toss the ball as you jump over the pillow.

  ▫ Do 10 jumping jacks.

  ▫ Crawl under the table.

Questions:

- What did you think about this activity?

- What was easy or hard for you?

- Were you surprised by something?

- Did you learn something new?

- What sensations did you notice?

Obstacle Course List

An obstacle course can be set up in a child's home with any of the following materials:

- Table placemats
- Colored paper
- Painter's tape
- Pillows
- Soft balls
- Pool noodles
- Trampoline
- Yoga mats
- Blankets
- Hula hoops
- Scooter
- Chair

Dr. Roseann-Capanna-Hodge

Technique Name:
Body Language Bingo

What Is It?

A way for children to evaluate different body language pictures and what they mean to them.

Materials:

Body Language Bingo Card

Chips, pennies, or rocks

Instructions:

- During the session, explain to the child that different body movements and expressions give us a clue about what people are feeling, and that if we pay attention to a person's body language, we can learn a lot.

- Call out different feelings and have the child place a chip, penny, or rock on the words that reflect that feeling.

Questions:

- What did you think about this activity?

- Was it easy or hard for you to match up the emotion to the picture?

- Were you surprised by something?

- Did you learn something new?

- What sensations did you notice?

BODY LANGUAGE

BINGO

Neutral	Disgust	Unsure	Irritated	Fear
Slouched	Desire	Surprise	Mad	Bored
Confusion	Worried	FREE SPACE	Hopeful	Sadness
Shy	Joyful	Calm	Embarrassment	Loving
Angry	Focused	Optimistic	Excitement	Pleased

© Roseann-Capanna-Hodge, 2020
© Global Institute of Children's Mental Health, 2020

Technique Name:
Metronome Matcher

What Is It?

A game that helps children give and follow directions, pay attention, gain impulse control, think ahead, and improve their timing. This technique is helpful for children who have no sense of time or trouble connecting to the moment, as well as those who over-rely on adults to transition them.

Materials:

Metronome app

Tennis ball

Instructions:

- You and the child download the metronome app.

- A metronome is the tool that is used to keep time in music to ensure that the beat stays in time. Set the metronome to a reasonable pace and ask the child to try to match the bouncing of the ball to the click of the metronome.

- Once the child gets the hang of using the metronome, you can make a fun competition out of it.

Questions:

- How did your body feel when you had to put the brakes on?

- Did it feel slow when you were trying to find the rhythm?

- What was easy?

- What was hard?

Technique Name:
Problem-Solving Decision Tree

What Is It?

A technique that helps children and teens identify the problem and come up with multiple solutions, as well as evaluate the pros and cons of each solution.

Materials:

SUDS Scale Handout

Problem-Solving Decision Tree Worksheet

Pencil, crayons, or markers

Instructions:

- Dialogue about whatever issue the child or teen presents.

- Fill out Problem-Solving Decision Tree Worksheet together using words or pictures.

- Use the SUDS scale before and after the activity.

Questions:

- What do you see as the issue?

- Can you think of a time when you had a problem before?

- How did you solve that problem?

- How did you feel when you solved that problem?

- Is there anything you learned from that to apply here?

- What advice would you give to a friend or another person about how to solve this problem?

- How do you feel about your solution to this problem?

- What sensations did you notice?

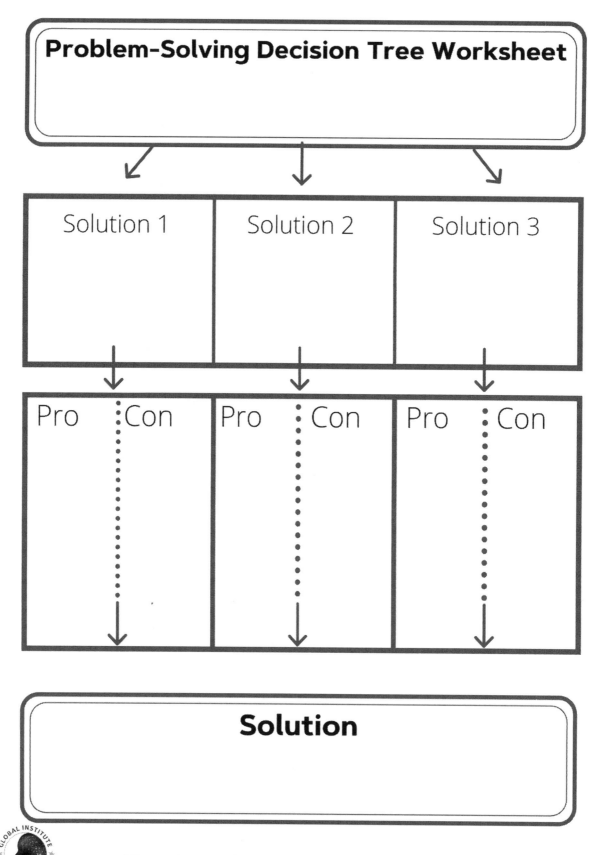

Problem-Solving Decision Tree Worksheet

Solution 1	Solution 2	Solution 3
Pro : Con	Pro : Con	Pro : Con

Solution

Technique Name:
Where Is My Focus?

What Is It?

A technique that helps children visualize when and how they get unfocused, understand what happens to their body, their triggers, how they are managing it, and what they can do to control it. It makes the focus more relatable—something they can better understand and address.

Materials:

Where Is My Focus? Worksheet

Pencils, crayons, or markers

Instructions:

- Walk the child or teen through the worksheet.

- Help him or her to recognize and connect to body sensations.

- Teach him/her about developing a window of tolerance.

Questions:

- What about this activity surprised you?

- Did you recognize where the focus was in your body?

- How can you use those body sensations in the future?

- What tools do you have to manage your focus?

- What do you see yourself doing in a month (or whatever appropriate time)?

- How do you see yourself getting there?

WHERE IS MY FOCUS? WORKSHEET

Where am I feeling a lack of focus in my body?

How/When did it start?

What is this lack of focus telling me?

What tools can I use to get through this lack of focus?

Technique Name:
Break It Down

What Is It?

A technique that helps children and teens complete big tasks by visualizing the end product and working backwards. Focusing on an obstacle and those micro-steps to solving the problem helps kids and teens see that they can break down a problem. This supports good executive functioning—a skill that can be developed with consistent practice.

Materials:

Break It Down Worksheet

Pencil, crayons, or markers

Instructions:

- Dialogue about the goal or project the child or teen wants to achieve.

- Fill out the Break It Down Worksheet together.

- Start with having him or her close his/her eyes and visualize the end result.

- Then, work out the steps.

- Lastly, write down the supplies needed to achieve the goal or project.

Questions:

- What do you see as the issue?

- Can you think of a time when you had a problem before?

- How did you solve that problem?

- How did you feel when you solved that problem?

- Is there anything you learned from that to apply here?

- What advice would you give to a friend or another person about how to solve this problem?

- How do you feel about your solution to this problem?

- What sensations did you notice?

BREAK IT DOWN WORKSHEET

GOAL or PROJECT

_____

_____

STEPS YOU NEED TO TAKE

Time Needed: _____

Time Needed: _____

Time Needed: _____

SUPPLIES

_____ _____ _____

_____ _____ _____

Chapter 16 – Teletherapy Techniques: Social Skills

Social Skills Teletherapy Techniques

Since I first landed in the world of pediatric mental health almost three decades ago, I have witnessed the steady decline of children's social skills. Long gone are the times of the double recess school days and unstructured play dates, and that is reflected in how children socialize today. It's hard to separate the chicken from the egg that landed us in this sticky situation, but kids today struggle with independent play.

Both in the classroom and on the playground, more and more kids need adults to moderate play with peers. And what's even more troubling is that even with adult intervention, many of these children go on to struggle with social skills throughout their lifetime. While we can't ignore the dramatic increase in children on the autism spectrum, which CDC data reports as one in 57 births, it is by no means the only source.

Kids today don't have as much opportunity to learn through play. When I met Catherine, she was a shy little girl who couldn't find her voice within the group of bossy girls in the second grade. Within the classroom, she could engage in any learning activity, but the playground was a different story. Catherine didn't like sports and didn't know how to start conversations with the other girls. After her teacher recommended that she come into my social skills group, I went to observe her on the playground. I saw a little girl riddled with anxiety sitting on the fringe of the activities.

In our counseling sessions, we worked on conversation starters and ways to engage kids in activities. I helped her plan out her idea of a good recess as well as what she can do at recess that feels good. And when we included her in our social skills group, she was able to feel comfortable enough to have conversations and play games with kids. Over the years, as she continued in her elementary school, I watched Catherine blossom and maintain the same friendships that started during that group.

Catherine is a great example of how intervening early can make all the difference in a child's social experiences at school. Developing social skills takes time and repeated intervention to reinforce what they've learned. Just like math, it can be taught. And social skills are so important in life (even more than academic grades).

This chapter of The Teletherapy Toolkit™ has activities that support children who need extra TLC with their social skills.

Technique Name:
Social Autopsy

What Is It?

A technique for examining a particular social event that occurred, so children can better understand their role and the expected behaviors of both parties.

Materials:

Social Autopsy Web Worksheet

Pen or pencil

Instructions:

- During the session, explain that together, you will look at what happened during a specific social situation.

- Dialogue about the event, but keep the child focused on the process, so s/he can get a better understanding of expected behaviors.

- Start with the center of the worksheet, and answer the following questions:

  □ What happened?

  □ What was the social mistake?

  □ Who did the social mistake affect? And how?

  □ How did you feel in this situation?

  □ How did others feel in this situation?

  □ What could you have done to correct the social mistake?

  □ What was the expected social behavior from you?

  □ What was the expected social behavior from the other person(s)?

Questions:

- What has changed in your thinking about what happened?

- Were you surprised by something?

- Did you learn something new?

- What sensations did you notice?

Social Autopsy Web Worksheet

What was the social mistake?

What was the expected social behavior from them?

Who did the social mistake affect? And how?

What happened?

What was the expected social behavior from you?

How did you feel in this situation?

What could you have done to correct the social mistake?

How did others feel in this situation?

Technique Name:
What Is a Friend?

What Is It?

A technique for children to visualize what a friend is and the qualities of a good friend.

Materials:

What Is a Friend? Picture Frame

Instructions:

- During the session, explain that the child will be drawing a picture of what a good friend does.

- Next, ask the child to list three things that make a good friend.

- Ask: *"What things do you do that make you a good friend?"*

- Ask: *"When was the last time you were a good friend? Can you tell me about it?"*

Questions:

- What did you think about this activity?

- Were you surprised by something?

- Did you learn something new?

- What sensations did you notice?

What Is a Friend? Picture Frame

Technique Name:
Why Does Everyone Like Them?

What Is It?

A technique for children to objectively see why some kids are more popular (or more liked) and the qualities of a good friend.

Materials:

Why Does Everyone Like Them? Worksheet

Pen or pencil

Instructions:

- During the session, explain that you will be looking at why some kids are more liked than others, and what kind of qualities they have, so you can learn more about them.

- Next, ask the child to list the names of popular children.

- Then, ask him or her to write down a quality about them s/he admires.

- Dialogue about the following questions:

    □ *"What are the qualities of good friends?"*

    □ *"How are these qualities alike or different?"*

    □ *"What qualities do you have?"*

    □ *"How can you develop qualities that others like?"*

Questions:

- What did you think about this activity?

- Were you surprised by something?

- Did you learn something new?

- What sensations did you notice?

Why Does Everyone Like Them? Worksheet

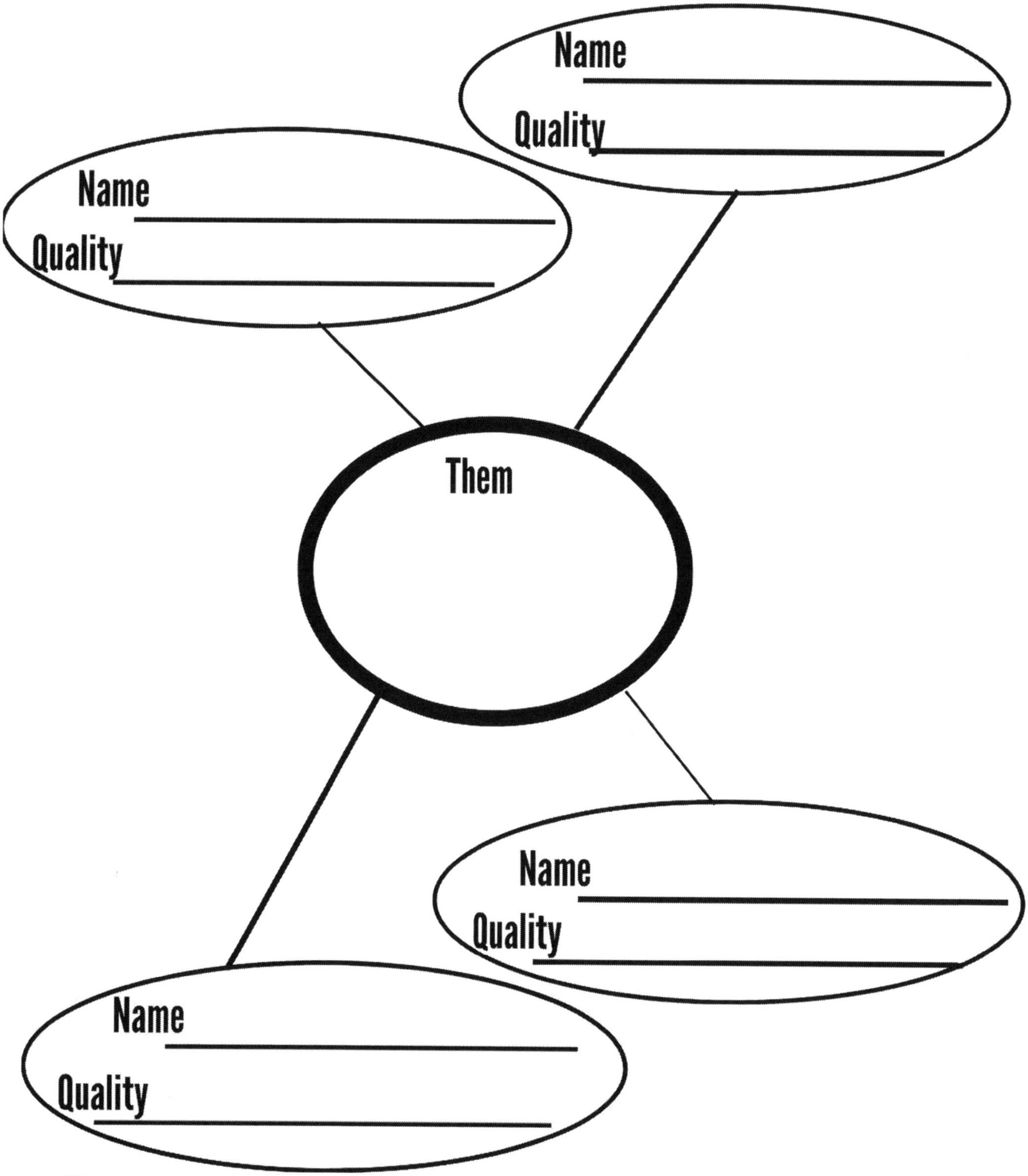

Name
_____

Quality
_____

Name
_____

Quality
_____

Them

Name
_____

Quality
_____

Name
_____

Quality
_____

Technique Name:
Picturing A Successful Recess

What Is It?

A way for children to visualize the social skills needed to get along with others at recess.

Materials:

Recess Picture Worksheet

Pen or pencil

Instructions:

- During the session, explain that you will look at what makes for a good recess.

- Next, ask the child to list three things that s/he needs for recess to feel good.

Questions:

- What did you think about this activity?

- Were you surprised by something?

- Did you learn something new?

- What sensations did you notice?

Recess Picture

Things you can do at recess:

Things others do at recess:

I feel good at recess when:

Technique Name:
What Is a Compliment?

What Is It?

A way for children to better understand the give-and-take required to build social relationships.

Materials:

What Is a Compliment? Worksheet

Markers, crayons, or pencil

Instructions:

- During the session, explain how everyone likes when someone says nice things to them.

- Ask the child to share the last time someone gave him/her a compliment, and what it was.

- Explain sometimes giving a compliment can be tricky, and that we only want to give a compliment when we really mean it.

- Fill out the What Is a Compliment? Worksheet together. A younger child can draw, while an older child can write.

Questions:

- What did you think about this activity?

- Were you surprised by something?

- Did you learn something new?

- What sensations did you notice?

What Is a Compliment? Worksheet

How do you know someone is giving you a sincere or real compliment?

What do you think someone feels when he or she gets a compliment?

How do you feel when you get a compliment?

Technique Name:
How to Get Along with Others

What Is It?

A way for children to better understand the give-and-take of friendship.

Materials:

How to Get Along with Others Worksheet

Markers, crayons, or pencil

Instructions:

- During the session, explain that the child will be drawing a picture or writing about a person he or she has a hard time getting along with.

- Talk about why it is sometimes hard to get along with other kids.

- Discuss ways to get along with others.

- Discuss ways to cope when stressed.

Questions:

- What did you think about this activity?

- Were you surprised by something?

- Did you learn something new?

- What sensations did you notice?

How to Get Along with Others Worksheet

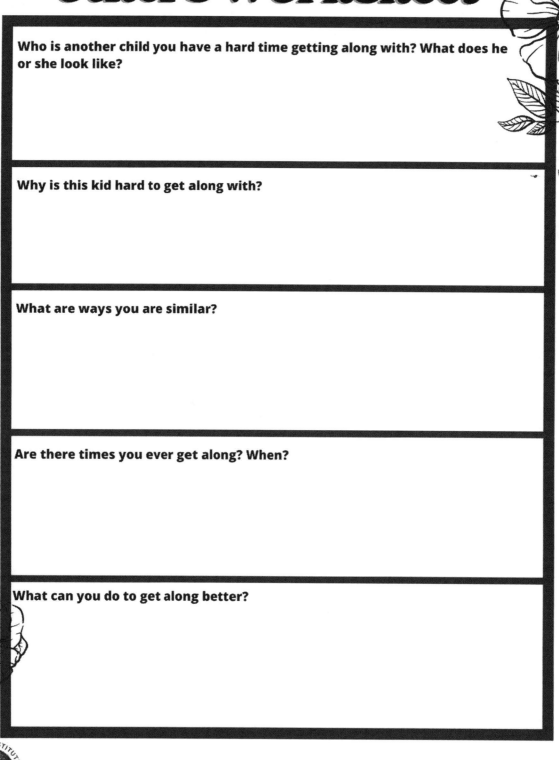

Who is another child you have a hard time getting along with? What does he or she look like?

Why is this kid hard to get along with?

What are ways you are similar?

Are there times you ever get along? When?

What can you do to get along better?

Technique Name:
My Friends and Me

What Is It?

A technique for children to examine issues that they and their friends have, so they can understand that we all have issues. This helps to normalize social issues, especially for those who blame others and lack insight into problem-solving.

Materials:

My Friends and Me Worksheet

Markers, crayons, or pencil

Instructions:

- During the session, fill out the My Friends and Me Worksheet.

- Dialogue about what is different and what is the same.

- Dialogue about ways to address his or her issues as well as his/her friend's.

Questions:

- What has changed in your thinking about your issue?

- What is different about your friend's issues from yours?

- How do your friends handle their issues?

- Were you surprised by something?

- Did you learn something new?

- What sensations did you notice?

My Friends and Me Worksheet

What are challenges my friends have?

What are challenges I have?

© Roseann-Capanna-Hodge, 2020
© Global Institute of Children's Mental Health, 2020

Technique Name:
Drawing Other People's Emotions

What Is It?

A technique to help children better identify emotions in others and themselves.

Materials:

Other People's Emotions Worksheet

Crayons, markers, or pencil

Instructions:

- Have the child draw faces that go with the different emotions.

Questions:

- Which emotion is the easiest to draw?

- Which emotion is the hardest to draw?

- When was the last time you had a hard time figuring out what someone was feeling? What did you do?

- When was the last time someone couldn't figure out what you were feeling? What happened?

Draw Other People's Emotions Worksheet

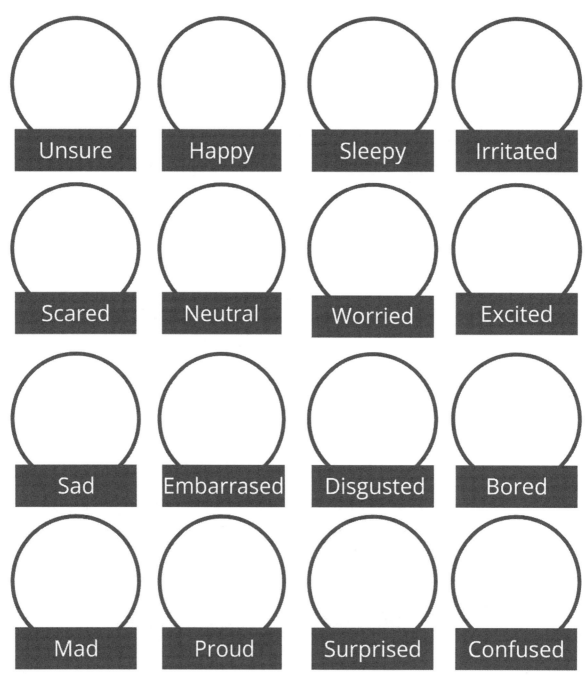

Unsure	Happy	Sleepy	Irritated
Scared	Neutral	Worried	Excited
Sad	Embarrased	Disgusted	Bored
Mad	Proud	Surprised	Confused

Chapter 17 – Teletherapy Techniques: Play and Expressive Arts

A Bridge to Therapeutic Change at Every Age

Riley was a senior in high school who was unsure of her purpose in life. Unlike her friends who all had college plans for the following year, Riley didn't even know if she wanted to go to college, let alone what she wanted to do in terms of a career. She was feeling aimless and sad, and her grades started to drop. By the time her dad called me, Riley was flunking three courses, and her graduation was in jeopardy.

Finding the words to define the issue was hard for her, so I knew she needed to spend time visualizing. Vision boarding is one of my favorite expressive arts techniques. It helps people to "see" the future, which makes setting goals so much easier. For weeks, Riley and I talked as she cut and pasted items related to what she could see herself doing in the future. She started off with fun things she enjoyed doing, and over time, she began to cultivate a vision board that married things she did for fun with a vocation.

Riley began to see the potential of what lay ahead of her instead of fear it. Before working on the vision board, she had been so 'stuck in the weeds,' she couldn't see the big picture, so she became immobilized.

Play and art therapy can help children and teens recognize and process feelings and sensations. For so many, it safely brings to the surface the things they couldn't see or put words to.

Even though we think of play and art therapy as only being for children, teens and adults can benefit from (and enjoy) these therapies, too. At the most basic level, these therapies help regulate the nervous system, so one can alert and process differently.

In this chapter of The Teletherapy Toolkit™, you'll discover play and art therapy activities that can be used virtually with children and teens.

Play Teletherapy Supply Checklist

The following is a list of items to purchase to support play therapy virtual sessions.

Setting Up a Space:

- ◻ Please remember the importance of privacy and confidentiality during these sessions.

- ◻ The use of headphones is encouraged.

- ◻ Your child can make a "Do Not Disturb" sign to hang during sessions.

Play Therapy Supply List:

- ◻ Paint and brushes

- ◻ White paper

- ◻ Lined paper

- ◻ Colored paper

- ◻ Paper plates

- ◻ Paper cups

- ◻ Markers

- ◻ Crayons

- ◻ Stickers

- ◻ Scissors

- ◻ Play-dough

- ◻ Air-drying clay

- ◻ Shaving cream

- ◻ Masking tape

- ◻ Duct tape

- ◻ Clear tape

- ◻ Glue

- ◻ Sparkles

- ▫ Popsicle sticks
- ▫ Pipe cleaners
- ▫ Yarn or string
- ▫ Fabric
- ▫ Old magazines
- ▫ Recycled items:
  - ▫ Egg carton
  - ▫ Cardboard
  - ▫ Newspaper
- ▫ Journal/small notebook
- ▫ Puppets
- ▫ Stuffed animals—aggressive and calm.
- ▫ Miniatures play people—workers, military, etc.
- ▫ Sand tray and miniatures
- ▫ Balloons
- ▫ Building blocks
- ▫ Cars
- ▫ Trains
- ▫ Train set
- ▫ Dolls and other toys that promote imaginative play
- ▫ Doll family
- ▫ Dollhouse
- ▫ Baby bottle
- ▫ Pacifier
- ▫ Doctor kit with Band-Aids
- ▫ Toy phone
- ▫ Play money
- ▫ Kitchen items
- ▫ Dress up clothing

- □ Mask
  - □ Hats and scarves
  - □ Everyday clothing
  - □ Worker clothing
  - □ Princess clothing
  - □ Superhero clothing
- □ Mirror
- □ Hairbrush or comb
- □ Dustpan and broom
- □ Sponge
- □ Dry erase board and markers
- □ Tinker or fidget toys
- □ Musical instruments
- □ Ring toss game
- □ Soft foam ball
- □ Bubbles
- □ Foam sword and shield

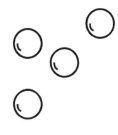

Technique Name:
Draw a Tree

What Is It?

Children's/teens' drawings are often reflections of what is happening in their life. Especially helpful for those who lack insight into their issues.

Materials:

Paper

Pencil, markers, or crayons

And/or virtual whiteboard

Instructions:

- Have the child/teen draw a tree—any kind he or she would like.

- Dialogue about it, analyzing the tree's roots, trunk, and branches.

Roots:

- Related to how connected the child is to him/herself, reality testing, and orientation.

Tree Trunk:

- Reflects the child's feelings of basic power, control, and inner strength.

- A slender trunk and large branches may suggest a need for satisfaction.

- Dark shadings of the trunk suggest anxiety about one's self.

Branches:

- Branches represent the child's felt resources for seeking satisfaction from the environment and how s/he manages frustration.

- Represent an individual's relationship with the external world.

- A tree drawn without branches might indicate social connections with others.

Ground:

- Related to a child's reality and stability.

Questions:

- Do you think the tree is weak or strong? What makes you think that?

- What could make the tree stronger?

- Is the tree familiar?

- Where does the tree provide shade?

- How did you organize your drawing?

Technique Name:
Draw a Person

What Is It?

Children's or teen's drawings are often a reflection of what is happening in their lives, as well as how they view themselves and others. Especially helpful for those who lack insight into their issues.

Materials:

Paper, Pencils, markers, or crayons; and/or virtual whiteboard

Instructions:

- Have the child/teen draw a person—any s/he would like, but with more detail than a stick figure.

- Dialogue about it.

- If it is the same gender as the child, it is often believed to be a reflection of his or her own self-concept.

- Analyze the drawing and its details:

  - Arms and Hands: Position of the hands, open versus closed fists, and specific gestures, if any, indicate behavioral traits, aggressiveness, and adaptation and integration with the social world.

  - Legs and Feet: Sense of stability, security, and support; contact with reality.

  - Head: Intelligence, communication, imagination, and sociability.

  - Hair: Sexuality and sensuality.

  - Face: Sense of identity:

    - Eyes: Social communication and perceived environment.

    - Mouth: Sensuality, sexuality, and verbal communication.

    - Nose: Phallic symbol.

Questions:

- Tell me about this person.

- Is this person familiar?

- What is this person doing?

- Where is this person's safe place?

- If this person had three wishes, what would they be?

Technique Name:
Draw a House

What Is It?

Children's or teen's drawings are often a reflection of what is happening in their life, as well as how they view themselves and others. Especially helpful for those who lack insight into their issues.

Materials:

Paper

Pencils, markers, or crayons

And/or virtual whiteboard

Instructions:

- Have the child draw a house—in any way s/he wants.

- Dialogue about it.

- Analyze the drawing and its details:

    - Roof: Represents the intellectual, fantasy, and spiritual life.

    - Wall: An indication of how strong one's personality is.

    - Doors and Windows: The relation of the person with the world outside, and how one interacts with others and integrates information.

    - Size: If the house is small, it might mean a rejection of one's life at home.

    - Sidewalks: Openness.

    - Ground: Stability and contact with reality.

Questions:

- Where is the safe place in this house?

- What needs to happen?

- What do you like about this house?

Technique Name:
Mandala

What Is It?

A mandala is a circle with a pattern inside it that represents the universe in Hindu and Buddhist symbolism. Drawing mandalas can help to create calm energy and promote focus. It is a great way to start a session or get a session going.

Materials:

SUDS Level Handout

Mandala Guide Handout

Paper

Pencils, markers, or crayons

Instructions:

Set guidelines:

- Draw in a plus sign to create a center and add a circle around it (trace around a can or cup) centered on the intersection as a visual guide. Draw these lines very lightly with a pencil, so they can be erased later.

Choose a center shape:

- Your center shape can be anything: a round dot, a geometric shape such as a triangle, diamond, or an octagon, or a symbol like a star or a petaled flower. Draw it in the center at the crisscross if you are using the Mandala Guide handout.

Build on the center shape:

- Draw a shape or symbol around your center, being consistent in size, shape, and color.

Continue to build outward:

- In the same way, continue to draw and develop your mandala outward, completing one layer or ring at a time, and then building upon that. If you do something that doesn't look or seem right, you can make it into something else, or just go with it. Give consideration to balancing color and proportions; the evenness of the design is a big part of what makes it so relaxing.

Questions:

- What sensations did you notice?

- What was your SUDS level before and after this task (use the SUDS Level Handout)?

Mandala Guide Handout

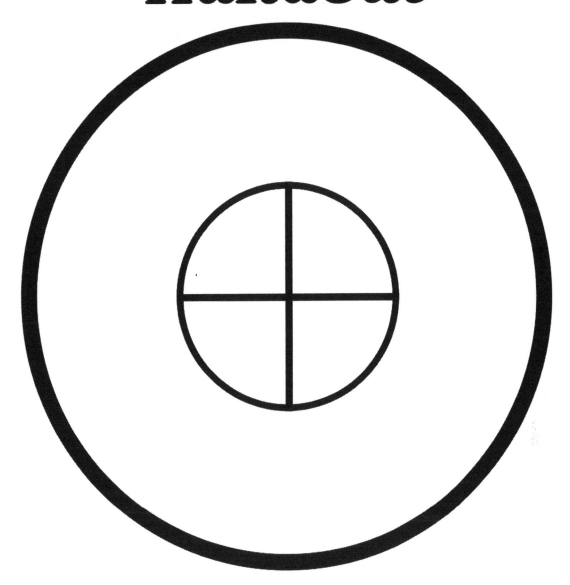

Technique Name:
Beat the Drum

What Is It?

Music helps children build a rhythm, facilitate a connection to the body, and construct a sense of control and safety. The use of the drum is a great way for children to develop cognitive and attentional skills, learn to self-regulate and release emotions, and increase self-awareness. Drumming is also an enjoyable and powerful way to deal with psychological stress.

Materials:

SUDS Level Handout

Paper or plastic cup

Dried beans, pasta, or rice (or anything that can make noise in the cup)

Plastic wrap

Rubber band

Paint or markers

Stickers

Instructions:

- Make the drum out of the plastic or paper cup.

- Have the child personalize it.

- Have the child explore the different sounds s/he can make.

- Have the child copy a series of drum movements and reinforce them.

- Have the child lead you in a series of drum movements.

- Explore relevant opposite concepts like soft and hard, quiet and loud, scary and safe, listening and not, etc.

Questions:

- Show me X emotion.

- What sensations did you notice?

- Did this make you think of anything?

- What was your SUDS level before and after this task (use the SUDS Level Handout)?

Technique Name:
Play That Song, D.J.

What Is It?

Helps teens identify things, people, or places in their life that make them feel safe, content, alert, anxious, sad, or alone through music.

Materials:

Smart phone or device to play music

Instructions:

- Ask the teen to make a list of songs that are important to him or her.

- Have him/her play the songs and explain why they are important.

- Dialogue about his/her values, family values, and how this music represents or affects them.

- If the teen relates to this activity and it assists with his/her therapeutic goals, create a theme-song list for each week focusing on emotional and stress-reduction needs.

Questions:

- What emotions came up?

- What things, people, or places surprised you as a stressor?

- What sensations did you notice?

Technique Name:
LEGO® Build Therapy Technique

What Is It?

Dr. Daniel LeGoff started experimenting with LEGO® therapy in 2003. His idea was to create an effective social skills program that could be used in multiple settings that would help children transfer their skills to the real world. While it is often used with children on the autism spectrum, it can be effective with any child with self-regulation issues. The goal of this play therapy technique is to improve relations with peers, share experiences, and collaborate.

Reference Citation:

LeGoff, Gomez de la Cuesta, Krauss & Baron-Cohen (2014). LEGO®-Based Therapy: How to build social competence through Lego®-Based Clubs for children with autism and related conditions. London: Jessica Kingsley Publishers.

Materials:

LEGOs®

Instructions:

This should be done with parents and siblings or peers, as the goal is to teach collaboration and social skills. It is also important for parents to learn these skills, so they can practice and reinforce them outside of the therapy session.

Children take turns in the following roles:

- **The Engineer:** Has a set of instructions for the model and has to request the bricks from the supplier and direct the builder to put the model together.

- **The Supplier:** Has the LEGO® bricks and supplies the engineer with the required items upon request.

- **The Builder:** Is given the bricks by the supplier and has to follow the instructions given by the engineer to make the model.

- **The Director:** This is the adult-facilitator role. The role of the facilitator is to direct the task with the goal of supporting socially appropriate and cooperative behavior.

The therapist encourages problem-solving, communication, and engagement throughout the session. It can be expanded to encourage creative play and collaboration through storytelling, dramatic activities, and innovation.

There can also be a focus on fine motor, visual-perceptual, cognitive, and auditory processing skills.

Work on verbally and nonverbally facilitating:

Social Skills:

- Take turns connecting the bricks.

- Learn to ask for help.

- Be courteous to each other.

- Learn not to interrupt others.

- Work on collaborative problem-solving activities.

- Regulate reactivity to disappointment.

- Encourage peers.

- Learn conversation starters.

- Make eye contact: look at the therapist and each other.

- Match body language and gestures.

- Stay in the building circle.

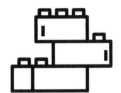

Fine Motor Skills:

- Reach for, grasp, and release bricks located below, at, and above waist level.

- Practice various prehension (grasp) patterns, such as picking up a LEGO with thumb and index finger, thumb and ring finger, etc.

- Move small bricks from one place to another within one hand while the other rests on a table or in the child's lap.

- Pick up and store bricks one at a time with and in one hand and then release them one by one using only that same hand.

- Lock the bricks together and take the project apart one brick at a time.

- Place bricks in containers using oversized tweezers, tongs, or hinged chopsticks.

Visual Perceptual Motor Skills:

- Copy body movements.

- Follow a diagram to build a project.

- Follow a model to build a project.

- Follow directors' step-by-step build.

- Correctly align the bricks, so all pieces fit together.

- Match bricks by size or shape.

- Create symmetrical projects.

- Find specific bricks when mixed in with others of varying colors, size, and shape.

- Trace around bricks with fingers and pencils.

- Identify the shape of a brick with eyes closed.

- Coordinate movement with a goal in mind.

Auditory Processing Skills:

- Follow directors' step-by-step verbal-build directions.

- Listen to verbal directions.

Cognitive Skills:

- Identify bricks by color, size, and shape.

- Create towers with largest bricks on the bottom (base) and smallest on top.

- Match bricks to pictures of a specific brick.

- Count total number of bricks or bricks by color.

- Find other objects in the clinic that are the same color or shape as a particular brick.

- Sort bricks correctly into containers identified by size or color.

- Follow directions to place bricks over, under, between, on top, on the right/left of a line, doll, or body part.

- Planning skills.

- Problem-solving skills.

- Collaborative problem-solving with others.

- Lead and follow.

Sensorimotor Skills:

- Lock bricks together.

- Find objects such as crayons, keys, coins, and marbles hidden in a bucket filled with bricks.

- Pick up and drop bricks into a bucket when laying on belly in a net swing.

- Dip bricks into a shallow tray of paint (bumpy side down) and stamp onto heavy paper secured to a tabletop or vertically along a wall.

Reference Citations:

LeGoff, Gomez de la Cuesta, Krauss & Baron-Cohen (2014). LEGO®-Based Therapy: How to build social competence through Lego®-Based Clubs for children with autism and related conditions. London: Jessica Kingsley

Publishers.

Wagenfeld (2017). LEGO® Therapy: How to Build Connections with Autism – One Brick at a Time. Autism Parenting Magazine. Retrieved on July 12, 2020.

For lessons for younger children, LEGO® Education has some great resources: education.lego.com/en-us/lessons/preschool

***For more information, purchase:

LeGoff, Gomez de la Cuesta, Krauss & Baron-Cohen (2014). LEGO®-Based Therapy: How to build social competence through Lego®-Based Clubs for children with autism and related conditions. London: Jessica Kingsley Publishers

Technique Name:
Using the Whiteboard

What Is It?

Using a whiteboard virtually or a real one in your office is a great way to get kids interacting and help them remain focused during a session. It can be used for psychoeducation about the brain or their particular issue in addition to playing games such as tic tac toe, for collaborative drawing, and squiggle drawing.

Materials:

Real whiteboard with dry erase markers

Access to HIPAA-compliant Zoom (which has whiteboard access). Alternatively, check your teletherapy platform to see if they have a whiteboard feature.

Download Skribbl.io

SUDS Scale

Instructions:

- Teach the child how to use the Zoom whiteboard feature or use a real whiteboard.

- Have him/her download Skribbl.io (a free multiplayer drawing and guessing game).

- Possible activities:

  ▫ Use a whiteboard for collaborative drawing.

  ▫ Use a whiteboard for games.

  ▫ Play Skribbl.io.

  ▫ Teach about the brain, stress activation, and neuroscience behind their issues.

Questions:

- What sensations did you notice?

- What was your SUDS level before and after this task (use the SUDS Level Handout)?

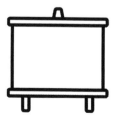

Technique Name:
What's on My Brain

What Is It?

A therapeutic technique that allows children or teens to draw what they are thinking about, processing, or dealing with. Especially helpful for children or teens who are having a hard time recognizing their issues.

Materials:

Paper

Pencils, markers, or crayons

Virtual whiteboard

What's on My Brain Worksheet

Instructions:

- Have the child or teen draw on the What's on My Brain Worksheet three things that are on his/her mind.

- Dialogue about it.

Questions:

- Did anything surprise you?

- Tell me about what is on your brain.

- What makes you think those thoughts that keep coming up?

- How do these things make your body feel?

What's On My Brain?
Worksheet

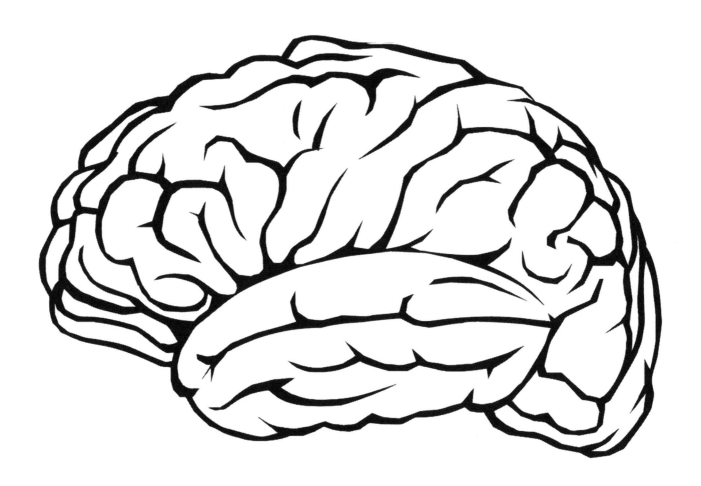

Technique Name:
Draw a Dreamcatcher

What Is It?

A therapeutic technique in which children or teens can draw things they are thinking about, processing, or dealing with. Especially helpful for children or teens who are having a hard time with motivation, may be stuck, are perfectionistic, or struggle with problem-solving.

Materials:

Draw a Dreamcatcher Worksheet

Paper

Pencil and markers or crayons

And/or virtual whiteboard

Instructions:

- Tell the child/teen to begin by drawing two circles, one within the other. This will form the hoop of the dreamcatcher.

- Begin to draw the flower-like design in the middle of the dreamcatcher.

  - For each "petal," use two curved lines. Enclose a shape that is pointed on both ends, with one point in the middle of the circle and one point on the edge of the hoop. Repeat until you have completed half the flower design.

- Draw the decorations of the dream catchers.

  - From each side of the hoop, extend several sets of long, curved lines, varying the length and design of each. From the bottom of the hoop, extend one set of curved lines. Enclose the lines by drawing three small circles at the bottom. These circles represent beads decorating the dream catcher.

- Draw feathers hanging from the dreamcatcher.

- Draw ribbons dangling from the hoop with beads attached to the end.

- Color the dream catcher (the central strands are often red).

Questions:

- Who do you know or admire who works toward their dreams?

- How do you think he or she achieved his/her dreams?

- What do you dream about?

- How do those dreams make your body feel?

- What dreams do you think your parents have for you?

Draw a Dreamcatcher Worksheet

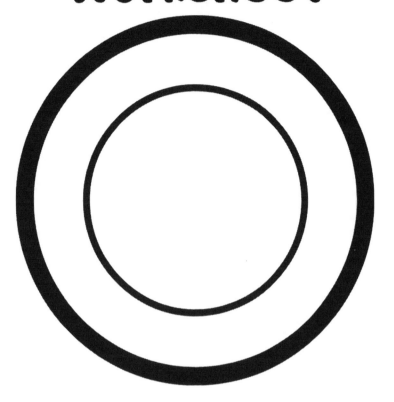

Technique Name:
The Masks We Wear

What Is It?

An art therapy technique that helps children or teens to see themselves and how others see them through the process of making two masks: one how they see themselves and another how others see them. Good for teens or children with low self-esteem, social anxiety, bullying or social difficulties, impulsive kids, or children or teens who struggle with self-concept or tend to misperceive events.

Materials:

The Masks We Wear Worksheet

Pencil, crayons, or markers

Glitter, paint, or any decorative items

SUDS Level Handout

Instructions:

- Have the child or teen decorate or color two masks.

- Give instructions informing him or her to make two masks: one how s/he sees him/herself, and another how others see him/her.

- Dialogue about whatever issue the child or teen presents.

- Use the SUDS scale before and after the activity (the SUDS Level Handout).

Questions:

- What did you think about this activity?

- Were you surprised by something?

- Did you learn something new?

- Was there anything that made you feel comfortable or uncomfortable?

- Did any thoughts, feelings, or memories come up?

- Did your body feel different when you were doing one mask or the other?

- What sensations did you notice?

The Masks We Wear Worksheet

1. How You See Yourself Mask:

The Masks We Wear Worksheet

2. How Others See You Mask:

Technique Name:
My Life in Photographs

What Is It?

Helps children or teens identify things, people, or places in their life that make them feel safe, content, alert, anxious, sad, or alone.

Materials:

Smart phone or device for pictures

Instructions:

- Ask the child or teen to take pictures of things that make him or her feel safe, content, alert, anxious, sad, or alone.

- Talk about the pictures and why they evoke the feelings they do.

- Discuss these photos in terms of which ones can be resources for him/her.

- Can use photos that represent resources in a collage, so the child or teen can have visual reminders in his/her room.

- This can be a regular homework assignment that you start with one emotion at every session.

Questions:

- What things, people, or places surprised you as a resource?

- What things, people, or places surprised you as a stressor?

- What sensations did you notice?

Technique Name:
Making Slime

What Is It?

An art therapy technique that helps soothe the nervous system and provide sensory support. Slime can be a tool to teach:

- Following directions: Following the recipe can help children follow a sequence.

- Impulse control: Controlling impulses while mixing and adding in color, glitter, etc.

- Flexibility: This experience provides the chance to manage stress, disappointment, and change the plan when it doesn't go as anticipated.

- Emotions: It can be a visual for big and small emotions.

- Stress relief: Slime releases tension, helps calm the nervous system, and meets sensory needs.

Materials:

Slime Recipe Handout

Bowl

White liquid glue

Baking soda

Food dye

Lens cleaner

SUDS Level Handout

Instructions:

- Teach the child how to make slime.

- Ask him or her how s/he wants to receive the directions: auditory or visually.

- Teach him/her about how using our strengths can help us learn information more easily.

- Teach him/her how to plan for a step-by-step task.

- Have him/her visualize the end product by asking, *"What does your slime look like?"*

- Ask guiding questions like, *"Ok, you want it to be blue and fluffy, so what should we get first?"*

Questions:

- What sensations did you notice?

- What was your SUDS level before and after this task (use the SUDS Level handout)?

Slime Recipe Handout

- Pour one cup of white glue into a mixing bowl.

- Add one tablespoon of baking soda.

- Mix the contents of the bowl thoroughly.

- Add more or less glue depending on your desired consistency.

- Squeeze eight drops of food coloring into a bowl.

- Mix.

- Add one tablespoon of lens cleaner.

- Stir your slime mixture with a spoon until it starts to thicken.

- Can add glitter.

© Roseann-Capanna-Hodge, 2020
© Global Institute of Children's Mental Health, 2020

Chapter 18 – Conclusion

As I wrote this book for my fellow therapists, I thought about all the challenges we face every day and the huge hurdles so many are dealing with during the pandemic. From working and learning at home to lost jobs and income, families are struggling … and the kids we work with are, too. Anxiety, panic, and social isolation are hitting our world hard. Children and teens are missing their friends, and even school! There seems to be no end in sight to mask wearing and social distancing.

We are all feeling the weight of these uncertain times, and as therapists, we are not immune to the stress. Virtual therapy session days can be long and isolating, especially without those lovely hallway chitchats with colleagues about this or that technique or the kid who declared, *"Your hair looks bad today."* I, for one, am truly missing those heart-to-hearts.

If you found yourself searching Amazon and Facebook groups looking for something … really *anything* that had effective and easy-to-use teletherapy activities for children and teens, you're not alone. I was doing the same thing and couldn't find anything! It was time to hunker down and pull from my almost 30 years of experience as a therapist to create the **Teletherapy Toolkit™**... and I'm so glad I did, because now, you can use these engaging therapeutic activities, too.

You may have felt like a first-year therapist again as you scrambled for resources, but I trust you are now enjoying renewed confidence with this handbook for virtual therapy with children and teens.

My goal with **The Teletherapy Toolkit™: Therapist Handbook for Treating Children and Teens** was to provide you everything you need to be a rockstar teletherapist for children and adolescents. I know how important it is to you to have clinically effective teletherapy activities in an easy-to-use format that will make your job easier, so you can focus on what you do best—providing great therapy. That is what I created, and I hope the included checklists and parent information sheets I've included go a long way in helping you conduct the most effective sessions possible.

Not only do you now have the infographics in the book, but you can also download them for free too, so you can share them on screen or give them to your clients in advance of a session or for homework. Go to **www.teletherapytoolkit.com/pdf** to access them. Simply enter your email address and show proof of purchase (with a picture of or scanned receipt or vendor order number) to receive a FREE copy of the activities and information sheets.

Because the world of teletherapy is still all so new, I have also created APA-approved CE-based courses to support your continued adaptation to teletherapy. You may be interested in **The Teletherapy Toolkit™: Virtual Therapy Activities for Children and Adolescents** course or our four-week intensive, **The Therapist Teletherapy Toolkit™ Bootcamp**, which includes three courses plus four Q&A sessions with APA-approved CEs. Visit **www.teletherapytoolkitcourses.com** today to register for a course, find more information, or even **submit a request** for a topic you would like to see me cover in my next course!

I work every day to create great resources for parents, schools, and professionals, so we can move the dial on children's mental health. Check out my **"YouTube"** channel all about this topic at *www. youtube.com/DrRoseann!*

There, you will find videos in which I dive into common issues children and teens face today, mental health related to the pandemic, and teletherapy. You can also listen to my podcast, **The Parent Coffee Talk**, at **www.parentcoffeetalk.com** on YouTube, or other major hosting platforms, including: Libsyn, iTunes, Spotify, etc.

Forbes Magazine just called me, *"A thought leader"* due to my ongoing commitment to *"changing the way we view and treat children's mental health."* That is what **The Global Institute of Children's Mental Health** is all about, and as therapists, psychologists, and school counselors, we can all lead the charge.

I welcome you to join me in our mission.

All my best,

Dr. Roseann

Made in the USA
Las Vegas, NV
17 June 2021